THE HIDDEN PLACES OF
THE LAKE DISTRICT
AND CUMBRIA

By Kat

Regional Hidden Places

Cornwall
Devon
Dorset, Hants & Isle of Wight
East Anglia
Lake District & Cumbria
Lancashire & Cheshire
Northumberland & Durham
Peak District and Derbyshire
Yorkshire

National Hidden Places

England
Ireland
Scotland
Wales

Country Living Rural Guides

East Anglia
Heart of England
Ireland
North East of England
North West of England
Scotland
South
South East
Wales
West Country

Other Guides

Off the Motorway
Garden Centres and Nurseries
  of Britain

Published by: Travel Publishing Ltd, Airport Business Centre, 10 Thornbury Road, Estover, Plymouth, Devon PL6 7PP

ISBN13   9781904434870

© Travel Publishing Ltd

First published 1990, second edition 1993, third edition 1996, fourth edition 1998, fifth edition 2001, sixth edition 2003, seventh edition 2005, eighth edition 2007, ninth edition 2009

Printing by: Latimer Trend, Plymouth

Maps by: ©MAPS IN MINUTES/Collins Bartholomew (2009)

Editor: Kate Daniel

Cover Design: Lines and Words, Aldermaston

Cover Photograph: Watendlath Tarn, Cumbria
© www.britainonview.co.uk

Text Photographs: © Bob Brooks, Weston-super-Mare
www.britainhistoricsites.co.uk

Foreword

This is the 9th edition of **The Hidden Places of the Lake District & Cumbria** taking you on a relaxed but informative tour of **Cumbria** and the "jewel in its crown", **The Lake District**. The guide has been been fully updated and in this respect we would like to thank the Tourist Information Centres in Cumbria for helping us update the editorial content. The guide is packed with information on the many interesting places to visit in one of England's most spectacular tourist destinations. In addition, you will find details of places of interest and advertisers of places to stay, eat and drink included under each village, town or city, which are cross referenced to more detailed information contained in a separate, easy-to-use section to the rear of the book. This section is also available as a free supplement from the local Tourist Information Offices.

The delightful county of **Cumbria** in which the Lakes reside is England's second largest county, but surprisingly has a relatively small population of only 490,000 people which is only slightly more numerous than the city of Leeds. The **Lake District** is most famous for its impressive mountain scenery but also encompasses green rolling hills, fast flowing rivers, deep lush forests and of course the enchanting and languid lakes. Below the fells, peaceful country lanes meander through beautiful little hamlets and tiny rural villages, many steeped in history. This wonderful scenery is of course celebrated by the "Lake Poets" - Wordswoth, Coleridge and Southey. Apart from the Lake District, Cumbria offers the visitor gentle moorland, craggy coastal headlands, scattered woodlands and a fascinating history and cultural heritage.

The Hidden Places of the Lake District & Cumbria contains a wealth of interesting information on the history, the countryside, the towns and villages and the more established places of interest. But it also promotes the more secluded and little known visitor attractions and places to stay, eat and drink many of which are easy to miss unless you know exactly where you are going.

We include hotels, bed & breakfasts, restaurants, pubs, bars, teashops and cafes as well as historic houses, museums, gardens and many other attractions throughout the area, all of which are comprehensively indexed. Many places are accompanied by an attractive photograph and are easily located by using the map at the beginning of each chapter. We do not award merit marks or rankings but concentrate on describing the more interesting, unusual or unique features of each place with the aim of making the reader's stay in the local area an enjoyable and stimulating experience.

Whether you are travelling around Cumbria on business or for pleasure we do hope that you enjoy reading and using this book. We are always interested in what readers think of places covered (or not covered) in our guides so please do not hesitate to use the reader reaction form provided to give us your considered comments. We also welcome any general comments which will help us improve the guides themselves. Finally if you are planning to visit any other corner of the British Isles we would like to refer you to the list of other *Hidden Places* titles to be found to the rear of the book and to the Travel Publishing website.

Travel Publishing

Did you know that you can also search our website for details of thousands of places to see, stay, eat or drink throughout Britain and Ireland? Our site has become increasingly popular and now receives over **200,000** visits annually. Try it!

website: **www.findsomewhere.co.uk**

Location Map

Contents

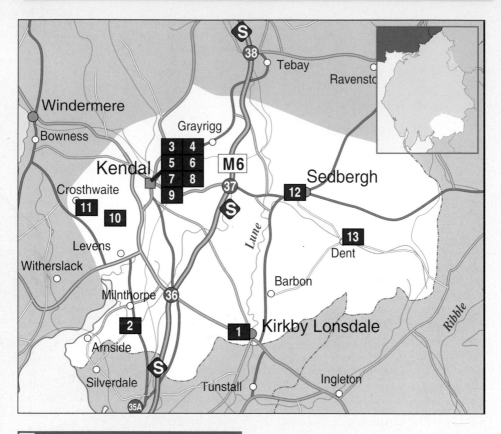

Gateway to the Lakes

The Lake District is renowned for the epic grandeur of its scenery; enchanting lakes and picturesque villages nestled among towering mountains. It is easy to see why millions of visitors flock to this most beautiful part of England every year. The region boasts England's highest mountain (Scafell Pike at an impressive 3,205 feet), its largest and deepest lakes (Windermere and Wast Water), along with hundreds of other mountains, another 14 lakes (known for the most part as 'meres' or 'waters'), challenging crags and lovely wooded valleys.

Despite its popularity with tourists and ramblers, much of the region still remains untouched, so many peaceful glades and windswept, isolated fells are as wild and beautiful as they have always been. The very same scenery which so inspired the romantic poet Wordsworth, writing such lines as

> *"Therefore am I still*
> *A lover of the meadows and the woods,*
> *And mountains; and of all that we behold*
> *From this green earth"*

and the other Lake poets Coleridge and Southey. Between them, this lyrical trio transformed the pervading 18th-century perception of this most northwesterly corner of England from that of an intimidating wilderness to an oasis of majestic scenery.

Cumbria is England's second-largest county in size, though its population numbers not half a million. The Lake District National Park, created in 1951 to protect the area from 'inappropriate development' and to provide 'access to the land for public enjoyment', holds almost one-third of the county's 2,636 square miles within its boundaries. It offers a wonderfully varied landscape, for a near endless range of outdoor activities and enjoyable walks.

Cumbria is much more than the Lake District National Park, however. It was here that the British Celts managed to preserve their independence from the Saxons; the Norse influence can still be detected in the place names here. This area has been so well preserved that not a single mile of motorway has been built past its borders, with only the very occasional stretch of dual-carriageway. Access to the area is very easy, however, as the M6 runs right along its eastern edge. For many visitors travelling from the south into Cumbria, their first experience of the county is the area around Kendal and Kirkby Lonsdale. These ancient settlements provide an excellent introduction to the history, people, culture and economy of Cumbria. Ideally placed for the Lake District National Park and the South Cumbrian coast, it is easy to forget that this area is also close to the northern Pennines and the Yorkshire Dales National Park.

Lune Valley, nr Kirkby Lonsdale

Kirkby Lonsdale

A charming, atmospheric Jacobean inn renowned for excellent cuisine, beer, wine and last but by no means least, superb accommodation.

🍴 🛏 *see page 134*

KIRKBY LONSDALE

"I do not know in all my country a place more naturally divine than Kirkby Lonsdale." John Ruskin said this when he came to Kirkby Lonsdale in 1875, after seeing a painting of JMW Turner's. "He stood on the stone terrace overlooking the valley of the River Lune, the view of which he had seen in this painting, and it took his breath away; *"one of the loveliest scenes in England, therefore in the world"*.

Turner himself had come in 1816 on the recommendation of William Wordsworth. These three artists and friends would have been sure to see the **Devil's Bridge,** a dramatic lofty structure of three fluted arches, bowing gracefully over the Lune. According to legend, the Devil's Bridge was built by Satan himself in just three days after an old woman unable to cross the deep river with her cattle made a deal with him. He agreed, but on the condition that in return he would have the soul of the first creature to cross. Cumbrian cunning outwitted him, however; the old woman threw a bun across the bridge for her dog to run and fetch; thus she cheated the Devil of a human soul.

The bridge is at least 700 years old. Its exact age is a mystery but we do know that some repairs were carried out in 1275, making it certainly the oldest surviving bridge in Westmorland. By the 1920s this narrow bridge, originally designed for pack-horses, proved quite inadequate for motorised transport. A new bridge was built and this, together with one of the country's first by-pass roads, has saved this lovely old town from further destructive road-widening schemes.

Kirkby's Main Street is a picturesque jumble of houses spanning several centuries, with intriguing passages and alleyways skittering off in all directions, all of them worth exploring. There are many individual shops, selling everything from fine cheeses to jewellery. Or there is, past the 16th-century weavers' cottages in Fairbank, the **Swine Market** with its 600-year-old cross where traders have displayed their wares every Thursday for more than 700 years. Even more admired is the **St Mary's Church** with its noble Norman doorway and massive pillars. Where, in the churchyard, a late Georgian gazebo looks across to the enchanting view of the Lune Valley as painted by Turner.

Devil's Bridge, Kirkby Lonsdale

AROUND KIRKBY LONSDALE

HALE

7 miles W of Kirkby Lonsdale off the A6

Lakeland Wildlife Oasis, Hale

This tiny village close to the Lancashire border is surrounded by woodland. It is the proud home to the **Lakeland Wildlife Oasis** which, much more than a zoo, provides a fascinating range of animals, birds, reptiles and insects many of whom you can have real hands-on interactions with. Visitors can drape a snake around their neck, exchange inquisitive glances with a ruffled lemur or a meerkat up on its haunches, and admire creatures rarely seen in captivity such as flying foxes and poison arrow frogs. The Tropical Hall is the home of numerous free-flying birds, bats and butterflies; other exhibits range from leaf-cutter ants to pygmy marmosets. The Oasis was established in 1991 by Dave and Jo Marsden, who were keepers at Chester Zoo before setting up this popular family attraction, which is open throughout the year.

About 3 miles south of the town, **Leighton Hall** is actually in Lancashire but well worth a short diversion. The Hall has been described as the most beautifully situated house in the British Isles, with the dramatic panorama of the Lakeland Fells providing a striking backdrop. The elaborate neo-Gothic façade cloaks an 18th-century mansion which in turn stands on the site of the original medieval house built in 1246 by Adam d'Avranches, whose descendants still live here. Leighton Hall is famed for its collection of Gillow furniture.

MILNTHORPE

8 miles W of Kirkby Lonsdale on A6

Just north of the Lancashire border, Milnthorpe has been a market town since the 14th century. It originally flourished as a port on the banks of the River Bela, but the harbour has long since silted up. The mill of the town's name refers to the waterfalls that once stood alongside the river. It is home to the beautiful **St Thomas' Parish Church** which was built in 1837, a real feature of which is its stained glass windows by a variety of artists. The first vicar of the church Nicholas Padwick stopped the Sunday hiring of farm labourers as their drunken revelry on the village green disrupted the congregation. Although the traditional cattle fairs ceased in 1929, Milnthorpe still holds Spring and Autumn fun fairs.

2 HERON CORN MILL

Beetham

Heron Corn Mill on the banks of the River Bela in South Cumbria, close to the Lancashire border, is one of the few working mills in the area.

see page 134

BEETHAM

8 miles W of Kirkby Lonsdale on the A6

The village of Beetham is rich in history with many interesting sights: an unusual 19th-century **Post Office** with a distinctive black-and-white studded door, the remains of the 14th century buildings Beetham Hall and Hazelslack Tower. Also there are the quaintly named "fairy steps" on a path climbing from the village to Beetham fell. The second of two flights of stone steps is so named due to a legend that if you climb the steps without touching the limestone sides of the narrow gully, the fairies will grant your wish.

The most outstanding feature of the village is its **Church of St Michael and All Angels**, a church approached through a pergola of rambling roses which dates back to Saxon times. Although the church was badly damaged during the Civil War, when its windows were smashed and effigies broken, a glass fragment of Henry IV in an ermine robe has survived the centuries. Also surviving the attack is a window commemorating St Lioba, a respected leader of a group of Nuns sent to Germany in AD748, whose life is celebrated each year on 28th September. During restoration work in the 1830s, a hoard of coins, minted in Norman times, was discovered inside the base of a pillar in the church.

Just outside the village lies **Heron Corn Mill**, a restored and working watermill with fully operational grinding machinery. A fine example of a traditional corn mill which operated for trade in the Westmorland farming area, the mill ceased trading as recently as the 1950s. Here you can enjoy watching flour ground from a 14 feet breast-shot water wheel, perfectly positioned on a ledge of rock created by the nearby waterfall, and even purchase some to take home. In the same location is the **Museum of Paper Making**, which was established in 1988 to commemorate 500 years of papermaking in England, where a history of paper making and ancient & modern tools are on exhibition.

ARNSIDE

10 miles W of Kirkby Lonsdale off the B5282

This quiet town on the Kent Estuary, with its short but elegant promenade, was once a busy port with its own shipbuilding and sea salt-refining industry. Sadly the port declined, but today it is still a busy town being a favourite retirement destination and a peaceful holiday resort. There are picturesque walks (the best way to experience Arnside and the surrounding countryside is on foot), and, on clear days, the views of the estuary and Lakeland mountains stretch on forever.

Inland from Arnside, down a quiet lane, **Arnside Tower** is one of the many pele towers that were built in the area in the 14th century and may have been part of the chain of towers designed to form a ring of protection around

Morecambe Bay. Pele towers, unique to the north of England, were usually three-storey buildings; about 90 were built in the region. It is easy to imagine how striking this tower must have been when it was built in the 1370s, even now as a shell of its former structure it is rousing.

KENDAL

Kendal, the unofficial capital of South Lakeland, has been found to have the highest quality of life of any town in England in a survey, which came as no surprise to the residents of this lively, bustling town. Here can be found the perfect balance between a celebrated rich history & heritage, and vibrant modern culture.

The Kendal woolen industry, which was once one of the most important woolen textile trades in northern England, was founded in 1331 by John Kemp, a Flemish weaver, and it flourished and sustained the town for almost 600 years until the development of competition from the huge West Riding of Yorkshire mills during the Industrial Revolution.

Kendal's motto "wool is my bread" reveals the extent to which the town's economy depended on the wool from the flocks of Herdwick sheep that roamed the surrounding fells. The fame of the local wool was so great that Shakespeare refers to archers clad in Kendal Green cloth in his play *Henry IV*. These archers were the famous **Kendal Bowmen** whose lethal longbows were made from local yew trees culled from the nearby limestone crags. It was these men who clinched the English victories at Agincourt and Crécy, and fought so decisively against the Scots at the Battle of Flodden Field in 1513.

Kendal has royal connections, too. The Parr family lived at **Kendal Castle** until 1483 – their most famous descendant being Katherine Parr, the last of Henry VIII's six wives. Today, the castle's gaunt ruins stand high on a hill overlooking the town, with most of

3 YE OLDE FLEECE INN

Kendal

An olde worlde property with a beautifully carved wooden interior serving a wide range of tasty food and drink all year round.

see page 135

4 BURGUNDY'S WINE BAR

Kendal

Popular town centre wine bar with excellent selection of wines, whiskeys, ales and real ales.

see page 136

Kendal Castle Ruins

5 DICKIE DOODLES

Kendal

For a wide variety of music and well kept ales, Dickie Doodles (open 8 till late) is the place to head for!

🍴 🏛 *see page 137*

6 HAMPERS TEA ROOMS

Kendal

A delightful tea room, just a short walk from Kendal's main thoroughfare, which specializes in traditional, home-cooked food.

🍴 *see page 136*

7 SAWYERS ARMS

Kendal

Situated in the heart of Stricklandgate; former coaching inn, Sawyers Arms offers a restful night's sleep for weary travellers.

🍴 🛏 *see page 138*

the castle wall and one of the towers still standing, and two underground vaults still complete. Castle Hill is a popular place for walking and picnics. In summer the hillside is smothered with wild flowers. From the hilltop there are spectacular views; a panorama panel here assists in identifying the distant fells.

The largest settlement in the old county of Westmorland, Kendal has always been a bustling town, from the days when it was on the main route to Scotland. Nowadays the M6 and a by-pass divert much of the traffic away from the town centre, but its narrow main streets, Highgate, Stramongate, and Stricklandgate, are always busy during the season. However, a new pedestrian priority zone through most of Highgate and Stricklandgate provides a much more pleasant ambience. The fine coaching inns of the 17th and 18th centuries, to which Bonnie Prince Charlie is said to have retreated after his abortive 1745 rebellion, still line these streets.

Anyone wandering around the town cannot help but notice the numerous alleyways, locally known as yards that are a unique architectural town planning feature of Kendal. An integral part of the old town, there were once about 150 of them leading off the main streets. In the late 18th century and early 19th century, when the woolen industry expanded, families worked together weaving, dyeing and tanning, all of which were carried out in the yards. Some of

these yards now provide place for shops and cafés.

A local product well worth sampling is **Kendal Mint Cake**, a tasty confection made from sugar, glucose and peppermint oil, which is cherished by climbers, walkers and adventurists for its instant infusion of energy. Ewan McGregor and Charley Boorman included mint cake in their supplies for their motorcycle trip around the world in "Long Way Round". The highly potent **Kendal Black Drop** is sadly (but not unsurprisingly!) no longer available. "A more than commonly strong mixture of opium and alcohol", Kendal Black Drop was a favourite of poets Samuel Taylor Coleridge and Thomas de Quincey.

Kendal's excellent sporting facilities include the **Lakes Leisure Centre**, which offers a pool and a wide selection of indoor activities (as well as a theatre which holds comedy, family and music shows); one of the highest indoor climbing facilities in the country at **The Lakeland Climbing Centre**; two local golf courses and a driving range. Drama, music and the visual arts are represented in a regularly changing programme of exhibitions, live music, theatre productions and craft workshops at the **Brewery Arts Centre**. The Centre also houses Kendal's cinemas, which present a mixture of mainstream, classic and art house films.

A number of interesting museums and galleries are also located in Kendal. The **Museum**

Museum of Lakeland Life, Kendal

8 CAFÉ 34

Kendal

Renowned for its large choice in light lunching and breakfasts served with a smile, Cafe 34 keeps diners coming to enjoy its relaxed and contemporary feel.

see page 140

of **Lakeland Life** takes as its theme the traditional rural trades of the region, and together with the **Abbot Hall Art Gallery** forms part of a complex within Abbot Hall Park. The museum, in re-created farmhouse rooms, contains a wide variety of exhibits, including Arthur Ransome memorabilia, craft workshops, a Victorian street scene, artefacts from the Arts and Crafts movement, nautical displays and Captain Flint's Locker, a pirate-themed activity area for children and families. The Gallery, in an elegant Georgian villa, houses a collection of society portraits by the locally born George Romney, and watercolour scenes by Ruskin and Turner, as well as works by 20th-century and contemporary artists such as Walter Sickert, Ben Nicholson, Paula Rego and Bridget Riley.

Kendal Museum, founded in 1796, is one of the oldest museums in the country and contains outstanding displays of archaeology, natural history, geology and local history (open Thursday, Friday and Saturday 12 noon - 5pm). Based on the collection first exhibited by William Todhunter in the late 18th century, the Museum takes visitors on a journey from prehistoric times, a trip which includes an interactive

Kendal Museum, Kendal

9

9 DUKE OF CUMBERLAND

Kendal

An 18th century coaching inn offering generous portions finely cooked complete with real ale and gorgeous beer garden to enjoy in.

🍴 see page 139

10 THE WHEATSHEAF

Brigsteer

This fine inn is almost 250 years old but has lost none of its charm and appeal.

🍴 🛏 see page 141

11 CROSTHWAITE HOUSE

Crosthwaite, nr Kendal

Offering a spectacular setting overlooking the fells, Crosthwaite House has a fantastic atmosphere and classical ambience.

🛏 see page 140

exhibit recounting the story of Kendal Castle.

The famous fellwalker and writer, Alfred Wainwright, whose handwritten guides to the Lakeland hills will be found in the backpack of any serious walker, was honorary clerk here between 1945 and 1974. Many of his original drawings are on display.

Adjacent to the elegant Georgian Abbot Hall and Museum is the 13th-century **Parish Church** of Kendal, 'the Church of the Angels', one of the widest in England, with five aisles and a peal of 10 bells. This amazingly light church has many interesting paraphernalia including, carved reredos of the Parr Chapel, stained glass windows, and a sculpture *The Family of Man* by Josephina de Vasconcellos. The church also contains a sword that is said to have belonged to Robert Philipson, a Cavalier during the Civil War.

Perhaps the most unusual attraction in Kendal is the **Quaker Tapestry Exhibition** at the Friends Meeting House in the centre of the town. This unique exhibition of 77 panels of community embroidery explores Quaker history from the 17th century to the present day. These colourful, beautifully crafted tapestries are the work of some 4,000 people aged between 4 and 90, from 15 countries. Many resources including Quaker costume display and large-screen video programme combine to provide a fascinating insight into the Quaker movement and its

development. You can even attend the popular embroidery demonstrations, workshops and courses and create your own tapestry (On tour during the winter, although the tea rooms here are open all year round).

AROUND KENDAL

BRIGSTEER
3 miles SW of Kendal off A591

This tiny hamlet lies under the limestone escarpment of Scout Scar. From this pretty settlement the road leads into the National Trust property of **Brigsteer Woods** where, as the climate is milder here due to its sheltered position, there is a flourish of wild daffodils in spring. These woods provide a picturesque, easy stroll (particularly lovely during daffodil season), and can be followed up to the Scout Scar for a longer, more challenging walk.

BURNESIDE
2 miles N of Kendal off the A591

The remains of an ancient stone circle can be seen close by Burneside, on **Potter Fell**. By the 15th century Burneside was a settled agricultural area, and a rich variety of mills sprang up along the River Sprint – corn, cotton, wool, bobbin and the original rag paper mill at **Cowan Head**. There has been a settlement at Burneside since Stone Age times.

Just south of Burneside is The

River Sprint, which meets the River Kent and has its own remarkably beautiful Longsleddale Valley which curves past Garnett Bridge deep into the high fell country. A bridle path climbs from the head of the valley into Kentmere, another spectacularly beautiful walk.

GRAYRIGG

5 miles NE of Kendal on the A685

This is a fine village with a cluster of almshouses, cottages and a simple church found in a lovely rural setting. It was the birthplace of Francis Howgill (1610-69), who was responsible for introducing founding Quaker father George Fox to the **Westmorland Seekers**, a group of radical Christians from the area.

LEVENS

5 miles S of Kendal off the A590

At the southern tip of Scout Scar, overlooking the Lyth Valley and the lower reaches of the River Kent stands **Levens Hall** with its unique topiary gardens. The superb Elizabethan mansion (described as 'one of the wonders of Lakeland') developed from a 14th-century pele tower. The gardens were first laid out in 1694, and were the work of Colonel James Grahme, a keen gardener who purchased the hall in 1688 and employed a Frenchman, Guillaume Beaumont, to create the amazing topiary work

(Beaumont also redesigned the gardens at Hampton Court for James II). Today there are many specimens, some almost 20 feet high, with the ancient yew trees cut into often surreal shapes. The topiary is by no means the only attraction in the grounds, however, which also include a Fountain Garden bordered with pleached limes, created in 1994 to mark the tercentenary of the gardens. A new addition is the living willow labyrinth; created from willow cuttings by Chris Crowder & his team of gardeners, in the summer its greenery provides paths for children and adults to explore as they hunt for the elusive hare in its centre, and a children's play area has also been added to the historic gardens. There is also a collection of working steam engines, a tea room, gift shop and plant centre. The interior of the house is equally rewarding – a wealth of period

Levens Hall, Levens

Sizergh Castle

12 ELLIE'S BAKERY AND TEAROOM

Sedburgh

A peaceful place to enjoy fine home-cooked food and baking with a holistic centre attached for total relaxation!

see page 142

furniture, fine panelling and plasterwork, a dining room with walls covered in goatskin, and paintings by Rubens, Lely and Cuyp. The Hall is said to be haunted by three ghosts: a black dog, a lady in pink, and a gypsy woman.

Only a couple of miles north of Levens Hall, just off the A591, is another stately old residence, **Sizergh Castle**, the impressive home of the Strickland family since 1239 (who still reside there, although the property is now administered by the National Trust). Originally a pele tower built to withstand border raiders, the house has been added to and altered over the intervening centuries to provide the family, as times became less violent, with a more comfortable home. It now boasts intricately carved chimney mantels, fine oak panelling and a collection of portraits of the Stuart royal family. The castle offers an additional 'attraction' in the form

of the ghost of a medieval lady. She is said to haunt the castle, screaming to be released from the room in which she was locked by her fiercely jealous husband. It was here that she starved to death while he was away in battle. More reliable (and less gruesome!) attractions at Sizergh are the well laid-out gardens and 1,500 acres of grounds which provide superb views over the Lakeland fells.

SEDBERGH

Sedbergh has been part of Cumbria since 1974, when it was brusquely removed from the West Riding of Yorkshire. However, it still lies within the Yorkshire Dales National Park – the surrounding scenery certainly belongs to the Dales, as the mighty **Howgill Fells**, great pear-shaped drumlins shaped by glaciers that soar to more than 2,200 feet (670 metres), attest. **Winder Hill**, which provides a dramatic backdrop to the little market town, is half that height, but with its sleek grassy flanks and domed top, seems much loftier. Four valleys and four mountain streams meet here. For centuries Sedbergh (pronounced Sedber) has been an important centre for cross-Pennine travellers. Long ago, the stage-coach would have been used frequently by the boys attending Sedbergh's famous **Public School**. Its founder was Roger Lupton, a Howgill boy who rose to become Provost of Eton: he established the school because he felt that one was desperately needed 'in the north country amongst the people rude in knowledge'. In later years Wordsworth's son studied here, and Coleridge's son, Hartley, became a master. The school's extensive grounds, through which visitors are welcome to wander, seem to place the old-world town within a park.

This impression is reinforced if you follow the path beside the River Rawthey to **Brigflatts**. Close to where George Fox stayed overnight with his friend Richard Robinson is the oldest **Quaker Meeting House** in the north of England. Built in 1675, and still with its original oak interior, this beautiful, simple building has changed little over the years (open daily, all year round).

This area is filled with Quaker history and **Firbank Knott**, on nearby Firbank Fell, can be said to be the birthplace of Quakerism: it was here, in 1652, that the visionary George Fox gave his great sermon to inspire a huge gathering from the whole of the north of England. This meeting was to lead to the development of the Quaker Movement. The simple boulder on the fell, from which Fox delivered his momentous words, is marked by a plaque and is now known as **Fox's Pulpit**.

Many of the town's older buildings have survived, in particular the stone-built cottages on both sides of the cobbled yard known as **The Folly**, just off Main Street, which have not only survived unscathed but remain dwellings rather than having been converted to other uses. Much of

the heart of Sedbergh has been deemed a Conservation Area.

To the east of town, on a small wooded hilltop, lies **Castlehaw**, the remains of an ancient motte-and-bailey castle. Built by the Normans in the 11th century, the castle guarded the valleys of the River Rawthey and the River Lune against the marauding Scots.

Also just outside town, on the A683 Garsdale road, is **Farfield Mill** Heritage and Arts Centre, where spinners, weavers, potters, woodcarvers and other craftspeople use traditional skills to produce high-quality goods, all of it for sale in the shop. Also on site are an arts and crafts gallery, a heritage display depicting the history of the mill, and a riverside restaurant. The mill is accessible to all visitors, with disabled facilities and a lift to all three levels.

AROUND SEDBERGH

DENT

4 miles SE of Sedbergh off the A684

This charming village (the only one in Cumbria's finest dale of Dentdale) gives visitors the feeling of being transported back in time with its delightful cobbled main street with tall rustic cottages lining the road. It is hard to believe this tranquil place was of greater importance than nearby Sedbergh in the 18th century. The impressive **St Andrew's Church** is Norman in origin, though it underwent almost complete renovation in the early 15th century. Inside can be seen a Jacobean three-decker pulpit that is

In 2006, Sedbergh was recognised as England's Book Town. The booktown movement, which started in Hay on Wye in Wales 40 years ago, is now an international phenomenon with towns, based on a love of books and trading in books, springing up from England and all over Europe to as far afield as Malaysia. Sedburgh's many different bookshops and other businesses based on writing, reading and publishing have been brought together, the main aim being to concentrate on selling hard-to-find second-hand books. Sedburgh now has a two-week Festival of Books and Drama that takes place in September each year, offering a mix of the latest book releases, original drama, famous authors and celebrates literary achievement by local people of all ages. Throughout the year the Book Town Literary Trust offers talks, courses and performances to help promote the love and use of language for everyone to enjoy.

13 STONE CLOSE TEA ROOMS AND BED & BREAKFAST

Dent

Stone Close offers delightful organic food and accommodation in stunning surroundings.

see page 142

still in use and also the local marble which paves the chancel.

Dent's most famous son is the 'Father of Geology', Adam Sedgwick. Born the son of the local vicar in 1785, Sedgwick went on to become the Woodwardian Professor of Geology at Cambridge University and also a friend of Queen Victoria and Prince Albert. The fountain of pinkish Shap granite in the village centre is Dent's memorial to the great geologist.

Farming has dominated the local economy for many years, though knitting, too, has played its part. During the 17th and 18th centuries the women, men and children on whom this work fell became known as the '**Terrible Knitters of Dent**', which may sound uncomplimentary but in fact, at that time, meant quite the opposite (like 'wicked' today!). They acquired this reputation not only because of the speed at which they knitted but also because of the curious method they employed of seeming to rock backwards and forwards as they worked. Large amounts of dressed wool were turned by the knitters into stockings and gloves which were then exported out of the dale to local towns.

Dent stone, with no iron pyrites likely to cause sparks, was popular for the millstones used in gunpowder works. The little valley of Dentdale winds from the village up past old farms and hamlets to **Lea Yeat** where a steep lane

hairpins up to Dent Station, almost 5 miles from the village. Dent is the highest railway station in Britain, over 1,100 feet above sea level, and it lies on the famous Settle-Carlisle railway line.

This is a marvellous place to begin a ramble into Dentdale or over the Whernside. In the shadow of Whernside itself, **Whernside Manor** is a famous house with associations with the slave trade. In the grounds of this 300 year old Grade II listed building, is accommodation in the form of a bunkhouse which sleeps up to 12 people and has a fully equipped kitchen.

GARSDALE

5 miles E of Sedbergh on the A683

Lying just north of Dentdale, Garsdale is both a dale and a village, both overlooked by the dramatic **Baugh Fell**. The River Clough follows down the dale from Garsdale Head, the watershed into Wensleydale where a row of Midland Railway cottages lies alongside the former junction station on the Settle-Carlisle line. This is now a surprisingly busy little place during the summer months when, from time to time, preserved steam locomotives pause to take water from a moorland spring. The pretty Garsdale Village hall, formerly the primary school, is regularly holding events and organized walks and interestingly can be used for overnight stay for walkers and visitors at prior arrangement.

Around Windermere and Ambleside

This southeastern corner of the extensive Lake District National Park, opened up to tourism as a result of the Victorians' growing interest in the natural world and their engineering ability in providing a railway service. Thus these villages, once little more than places where the fell farmers congregated to buy and sell their livestock and exchange gossip, grew into inland resorts with fine Victorian and Edwardian villas, houses and municipal buildings.

The region is Cumbria's best known and most popular area, with the main resort towns of Windermere, Bowness-on-Windermere and Ambleside – and, of course, Lake Windermere itself. The area is certainly busy with tourists during the summer months, but this does not in any way detract from its charm. Also, with the unpredictability of Lakeland weather, the region is well equipped with a host of indoor amusements to appeal to all ages.

For a retreat from the bustling and crowded towns there are many beautiful places close by which provide some peace and solitude. To the southeast lies Cartmel Fell, while further north is isolated Kentmere.

Lake Windermere at Dusk

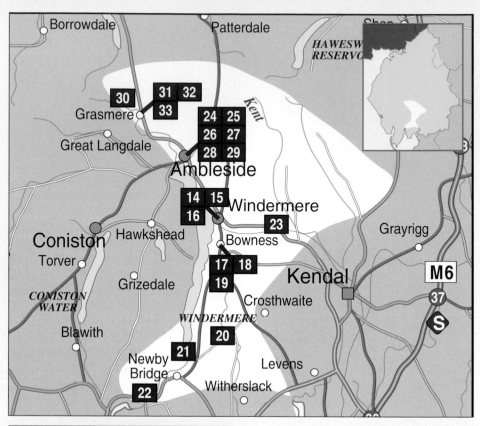

WINDERMERE

Windermere is a lovely tourist town, centred on a compact shopping area with art galleries and cafés alongside traditional shops such as butchers, bakers and a well-stocked ironmongery store.

The town began life as the village of **Birthwaite**, this change of name is due to the Kendal and Windermere Railway Company which built a branch line to it in 1847. With an eye on tourist traffic, and considering the name Birthwaite had little appeal, they named the station 'Windermere' despite the lake being over a mile away from the actual settlement. In the early days carriages and, in later years, buses linked the station with the landing stages in the village of Bowness on the shores of the lake. As the village burgeoned into a prosperous Victorian resort, it became popularly, and then officially, known by the name of its station, while Windermere Water was given the redundant prefix of Lake.

The town's Victorian heritage is still predominant here in the many large houses, originally built as country retreats for Manchester businessmen – the railway made it possible for them to reach this idyllic countryside in just over two hours. Hotels, boarding houses, comfortable villas and shops sprang up around the station and spread rapidly down the hill towards the lake until Birthwaite and Bowness were linked together.

Windermere's railway is still operating, albeit now as a single track branch line. Diesel railcars run along the **Lakes Line**, providing a busy shuttle service to and from the main line at Oxenholme. The route, through Kendal, Burneside and Staveley, is a delight and provides a very pleasant alternative to the often-crowded A591. The Lakes Line is now the only surviving Railtrack line to run into the heart of the Lake District.

Within a few yards of Windermere Station, just across the busy main road, is a footpath that leads through the woods to one of the finest viewpoints in Lakeland, **Orrest Head**. This spectacular vantage point provides a 360-degree panoramic view that takes in the ten-mile length of Windermere, the Cumbrian hills and even the fells of the Yorkshire Pennines. There is a plaque of remembrance for the well known author and walker Alfred Wainwright here. He was greatly inspired when he walked to the summit of Orrest

14 THE LAKES HOTEL

Windermere

The Lakes House is a comfortable, well-equipped B&B and is also the headquarters of Lakes Supertours.

 see page 143

15 WINSTER HOUSE

Windermere

Three luxury self catering apartments with charming gardens and quality kitchen and bathroom facilities set just a short walk from Lake Windermere.

see page 143

Cumbrian Mountains across Lake Windermere

16 WICKED WINDERMERE

Windermere

Local, Traditional, Cumbrian food, which has been transformed in to mouth-watering works of art.

🍴 see page 144

17 BLENHEIM LODGE

Bowness-on-Windemere

With stunning lake and mountain views Blenheim Lodge, nestled in the heart of the Lake District, provides the ideal getaway.

🛏 see page 145

head in 1930 ("those few hours at Orrest Head cast a spell that changed my life"), and today as then this remains exceptional, even in a region where glorious views open up at every turn.

In Victorian times, visitors wandered through such ravishing scenery carrying, not cameras, but small, tinted mirrors mounted in elaborate frames known as **Claude Glasses,** after the painter Claude Lorraine's romantic landscapes. They would place themselves with their back to the view, hold the mirrors above them and so observe the view framed, as in a painting.

AROUND WINDERMERE

BOWNESS-ON-WINDERMERE

2 miles S of Windermere on the A592

Although the towns of Windermere and Bowness-on-Windermere have grown together, they both retain distinguishable town centres and are quite different in atmosphere. Bowness is a seasonally busy lakeside town, where a whole range of water-activities, such as sailing, canoeing, kayaking, rowing, windsurfing, and even wakeboarding and wakesurfing, can be enjoyed as well as the cosmopolitan mix of shops, restaurants and affordable accommodation.

It is from this attractive town that most of the lake cruises operate. Lasting between 45 and 90 minutes, the cruises operate daily. There are evening food and

champagne cruises during the summer months, and rowing boats and self-drive motor boats are also available for hire all year round. These provide connections to several attractions and idyllic spots. For example the **Visitor Centre** at Brockhole, **Lakeside & Haverthwaite Steam Railway** where you can travel along the river Leven on authentic steam trains to other locations in the area, **The Lakes Aquarium**, and the **Fell Foot Country Park**, with Victorian lawns and views of the lake.

Windermere boasts not just being the largest lake in Cumbria but also, at 11 miles long, the largest in England. Formed in the Ice Age by the action of moving glaciers, the lake is fed by the Rivers Brathay and Rothay at the northern end, while the outlet is into the River Leven, at Newby Bridge. Technically a public waterway, Windermere with its thickly wooded banks and scattered islands has been used since Roman times as a means of transporting stone to their fort at *Galava*, near present-day Ambleside at the head of the lake.

Across from Bowness, the lake is almost divided in two by **Belle Island,** Windermere's largest island. It is home to the Belle Isle Round House, visible from the shore of Bowness, yet mostly cloaked by a thick layer of trees. In the midst of this open and glassy lake bustling with activity, the round house remains a still and mysterious monument,.; with the house and its 40 acres of land privately owned and not open to the public. It was built in 1774 by John Plaw to the instructions of the island owner, Mr. English, a yachting enthusiast who named the island after his wife Isabella.

Fishermen find great enjoyment practicing their skills on this well-stocked lake. Once considered a great delicacy in the 17th and 18th centuries, the char, a deep-water trout, is still found here – though catching it is a special art.

Away from the marinas and car parks is the old village where **St Martin's Church** is of particular interest. It has a magnificent east window filled with 14th and 15th century glass, and an unusual 300-year-old carved wooden figure of St Martin depicted sharing his cloak with a beggar. There has been a church here from as early as 1203 and, although it was burnt down in 1480, the octagonal sandstone font survived and

View down Lake Windermere

remains in the present church as a stunning relic.

On the lake shore just to the north of the village is the Old Laundry Visitor Centre, the home of **The World of Beatrix Potter**, established in 1991 it is one of the most popular visitor attractions in the country. Here visitors can enjoy fascinating re-creations of the Lakeland author's books, complete with the sounds, sights and even the smells of the countryside. A delightful new addition is the organic Peter Rabbit garden, which allows you to walk right into Beatrix Potter's enchanting stories, with gooseberry bushes, fruit trees and of course rows of lettuce and carrots. This garden also has a weather station, bumble bee & ladybird homes, and puzzles so young ones can learn while they enjoy roaming through the paths and trails. The centre also hosts fun events in the spirit of Beatrix Potter; the afternoon tea with Peter

18 ST MARTIN'S COFFEE HOUSE

Bowness-on-Windermere

Popular family run town centre coffee shop serving delicious home-made meals and snacks.

see page 145

The World of Beatrix Potter

19

19 ROYAL OAK INN

Bowness-on-Windemere

A friendly, family run country Inn serving fine home cooked food with gorgeous guest accommodation just a stone's throw from Lake Windermere.

🍴 🛏 *see page 146*

Rabbit is a firm favourite (and is essential to book in advance), and other events such as the fluffy Halloween, where ghouls and witches are replaced by heaps of fluffy bunting and pumpkins with smiley faces (much more appropriate for young children than the normal creepy fare) are regularly being held. Open all year, the complex also includes the Tailor of Gloucester Tea Room (children's menu and colouring sheets available) and the Beatrix Potter shop.

About a mile and a half south of Bowness, just off the A5074 on the B5360, **Blackwell** is a treasure trove of the Arts and Crafts Movement. Completed in 1900, it is the largest and most important surviving masterpiece of the

architect MH Baillie Scott (1865-1945). Inspired by Lakeland flora and fauna, he designed every last detail of this outstanding house, creating a symphony of Art Nouveau stained glass, oak panelling, intricate plasterwork and fanciful metalwork. The aim of the £3.5 million rejuvenation done in 1998 on this site was not to create a static museum, but to bring back to life a very special house that was designed as a place to be enjoyed. For this reason, Blackwell has become a blossoming and exciting exhibition to visit, and its position and beautiful views of Windermere and the Coniston fells (especially lovely seen from the restore garden terraces) will leave you feeling content and in awe.

WINSTER

4 miles S of Windermere on the A5074

This charming hamlet has an old post office, originally built in the early 17th century as a cottage, which is much photographed. South from the village runs the Winster Valley, which provided Wordsworth with one of his favourite walks. It was at **Low Ludderburn**, a couple of miles to the south that Arthur Ransome settled in 1925 and here that he wrote his classic children's novel *Swallows and Amazons*. The house is still there, but is not open to the public.

While living here, Ransome discovered the peaceful St Paul's churchyard at **Rusland** and decided that was where he wanted to be

Blackwell House, Bowness-on-Windermere

buried. When he passed away in 1967, he was duly buried here, to be joined later by his second wife Eugenia.

NEWBY BRIDGE

8 miles S of Windermere on the A592

The bridge here crosses the River Leven which runs from the southern tip of Windermere to Morecambe Bay. According to geologists, the mass of end moraines seen here show clearly that the village lay at the southernmost point of Windermere, since they were deposited by the glacier while it paused, having carved out the lake. Today, however, the village is some distance from the water's edge, which can be reached on foot, by car or by taking the steam train on the Lakeside & Haverthwaite Railway.

One mile north of the village, **Fell Foot Country Park** (National Trust) is a delightful 18-acre site of landscaped gardens and woodland laid out in late-Victorian times. Admission is free (although there's a car parking charge), and the grounds include picnic areas, a children's adventure playground, a splendid rhododendron garden, a gift shop and a tea room with outside tables where you can watch the lake traffic and also the steam trains chugging into Lakeside on the western bank. Rowing boats can be hired at the piers from which there are regular ferries across to Lakeside, and pleasure cruises operate during the summer school holidays.

WITHERSLACK

9 miles S of Windermere off the A590

On the edge of the village is the **Latterbarrow Reserve** of the Cumbrian Wildlife Trust, a relatively small reserve that is home to some 200 species of flowering plants and ferns. Butterflies and birds, including the spotted flycatcher, are a common sight among the plants that grow in the thin soil between the rocky outcrops. Further from the village is **Witherslack Hall**, once the summer residence of the Earls of Derby, now a school.

BACKBARROW

9 miles S of Windermere on the A592

This small village in the valley of the River Leven, which drains Windermere, was a hive of industry at one time. In 1711, the most ambitious iron furnace in Cumbria was built here, its remains can still be seen, along with the relics of the heyday of water power in the village.

LAKESIDE

10 miles S of Windermere off the A590

Located at the southwestern tip of Windermere, Lakeside sits beneath gentle wooded hills. It's the northern terminus of the **Lakeside & Haverthwaite Railway**, a 4-mile route through the beautiful Leven Valley which was once part of a line stretching to Ulverston and Barrow-in-Furness. Throughout the season, hard-working steam locomotives chug along the track, their departure times set to coincide with boat arrivals from

20 THE HARE & HOUNDS

Bowland Bridge, nr Grange-over-Sands

This is a lovely inn offering wonderful food and drink in a beautiful location.

see page 147

The Lakes Aquarium, Lakeside

21 STOTT PARK BOBBIN MILL

Lakeside

Guided tours are offered at this working historic mill.

🏛 see page 146

22 THE ANGLERS ARMS

Haverthwaite

Ten real ales and great food brings visitors from near and far to the Anglers Arms.

see page 148

swimming right over your head – just like really being beneath the lake! It is open from 9am all year round.

A mile or so north of Lakeside, **Stott Park Bobbin Mill** (English Heritage) is a must for anyone interested in the area's industrial heritage. One of the best preserved in the country, it's a genuine working 19th-century mill and stands in a lovely woodland setting at the southern end of the Lake. Visitors can join the inclusive 30-minute tour (run on the hour and at half past), watch wooden bobbins being made as they were 200 years ago, and browse over the informative exhibition.

Bowness – a joint boat and train return ticket is available.

Nearby lays **The Lakes Aquarium,** which can be travelled to by road, steam train or boat (take your pick!) and for the latter two special all inclusive tickets can be arranged. Britain's only freshwater aquarium, it shows amazing exhibits of aquatic creatures:.; from exotic eyeless fish from the caves of Mexico to the adorable Asian otters Mia and Smudge. Most endearing about this Aquarium however comes from slightly closer to home; the animals of Morcambe Bay Leven Estuary and the rest of the Lake District, such as brown trout, pike and lobsters (and some un-nautical harvest mice & pole cats) are on display here, showing the abundance of wildlife from this area not usually seen. Another interesting feature is the aquariums re-created journey underneath Lake Windermere, where you can see diving ducks, carp and perch

HAVERTHWAITE

12 miles S of Windermere on the A590

Haverthwaite is the southern terminus of the **Lakeside & Haverthwaite Railway**, a branch of the Furness railway originally built to transport passengers and goods to the steamers on Lake Windermere. It was one of the first attempts at mass tourism in the Lake District. Passenger numbers peaked in the 1920s, but the general decline of rail travel in the 1960s led to the railway's closure in 1967. However, a group of dedicated rail enthusiasts rescued this scenic stretch, restored its engines and rolling stock to working order. The station now provides a full service of steam trains throughout the season; a useful and picturesque connection between the towns of this area (and the landing place for boat trips on Lake Windermere)

Lakeside & Haverthwaite Railway

23 WILF'S CAFE

Staveley, nr Kendal

Wilf's offer fantastic food to eat in or take away, as well as a great eating experience.

see page 149

and many attractions, for which all-inclusive tickets can be purchased.

INGS

3 miles E of Windermere off the A591

A pleasant little village set alongside the River Gowan, Ings owes its fine Georgian church and charming almshouses to a certain Robert Bateman, who was born here in the late 1600s. Wordsworth commemorated Bateman in a poem that recounts how the villagers made a collection so that the young boy could travel to London. He prospered greatly, became a major ship owner and devoted a sizeable portion of his wealth to the benefit of his native village. Sadly, he never saw the completed church: less than a year after building began, he was murdered by pirates.

TROUTBECK BRIDGE

1 mile NE of Windermere on the A591

This small village in the valley of Trout Beck takes its name from the bridge here over the Beck, just before the water runs into Windermere. During the 17th century, **Calgarth Hall** was owned by Myles Phillipson, a local Justice of the Peace who wished to gain possession of nearby farmland. He duly invited the landowner and his wife to a banquet at the Hall and then, having hidden a silver cup in their luggage, accused them of stealing.

At the resulting trial, Phillipson, who was the presiding judge, sentenced the couple to death as well as appropriating their land. As she was led away, the wife placed a curse on the judge, saying that not only would his victims never leave him but that his family would also perish in poverty. The couple were executed, but their skulls reappeared at Calgarth Hall and, no matter what Phillipson did (including burning them and throwing them into Lake Windermere) the skulls kept

Townend Farm, Troutbeck

However, perhaps the best-known building at Troutbeck is **Townend** (National Trust), another enchanting example of Lake District vernacular architecture. Built in 1626, the stone-and-slate house contains some fine carved woodwork, books, furniture and domestic implements collected by the Browne family, wealthy farmers who lived here for more than 300 years until 1944.

Of interest to gardeners is the **Holehird Gardens,** a demonstration garden managed by the Lakeland Horticultural Society. It lies in the grounds of the Holehird estate, the building of which is leased as a nursing home, and so is not open to the public. The five acres of gardens, however are, and demonstrate an amazing array of plants which flourish in this area; there is an herbaceous walled garden in addition to alpine and heather beds and collections of rhododendrons, azaleas, astilbes, polystichum ferns and hydrangeas.

returning to the Hall. Moreover, the Phillipson family grew poorer and poorer. Finally, in 1705, the family died out altogether.

TROUTBECK

3 miles NE of Windermere off the A592

Designated a conservation area, Troutbeck has no recognisable centre, as the houses and cottages are grouped around a number of wells and springs which, until recently, were the only form of water supply. Dating from the 16th, 17th and 18th centuries, the houses retain many of their original features, including mullioned windows, heavy cylindrical chimneys and, in some cases, exposed spinning galleries, and are of great interest to lovers of vernacular architecture. **Troutbeck Church**, too, is worthy of a visit as there is a fine east window, dating from 1873, that is the combined work of Edward Burne-Jones, Ford Maddox Brown and William Morris.

KENTMERE

8 miles NE of Windermere off the A591

This hamlet, as its name implies, lies in part of the valley that was once a lake, later drained to provide precious bottom pasture land. A large mill pond remains to provide a head of water on the River Kent for use at a paper mill.

The beautiful valley of the River Kent is best explored on foot. A public footpath runs up its western side, past Kentmere Hall (now a privately owned farmhouse).

Following the river southwards, the **Dales Way** runs down into Kendal and on into the Yorkshire Dales.

BROCKHOLE

3 miles NW of Windermere off the A591

The **Lake District Visitor Centre** at Brockhole is a vibrant centre with much to do; 30 acres of beautiful gardens, two floors of interactive exhibitions covering the Lake District of the present and of the past, and what can be done to conserve this most beautiful slice of England. For families there are organized "adventure out" activities, covering everything from archery, to painting or walking & map reading, and there are festive events held regularly. The visitors centre is easily reached by road as well as by water.

Lake cruises depart from the jetty here for 45-minute circular trips – groups of 20 or more can organise their own private boat.

Within the beautifully landscaped grounds at Brockhole visitors can join an organised walk accompanied by one of the gardening team, while their children can enjoy the well-equipped adventure playground. There are also lakeside picnic areas. Brockhole itself is a fine Victorian mansion, originally built for a Manchester silk merchant. Here visitors can watch an audio-visual presentation about the area, browse in the gift shop (which stocks an excellent range of books, guides and maps), or take a break in the comfortable café which has an outdoor terrace overlooking the lake. Home baking to traditional Cumbrian recipes is the speciality, and many dishes feature local produce. There is good wheelchair access to all parts of the Visitor Centre and most of the grounds.

AMBLESIDE

5 miles NW of Windermere on the A591

Standing less than a mile from the head of Lake Windermere, Ambleside is one of the busiest of the Lakeland towns, a popular centre for walkers and tourers, with glorious walks and drives radiating from the town in all directions. Ambleside offers a huge choice of pubs, restaurants, cafés, hotels and guest houses, as well as art galleries, two 2-screen cinemas and a mix of traditional family-run shops supplemented by a modern range of retailers in the **Market Cross Centre**. Because of its many shops specialising in outdoor clothing, the town has been described as 'the anorak capital of the world'. It would certainly be hard to find a wider selection anywhere of climbing, camping and walking gear.

Lucy's of Ambleside is a quirky mixture of delicatessen, café, wine bar, restaurant, and also has a mail order catalogue, runs cookery schools and provides outside catering - quite typical of the interesting and individual shops and restaurants in Ambleside. The mail order menu includes rather special gift baskets; such as the "champagne breakfast" which carries champagne, delicious chocolates, everything you need for

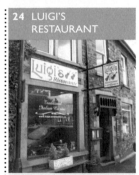

24 LUIGI'S RESTAURANT

Ambleside

Long-established and popular town centre restaurant serving authentic Italian cuisine and wines.

🍴 see page 150

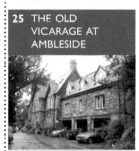

25 THE OLD VICARAGE AT AMBLESIDE

Ambleside

This charming detached Victorian House, set in its own wooded gardens, is an oasis in the heart of the village.

🛏 see page 151

26 STAMPERS RESTAURANT

Ambleside

Simply *the* place to dine in Cumbria – innovative and truly delicious menu served in an intimate and historic setting with plenty of character.

🍴 see page 152

27 THE GIGGLING GOOSE CAFÉ AT THE OLD MILL

Ambleside

Good food served with a hospitable and friendly service set in the charming community of Ambleside.

🍴 see page 153

a luxury breakfast (including the juice!), and balloon & personalised card.

Many of Ambleside's buildings are constructed in the distinctive grey-green stone of the area that blends in well with the green of the fields and fells all around. The centre of the town is a conservation area; its most picturesque building perhaps being **The Bridge House**, a tiny cottage perched surreally on a packhorse bridge across Stock Ghyll. Today it's a National Trust shop and information centre, but during the 1850s it was the home of Mr and Mrs Rigg and their six children (so built to escape land tax). The main room of this one-up, one-down residence measures just 13 feet by 6 feet, so living chez Rigg must have been quite cosy!

The **Armitt Museum** and Library is dedicated to the area's history, it has changing exhibitions,

Bridge House, Ambleside

and interactive displays on 2000 years of local past. Everything is covered from the Roman's, to the areas most famous literary luminaries, John Ruskin and Beatrix Potter. Among the highlights are Beatrix Potter's early watercolours – over 450 exquisite studies of fungi and mosses, which are presently available to adopt, with your name recorded in a register alongside, in aid of the museums funding. Also on display are a fascinating collection of photographs by Herbert Bell, an Ambleside chemist who became an accomplished photographer. The shop has a selection of Cumbria-made merchandise and their own specially made gifts. It is open 7 days a week, except at Christmas.

The popular panoramic view of Ambleside, looking north from the path up **Loughrigg Fell**, reveals the town cradled within the apron of the massive Fairfield Horseshoe, which rises to nearly 3,000 feet. Within the townscape itself, the most impressive feature is the window-adorned, rocket-like spire, 180 feet high, of **St Mary's Church**. The church was completed in 1854 to a design by Sir George Gilbert Scott, the architect of London's St Pancras Station and the Albert Memorial. Inside the church is a chapel devoted to the memory of William Wordsworth, and an interesting 1940s mural depicting the ancient ceremony of rush-bearing. This ceremony dates back to the days when the floor of the church was covered by rushes, and is still

Loughrigg Tarn, nr Ambleside

Every July, the famous Ambleside Sports take place, an event distinguished by the variety of local traditional sports it features. The Sports include Cumberland and Westmorland wrestling (a little like Sumo wrestling but without the rolls of fat), fell-racing and hound-trailing, as well as various events for youths and seniors.

28 STAGSHAW GARDEN

Ambleside

A steep woodland garden noted for its flowering shrubs.

🏛 *see page 154*

29 QUAYSIDERS CLUB LIMITED

Waterhead

Self catering apartments in beautiful surroundings, right next to Lake Windermere

🛏 *see page 154*

enacted on the first Saturday in July. Some 400 children process through the town bearing colourful decorated rushes and singing the specially-commissioned Ambleside Rushbearer's Hymn.

Another experience not to be missed while at Ambleside is a boat cruise on Lake Windermere to Bowness. There are daily departures from the pier at **Waterhead**, about a mile south of the town. At Bowness there are connections to other lakeland attractions and, during the summer months, evening wine cruises. Rowing boats and self-drive motor boats can also be hired. Just to the west of the pier is **Borrans Park**, a pleasant lakeside park with plenty of picnic spots, and to the west of the park, the site of Galava Roman Fort. There is little to be seen of the fort, but the setting is

enchanting. Also well worth a visit is nearby **Stagshaw Gardens** (National Trust), a spring woodland garden which contains a fine collection of shrubs, including some impressive rhododendrons, azaleas and camellias. Parking is very limited and vehicular access is hazardous, so it's best to park at Waterhead car park and walk. The gardens are open all week 1st April-30th June (July to end of October can be visited by prior arrangement).

Perhaps the most unusual visitor attraction in Ambleside is the **Homes of Football**, described by the *Sunday Times* as a national treasure. It began as a travelling exhibition of football photographs and memorabilia, but now has a permanent home in Lake Road. Photographer Stuart Clarke recorded games and grounds at every kind of venue from the

27

Kirkstone Pass, nr Ambleside

30 LANCRIGG COUNTRY HOUSE HOTEL & THE GREEN VALLEY RESTAURANT

Grasmere

Haven of tranquillity and vegetarian food in 30 beautiful acres of gardens and woodland.

see page 155

Premier League down to amateur village teams. There are now 60,000 photographs on file and a massive selection on show, framed and for sale.

From Ambleside town centre, a steep road climbs sharply up to the dramatic **Kirkstone Pass** and over to Ullswater. Rising to some 1,489 feet above sea level, the road is the highest in the Lake District and, though today's vehicles make light work of the climb, for centuries the Pass presented a formidable obstacle (once known by the unambiguous title of "The Struggle").

RYDAL

7 miles NW of Windermere on the A591

In 1813, following the deaths of their young children Catherine and Thomas, William and Mary Wordsworth were too grief-stricken to stay on at the Old Rectory in Grasmere. They moved a couple of miles down the road to **Rydal Mount**, a handsome house overlooking tiny **Rydal Water**. By now, the poet was well established and comparatively prosperous. A salaried position as Westmorland's Distributor of Stamps (a tax official) supplemented his earnings from poetry. Although Wordsworth only ever rented the house, it is now owned by his descendants and has been open to the public since 1970. The interior has seen little change, retaining a lived-in atmosphere. It contains first editions of the poet's work and many personal possessions, among them the only surviving portrait of his beloved sister, Dorothy.

William Wordsworth was a keen gardener, and the 4-acre garden at Rydal Mount remains very much as he designed it.

GRASMERE

9 miles NW of Windermere on the A591

In 1799, Wordsworth described Grasmere as *"the loveliest spot that man hath ever found"*. Certainly Grasmere enjoys one of the finest settings in all Lakeland, its small lake nestling in a natural scenic amphitheatre beside the compact, rough-stone village.

For lovers of Wordsworth's

poetry, Grasmere is the pre-eminent place of pilgrimage. They come to visit **Dove Cottage** where Wordsworth lived in dire poverty from 1799 to 1808, obliged to line the walls with newspaper for warmth. The great poet shared this very basic accommodation with his wife Mary, his sister Dorothy, his sister-in-law Alice and, as almost permanent guests, Coleridge and De Quincey. (Sir Walter Scott also stayed, though he often sneaked off to the Swan Hotel for a dram, since the Wordsworths were virtually teetotal.) Located on the outskirts of the village, Dove Cottage has been preserved intact: next door is an award-winning museum dedicated to Wordsworth's life and works. Dove Cottage, Rydal Mount (another of the poet's homes near Grasmere), and his birthplace, Wordsworth House at Cockermouth, are all owned by the **Wordsworth Trust**.

In 1808 Wordsworth moved to **The Rectory** (private) opposite St Oswald's Church. In his long poem *The Excursion*, he describes the house and its lovely garden beside the River Rothay. The church, too, is remembered in the same poem:

Not raised in nice proportions
was the pile
But large and massy, for duration built,
With pillars crowded and the roof upheld
By naked rafters intricately crossed,
Like leafless underboughs in some
thick wood.

In 1850 the Poet Laureate was buried beneath yew trees he himself had planted in **St Oswald's** churchyard. He was joined there by his sister Dorothy in 1885, and his wife Mary in 1889. In Grasmere town cemetery is the grave of **William Archibald Spooner**, sometime Warden of New College, Oxford. He gave his name to Spoonerisms, in which the initial letters of two words are transposed, with amusing results. Here are a few of his gems, some genuine, others perhaps apocryphal, such as "*You have hissed all my mystery lessons*" and "*Yes indeed: the Lord is a shoving leopard.*" Spooner spent many holidays in Grasmere with his wife at her house, How Foot.

Like Ambleside, Grasmere is famous for its **Sports**, first recorded in 1852, which still take place in late August. The most celebrated event in the Lake District, they attract some 10,000 visitors and feature many pursuits unique to Cumbria, such as Cumberland and Westmorland wrestling as well as the more straightforward, if arduous, fell-running.

Collectors of curiosities who happen to be travelling north on the A591 from Grasmere should look out for the vintage black-and-yellow AA telephone box on the right-hand side of the road. Still functioning, **Box 487** has been accorded Grade II listed building status by the Department of the Environment.

31 DALE LODGE HOTEL

Grasmere

This luxurious hotel invites guests to truly unwind and indulge in some of the finest scenery, food and drink in the Lake District.

🛏 🍴 see page 156

32 GREEN'S CAFÉ AND BISTRO

Grasmere

All kinds of diets can be catered for in this charming café and bistro

🍴 see page 157

33 OAK BANK HOTEL

Grasmere

Grand Victorian Lakeland House in the heart of Grasmere, with amazing accommodation and delicious seasonal menus.

🛏 🍴 see page 158

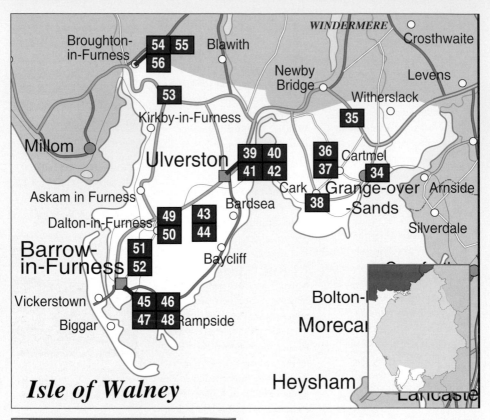

The Cartmel and Furness Peninsulas

This area on the southernmost coast of Cumbria, with its gentle moorland, craggy headlands, scattered woodlands and vast expanses of sand, is sadly sometimes overlooked by visitors rushing to more central locations in the lakes. This is a pity because of all it has to offer, and its stunning location between the lakes and mountains of the Lake District and the sandy estuaries of Morecambe Bay.

The buildings and fabric of the landscape was heavily influenced by Cistercian monks, for whom this was once a stronghold, several monasteries still remain. Two in particular are well worth visiting today: Cartmel Priory and Furness Abbey.

Before the great boom of the local iron-ore mining industry, the peninsular villages and market towns relied on farming and fishing and, before some of the river estuaries silted up, there was also some import and export trade.

The arrival of the railways in the mid-19th century saw the development of genteel resorts such as Grange-over-Sands overlooking the treacherous sands of Morecambe Bay. Grange is still an elegant little town and has been spared the indignity of vast amusement parks and rows of slot machines, retaining its character as a quiet and pleasant holiday centre.

Furness Abbey

The route to Grange, across the sands of Morecambe Bay, is a treacherous one, though it was used not only by the Romans but also by the monks of Furness Abbey and, later, even by stage coaches looking to shorten their journey time. Avoiding the quicksands of the bay, which have taken many lives over the centuries, is a difficult task. Back in the 16th century, the Duchy of Lancaster appointed an official guide to escort travellers over the shifting sands, and also provided him with a house at Grange. The town still has an official guide who takes groups on a three-hour walk across the bay. The sands are extremely dangerous since 'the tide comes in with the merciless speed of a galloping horse' – a crossing should never be attempted without the help of a qualified guide.

GRANGE-OVER-SANDS

Grange, as its known locally, is an attractive little town set in a natural sun-trap on the north shore of Morecambe Bay. Much of its Victorian charm can be credited to the **Furness Railway Company** which developed the town after building the Lancaster-to-Whitehaven line in 1857. At that time, the whole of the Cartmel and Furness Peninsulas were part of Lancashire, a detached area whose main link with the rest of the county was the dubious route across Morecambe Sands. The railway provided a safe alternative to this hazardous journey. At Grange the company built an elegant mile-long promenade (now traffic free) and set out the colourful ornamental gardens. Prosperous merchants built grand country homes here, and it wasn't long before local residents began referring to their town as 'the Torquay of the North'.

Though Grange doesn't have a beach to rival that of its neighbour across Morecambe Bay, it does enjoy an exceptionally mild climate, the mildest in the northwest, thanks to the Gulf Stream. It is still a popular place, particularly with people who are looking for a pleasant and quiet place to retire. It was a favourite with Beatrix Potter, who recorded that on one visit to the town she met a 'friendly porker', a meeting that inspired *The Tale of Pigling Bland*. There's no connection, of course, but today the town boasts a butcher's shop, Higginsons, which has been voted the Best Butcher's Shop in England. The traffic-free **promenade** at Grange, runs alongside lovely ornamental gardens and provides a host of activities such as a children's playground, bowls & putting, also a café. The promenade is wheel-chair friendly.

The **Park Road Gardens** in Grange offer a tranquil environment of well-maintained manicured lawns and ornamental gardens, perfect for sitting and absorbing the atmosphere of the town. They recently celebrated the 80th anniversary of the gardens, at which 430 people flocked to hear a concert including the world famous "Besses o' th' Barn" brass band.

Another location in Grange to see beautiful gardens is at **Yewbarrow House**. Tired of their overgrown garden that obscured spectacular views over the bay, the owners undertook the massive task of changing it into an Eden-like four and a half acres terraced into the hillside, which invites you to take leave of your senses. Surrounded by woodland the gardens here include a Victorian kitchen garden, Italian terrace, Japanese garden with moon terrace and "hot spring pool" (actually a heated swimming pool), and trial beds where they are experimenting with Dahlias, creating varieties completely unique to these gardens. Two pre-Raphaelite stained glass windows, rescued from a church in

Yorkshire, and an arch planted with sempervivums made from stone reclaimed from the now demolished ancient Meathop Bridge, are among the beautiful features to be seen here. The gardens are available for public viewing on open days held the first Sunday of the month between June and September.

Away from the hotels, shops and cafés of the town, there are some lovely walks, and none is more pleasant than the path behind Grange which climbs through magnificent limestone woodlands rich in wildflowers. The path finally leads to the 727 feet **Hampsfell Summit** and **The Hospice**, a little stone tower from which there are unforgettable views over the bay and, in the opposite direction, the craggy peaks of the Lake District. The Hospice was provided by Grange's Vicar, the Reverend Thomas Remington, in 1834 to provide a refuge for travellers who found themselves stranded on the fell overnight. An external flight of stairs leads to a flat roof and, as the Vicar observed in a poem attached to the wall:

The flight of steps requireth care,
The roof will show a prospect rare.

AROUND GRANGE-OVER-SANDS

LINDALE

2 miles NE of Grange-over-Sands off the A590

This small village was the birthplace of a man who defied the scepticism of his contemporaries

and built the first successful iron ship. 'Iron Mad' John Wilkinson also built the first cast-iron barges, and later created the castings for the famous Iron Bridge at Coalbrookdale. After his death in 1808 he was buried in an iron coffin (naturally) in an unmarked grave, and the lofty **Wilkinson Obelisk** to his memory that stands near the village crossroads is also cast in iron. The admirers who erected it, however, omitted to provide the iron column with a lightning conductor. A few years later it was struck to the ground by a lightning bolt. The obelisk lay neglected in shrubbery for some years, but has now been restored and towers above the village once again. Just outside Lindale, at **Castle Head**, is the imposing house that Wilkinson built by the River Winster.

CARTMEL

2 miles W of Grange-over-Sands off the B5278

One of the prettiest villages in the Peninsula, Cartmel is a delightful cluster of houses and cottages set around a square from which lead winding streets and arches into back yards. This square and its surrounding winding streets holds some lovely village shops and public houses. This village is home to the famously delicious **Cartmel sticky toffee pudding,** and Cartmel village shop (its flag-ship store) is still located here in the heart of the village as ever it was. In addition to this sugary treat, they sell an exquisite range of locally sourced savory chutneys and

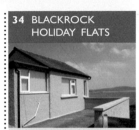

34 BLACKROCK HOLIDAY FLATS

Grange-over-Sands

Overlooking the fabulous Morecambe bay, Blackrock offers extremely cosy and comfortable accommodation comprising of two flats and one cottage.

see page 159

35 CROWN INN

Newton-in-Cartmel

This inn provides warm and comfortable accommodation, great food and a wonderful atmosphere.

see page 159

36 THE CAVENDISH ARMS AT CARTMEL

Cartmel

Charming retreat offering excellent British food, real ales and quality en suite accommodation.

 see page 160

37 THE ROYAL OAK INN

Cartmel

This old fashioned village inn offers excellent cuisine, fine ales, quality accommodation and an unbeatable welcome.

 see page 161

preserves, fresh baked bread, fine cheeses and ales from local breweries. A paradise for food fanatics, this shop was even included on the BBC's recent "Great British menu" program, which showcases the best of regional food in the country.

Cartmel Priory, founded by Augustinian canons, has been a focus for Christian worship for 800 years. A unique feature of the priory is its square belfry tower, constructed diagonally across the original lantern tower. Inside this ancient building is a hive of activity, holding regular music and choir concerts, and various events throughout the year. It is easy to see why the Cartmel Priory, described as 'the most beautiful church in the northwest', attracts around 60,000 pilgrims and visitors every year.

Cartmel is also famous for its attractive **Racecourse**, set beside the River Eea, on which National Hunt meetings are held in May, July and August. Located close to the village, the course must be one of the most picturesque in the country; it is certainly one of the smallest.

FLOOKBURGH

3 miles SW of Grange-over-Sands on the B5277

An ancient Charter Borough, Flookburgh is still the principal fishing village on Morecambe Bay. Roads from the square lead down to the shore where fishermen still land their catches of cockle, shrimps and (less often nowadays) flukes, the tasty small flat fish from which the village takes its name. The **Lakeland Miniature Village** contains over 100 houses, farms and barns made of local Coniston slate which are accurate down to the last detail. There is also an oriental garden which is overlooked by their gift shop. The village is open 10:30am – 6pm in the summer months, and until dusk in the winter.

Cartmel Priory Church

Ducky's Farm Park provides a fun day out for all the family with a variety of animals to see and stroke, such as lambs, goats, ducks, and the newly introduced capybara, raccoon and fallow deer. And of course there is the big bright yellow "Ducky" around for the children to meet. Another new addition is the indoor play area, which provides much for the children to do while those a little older can relax at the café/bar; there is also a safe completely soft play environment for toddlers.

For the dare-devils among you, Flookburgh is home to **Skydiving North West,** where you can skydive from a white-knuckle, adrenaline-rushing 14,500 feet (there is an option to be attached to a professional for beginners). I cannot think of a better way to capture the views of Cumbria!

CARK-IN-CARTMEL

3 miles SW of Grange-over-Sands on the B5278

Cumbria's premier stately home, **Holker Hall** is one of many belonging to the Cavendish family, the Dukes of Devonshire. An intriguing blend of 16th-century Georgian and Victorian architecture, a visitor-friendly place with no restraining ropes keeping visitors at a distance, a fire burning in the hearth and a lived-in, family atmosphere. There's an impressive cantilevered staircase, a library with some 3,500 leather-bound books (plus a few dummy covers designed to hide electricity sockets) and an embroidered panel said to be the work of Mary, Queen of Scots.

There is a food hall which sells the very best of seasonal local produce, including the delicious saltmarsh lamb, ewes milk cheeses, venison and beef all produced right there on the Holker estate. The food hall has started establishing a monthly producers market through the summer months at Holker Hall, showing off their broad range of regional produce.

Each year, Holker's 25 acres of award-winning gardens host the **Holker Garden Festival** which has been hailed as the 'Chelsea of the North'. The gardens are the pride of Lord and Lady Cavendish, who developed the present layout from the original 'contrived natural landscape' of Lord George Cavendish over 200 years ago. The Great Holker Lime (a magnificent 72 feet high and 25 feet wide) and the stunning spring display of rhododendrons are among the delights not to be missed. Here, too, are a wonderful rose garden, an azalea walk and a restored Victorian rockery. Lord and Lady Cavendish have put their pride of Holker into words: 'If you gain from your visit a small fraction of the pleasure that we ourselves get from them, then the work of generations of gardeners will not have been in vain.' The gardens at Holker Hall have featured in BBC-TV's *An English Country Garden.*

38 LAKELAND MOTOR MUSEUM

Cark-in-Cartmel

A nostalgic reminder of transport bygones, the **Lakeland Motor Museum** has more than 100 vehicles on show.

🏛 *see page 162*

Holker Hall Gardens

35

The Holker Hall estate contains a wide variety of other attractions: formal gardens, water features, a 125-acre deer park, picnic and children's play areas, a gift shop and café. As well as within the **Lakeland Motor Museum**, which boasts a completely restored 1920s garage, with more than 100 vehicles on show and well over 20,000 well-presented exhibits. The cars may hold centre stage, but there's a great deal more, including 'magnificent motorbikes, superb scooters, bygone bicycles and triumphant tractors'. Housed in a quaint former Shire horse stable and its courtyard, the Lakeland Motor Museum also honours leading figures from the world of motoring.

ULVERSTON

Ulverston is a pretty market town, only 10 miles from the shores of Lake Windermere, with many unique specialist shops, cafés and restaurants, and well priced accommodation perfect for visitors. The market is still held here every Thursday (and a smaller one on Saturdays) like it has for over 700 years, filling the narrow streets and cobbled market square with its many crowds of colourful stalls. It's a picturesque scene, but a walk up nearby **Hoad Hill** is rewarded with an even more striking view of the town. The great expanse of Morecambe Bay with a backdrop of the Pennines stretches to the south, the bulk of Ingleborough lies to the east, Coniston Old Man and the Langdale Pikes lie to the west and north. Crowning another hill, to the north of the town centre, is the **Barrow Monument**, a 100-feet replica of the Eddystone Lighthouse erected in 1850 to honour explorer, diplomat and author Sir John Barrow.

A famous son of Ulverston was Stanley Jefferson, born at number 3, Argyle Street on June 16th, 1890. Stanley is far better known to the world as Stan Laurel. His 30-year career in more than 100 comedy films with Oliver Hardy is celebrated in the town's

Hoad Hill, Ulverston

Laurel and Hardy Museum, Ulverston

Laurel and Hardy Museum in Upper Brook Street. The museum was founded in 1976 by the late Bill Cubin, who devoted his life to the famous duo and collected an extraordinary variety of memorabilia, believed to be the largest in the world. Everything is here, including letters, photographs, personal items and even furniture belonging to the two greats of cinema comedy. A large extension has been added to the modest 17th-century house and there is also a small cinema showing films and documentaries throughout the day. The museum is open seven days a week all year round except during January.

Another great man associated with the town is George Fox, founder of the Quakers. Despite an extremely rough reception from the citizens of Ulverston when he preached here in the 1650s, Fox later married Margaret, widow of Judge Fell of nearby **Swarthmoor Hall**. This lovely late 16th-century manor house, set in extensive gardens, was the birthplace of the Quaker movement and was for a time George and Margaret's home and the first settled centre of the Quaker movement.

Ulverston itself, with its fascinating alleys and cobbled streets, is a delightful place to wander around. The oldest building in the town is the **Church of St Mary** which dates, in parts, from 1111. Though it was restored and rebuilt in the mid-19th century and the chancel was added in 1903, it has retained its splendid Norman door and some magnificent stained glass, including a window designed by the painter Sir Joshua Reynolds. The present tower dates from the reign of Elizabeth I, as the original steeple was destroyed during a storm in 1540.

Ulverston also boasts England's shortest, widest and deepest **Canal**. Visitors can follow the towpath walk alongside, which runs dead straight for just over a mile to Morecambe Bay. Built by the famous engineer John Rennie and opened in 1796, the canal ushered in a half-century of great prosperity for Ulverston as an inland port. At its peak, some 600 large ships a year berthed here, though those good times came to an abrupt end in 1856 with the arrival of the railway. The railway company's directors bought the

39 THE KINGS HEAD HOTEL

Ulverston

A majestic listed building offering hospitality, food and ale second to none.

see page 162

40 OLD FRIENDS

Ulverston

This great local provides a great atmosphere with excellent food and drink.

see page 163

41 GILLAM'S TEAROOM AND RESTAURANT

Ulverston

Serving fine wine, wholesome organic food and homemade cakes Gillam's provides a quality environment to take some respite.

see page 163

42 THE STAN LAUREL

Ulverston

Named after Ulverston's most famous son, this delightful pub offers top notch cuisine alongside comfy accommodation.

see page 164

The open area to the north of Ulverston, known as The Gill, is the starting point for the 70-mile Cumbria Way. The route of the Cumbria Way was originally devised by the Lake District area of the Ramblers Association in the mid-1970s, and provides an exhilarating journey through a wonderful mix of natural splendour and fascinating heritage. The first section is the 15-mile walk to Coniston.

canal and promptly closed it.

The town's other attractions include **The Lakes Glass Centre**, which features the high-quality Heron Glass and Cumbria Crystal. Also at the Centre is the **Gateway to Furness Exhibition**, providing a colourful snapshot of the history of the Furness Peninsula.

AROUND ULVERSTON

SWARTHMOOR

1 mile S of Ulverston off the A590

This small village of whitewashed cottages, now almost entirely incorporated into Ulverston, also has a curious 16th-century hall. **Swarthmoor Hall** stands in well-kept gardens and, although a cement rendering disguises its antiquity, the mullion windows and leaded panes give a clue to its true age. The hall is recognised as the "birth" place of Quakerism; George Fox was offered protection and shelter here by Judge Thomas Fell (the son of George Fell, a wealthy landowner), and settled here his first centre of the Quaker Movement. There is opportunity for visitors to seek there own shelter at Swarthmoor now, with comfortable bed & breakfast or self-catering cottages available in the grounds all year round, and being only a 10 minute walk from Ulverston makes it an ideal base to explore the town and surrounding areas.

Swarthmoor Hall offers toured guides for the public and for schools, and also hosts a variety of events throughout the year giving visitors a fascinating insight into the history of the early Quakers.

BARDSEA

2 miles S of Ulverston off the A5087

The village stands on a lovely green knoll overlooking the sea and, as well as having a charming, unhurried air about it, there are some excellent walks from here along the coast either from its Country Park or through the woodland.

Just up the coast, to the north, lies **Conishead Priory**, once the site of a leper colony that was established by Augustinian canons in the 12th century. After the Dissolution, a superb private house was built on the site and the guide service was continued by the Duchy of Lancaster. In 1821, Colonel Braddyll demolished the house and built in its place the ornate Gothic mansion that stands here today. He was also responsible for the atmospheric ruined folly on **Chapel Island** that is clearly visible in the estuary. The monks from Conishead Priory used to act as guides across the dangerous Cartmel Sands to Lancashire.

Latterly, **Conishead Priory** has been a private house, a hydropathic hotel, a military hospital and a rest home for Durham miners; it is now owned by the Tibet Buddhist Manjushri Mahayana Buddhist Centre, who came here in 1977. During the summer months visitors are welcome to the house, which is open for tours, and there is a delightful woodland trail to follow through the grounds. A new

Buddhist temple was opened in 1998, based on a traditional design which symbolises the pure world (Mandala) of a Buddha.

GREAT URSWICK

3 miles S of Ulverston off the A590

Lying between Great Urswick and Bardsea and overlooking Morecambe Bay is **Birkrigg Common**, a lovely area of open land. On the east side of the common is the **Druid's Circle**, with two concentric circles made up of 31 stones, some of them 3 feet high. The cremated remains found around the site in 1921 indicated that it was used for burials.

The ancient village **Church of St Mary and St Michael** is noted for its unusual and lively woodcarvings that were created by the Chipping Campden Guild of Carvers. As well as the figure of a pilgrim to the left of the chancel arch, there are some smaller carvings in the choir stall of winged children playing musical instruments. Also worthy of a second look is the 9th-century wooden cross which bears a runic inscription.

LINDAL-IN-FURNESS

3 miles SW of Ulverston on the A590

The **Colony Country Store** combines the aromatic character of an old-fashioned country general stores with the cost-cutting advantages of a Factory Shop. There's a huge range of textiles, glassware, ceramics and decorative accessories for the home, but the Colony is also Europe's leading manufacturer of scented candles, supplying millions of scented and dinner candles every year to prestigious shops around the world. From a viewing gallery visitors can watch the traditional skills of hand-pouring and dipping being used to create a variety of candle styles.

43 THE DERBY ARMS

Great Urswick

The Derby Arms is the social hub of the picturesque village of Great Urswick offering welcoming guest accommodation, great food and ale every day.

 see page 163

44 GENERAL BURGOYNE

Great Urswick

This convivial pub offers wonderful food and great drink with excellent service.

see page 165

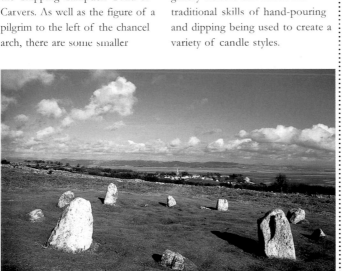

Druid's Circle, Birkrigg Common

45 THE BRIDGE CAFE

Barrow-in-Furness

The **Coffee Shop** in the Dock Museum provides an excellent break while visiting one of the North of England's best attractions.

see page 166

46 THE DOCK MUSEUM

Barrow-in Furness

Explore the history behind the transformation of a small farming village into a major industrial town at The Dock Museum.

see page 166

The Dock Museum, Barrow-in-Furness

BARROW-IN-FURNESS

Barrow- in-Furness on the southern most tip of Cumbria, presents a huge variety for visitors to see and do; the history of the small villages, picturesque walks, lively culture, and the striking expanses of beaches.

Undoubtedly the best introduction to Barrow is to pay a visit to the **Dock Museum** (free admission), an impressive glass-and-steel structure which hangs suspended above a Victorian Graving Dock. This wonderfully modern museum explores the maritime, industrial and social heritage of Barrow, giving a more in-depth understanding of the area. It also has a children's play area. Closed on Mondays (except bank holidays; also closed Tuesdays in winter months)

Today, Barrow is the Peninsula's prime shopping centre, with all the familiar High Street stores mingling with local specialist shops, and the largest indoor traditional market in the area which is open on Mondays, Wednesdays, Fridays and Saturdays. There is a vibrant night-life, with places such as the Blue Lagoon (an unusual floating night club aboard the Princess Selandia) perfect for a celebration or just letting your hair down for a night. Adding to the lively, much-layered culture here are two art and entertainment venues; **Forum 28**, the main theatre showing a variety of music, dance, comedy and drama events from local & touring companies, and **The Canteen Media & Arts Centre**, a smaller more alternative venue of music and arts events.

The Edwardian **Barrow Park** near the centre of the town has been voted the best park in the

North West and awarded a Green Flag. And no wonder with their wonderful displays of landscaped grounds, ornamental flower beds, a pavilion, display glasshouse and bandstand. Far from being just pretty to look at, the park is a hot-bed of constant activity with bowling, miniature railway, putting, play areas and it features the first "iPlay" interactive play equipment in the country (as featured on the BBC) and a new skate park.

Barrow is also the western starting point of the **Cistercian Way**, a 33-mile-walk to Grange-over-Sands through wonderfully unspoilt countryside. En route it passes Furness Abbey in the Vale of Deadly Nightshade, prehistoric sites on the hills surrounding Urswick Tarn and many other historical places of interest. The Way is marked on public roads and footpaths, and a fully descriptive leaflet is available from Tourist Information Centres.

AROUND BARROW-IN-FURNESS

GLEASTON

3 miles E of Barrow-in-Furness off the A5087

This village is typical of the small, peaceful villages and hamlets that can be found in this part of the peninsula. Here, standing close by the ruins of **Gleaston Castle**, can be found **Gleaston Water Mill**. The present buildings date from 1774, with the massive original wooden gearing still in place. The machinery is operational most days – an 18 feet water-wheel and an 11 feet wooden pit wheel serviced by an intriguing water course.

Evening tours with supper are available by prior arrangement. To reach Gleaston Water Mill, follow the signs from the A5087. Guided talks, walks and tours can be arranged.

47 THE KINGS ARMS

Barrow-in-Furness

The Kings Arms is a thriving live music pub offering good food and drink all at very reasonable prices.

🍴 *see page 167*

48 THE CONSERVATORY CAFÉ & QUICHE'S QUALITY CATERING

Barrow-in-Furness

The Conservatory Café in the seaport town of Barrow-in-Furness, seats 27 people inside and 16 outside and has a five star rating from Barrow Borough Council Environmental Health

🍴 *see page 168*

Gleaston Water Mill

FOULNEY ISLAND

5 miles E of Barrow-in-Furness off the A5087

The island, like its smaller neighbour Roa Island, is joined to the mainland by a man-made causeway, built in the 19th century to prevent the Walney Channel from silting up. The site of the local lifeboat station, the island is small and sheltered from the Irish Sea by Walney Island. It provides a nesting place for a variety of terns in the summer who are watched over and protected by a warden; it is also home to important vegetation including sea kale, sea campion and yellow horned poppy.

PIEL ISLAND

5 miles SE of Barrow-in-Furness via foot ferry from Roa Island

Piel Castle, on the island, was a house fortified in the early part of the 14th century and at the time it was the largest of its kind in the northwest. Intended to be used as one of Furness Abbey's warehouses and to offer protection from raiders, in later years the castle also proved to be a useful defence against the King's Customs men, and a prosperous trade in smuggling began. The castle has, over many years, been allowed to fall into ruin and now presents a stark outline on the horizon.

WALNEY ISLAND

2 miles W of Barrow-in-Furness on the A590

This 10-mile-long island is joined to the Furness Peninsula by a bridge from Barrow docks and is home to two important nature reserves situated at either end of the island. **North Walney National Nature Reserve** covers some 350 acres within which are a great variety of habitats including sand dunes, heath, salt marsh, shingle and scrub. As well as having several species of orchid and over 130 species of bird either living or visiting the reserve, there is also an area for the preservation of the Natterjack toad, Britain's rarest amphibian. Unique to the Reserve is the Walney Geranium, a plant that grows nowhere else in the world. North Walney also boasts a rich prehistoric past, with important archaeological sites from Mesolithic, Neolithic, Bronze and Iron Age times. **South Walney Nature Reserve** is home to the largest nesting ground of herring gulls and lesser black-backed gulls in Europe.

Walney Island's southernmost tip, **Walney Point**, is dominated by a 70 feet lighthouse which was built in 1790 and whose light was,

Piel Castle from Isle of Walney

Dalton Castle

49 THE NEWTON

Dalton-In-Furness

This spacious family run pub offers a fun and relaxed family atmosphere for all.

see page 169

50 HARTLEY'S RESTAURANT

Dalton-In-Furness

A great Mediterranean themed restaurant with spectacular food.

see page 170

originally, an oil lamp.

Events are held on Walney, including an exciting annual air show, boat race and even a carnival. Recently the British Kite-Surfing championship was hosted here; Walney's unsheltered position, length and expanse of beach make...ing the conditions perfect for this increasingly popular and spectacular sport.

DALTON-IN-FURNESS

5 miles N of Barrow-in-Furness off the A590

Lying in a narrow valley on the part of Furness that extends deep into Morecambe Bay, it is difficult to imagine that this ancient place was once the leading town of Furness and an important centre for administration and justice. The 14th-century pele tower, **Dalton Castle**, was built with walls 6 feet thick to provide a place of refuge for the monks of Furness Abbey against Scottish raiders and it still looks very formidable. Over the centuries, in its twin role as both prison and court, it has been substantially altered internally although it still retains most of its original external features. It is now owned by the National Trust and houses a small museum with an interesting display of 16th- and 17th-century armour, along with exhibits about iron mining, the Civil War in Furness, and the life and work of George Romney, the 18th-century portrait painter.

Dalton became established as a market town in the 13th century when the Cistercians began to hold fairs and markets in the town. Visitors will find that it is time well spent looking around the many fascinating façades in and close to the market place, such as the unique, cast-iron shop front at **No 51, Market Street**. In the market place itself is an elegant, **Victorian**

43

51 FURNESS ABBEY

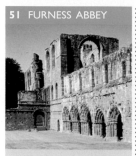

Furness, nr Dalton-in-Furness

The impressive remains of an abbey founded by Stephen, later King of England.

 see page 170

52 ABBEY MILL COFFEE SHOP

Furness, nr Dalton-in-Furness

Unique coffee shop in former medieval Abbot's cottage set in idyllic surroundings.

 see page 171

53 THE GREYHOUND COMMUNITY PUB

Grizebeck

Village hostelry saved from closure by locals; now offering good home-made food, real ales and en suite rooms.

see page 171

Drinking Fountain with fluted columns supporting a dome of open iron work above the pedestal fountain. Nearby stand the market cross and the slabs of stone that were used for fish-drying in the 19th century.

From the mostly pedestrianised Tudor Square, visitors can board a bus to the award-winning **South Lakes Wild Animal Park** which has been designated the Region's Official Top Attraction by the Cumbria Tourist Board. It's the only place in Britain where you can see rare Amur and Sumatran tigers (the world's biggest and smallest tigers). At feeding time (2.30pm each day) they climb a 20 feet vertical tree to 'catch' their food. Ring-tailed lemurs wander freely through the park; visitors can walk with emus and hand-feed giraffes, penguins and the largest collection of kangaroos in Europe. The 17 acres of natural parkland are also home to some of the rarest animals on earth, among them the red panda, maned wolves and tamarin monkeys as well as some 150 other species from around the world, including rhinos, condors, tapirs, coatis and the ever-popular meerkats. Other attractions include a Safari Railway, adventure play area, many picnic spots, a gift shop and café.

To the south of the town lies **Furness Abbey** (English Heritage), a magnificent ruin of eroded red sandstone set in fine parkland, the focal point of south Cumbria's monastic heritage. Among the atmospheric remains can still be

seen the canopied seats in the presbytery and the graceful arches overlooking the cloister, testaments to the abbey's former wealth and influence. Furness Abbey stands in the **Vale of Deadly Nightshade**, a shallow valley of sandstone cliffs and rich pastureland. It is now owned by English Heritage, who has a small Interpretative Centre nearby detailing its history, from its founding in 1123 to its decline into a picturesque and romantic ruin after the Dissolution in 1537. Off the A595 Dalton-to-Askam road, **Sandscale Haws** is one of the most important sand dune systems in Britain, supporting an outstanding variety of fauna.

GRIZEBECK

15 miles N of Barrow-in-Furness on the A595/A5092

This small village on the edge of the Lake District National Park nestles against the flanks of the **Furness Fells**. Although it stands at the junction of roads leading to the Furness Peninsula and the South Cumbria coast, the village and the area around is peaceful and unhurried, offering the visitor an inviting alternative to some of the busier and more crowded Lakeland towns.

BROUGHTON-IN-FURNESS

19 miles N of Barrow-in-Furness on the A595/A593

At the heart of this attractive, unspoilt little town is the **Market Square** with its tall Georgian houses, commemorative obelisk of

1810, village stocks, fish slabs and some venerable chestnut trees. The old Town Hall, occupying the whole of one side, dates back to 1766 and now houses the town's Tourist Information Centre and the Clocktower Gallery, which exhibits paintings, ceramics, mirrors and glassware. On August 1st each year, Broughton's Lord of the Manor comes to the Square to read out the market charter granted by Elizabeth I, while Councillors dispense pennies to any children in the crowd.

One of the town's famous short-term residents was Branwell Brontë, who was employed here as a tutor at **Broughton House**, a splendid double-fronted, three-storey town house just off the Square. Branwell apparently found time both to enjoy the elegance of the town and to share in whatever revelries were in train. Wordsworth often visited Broughton as a child. Throughout his life he loved this peaceful corner of Lakeland and celebrated its charms in some 150 poems; his 20th-century poetical successor, Norman Nicholson, was similarly enchanted.

About 3 miles north of the town, the peaceful hamlet of **Broughton Mills** will attract followers of the Coleridge Trail. During the course of his famous 'circumcursion' of Lakeland in August 1802, the poet stopped to refresh himself at the **Blacksmith's Arms** where he 'Dined on Oatcake and Cheese, with a pint of Ale, and 2 glasses of Rum and water sweetened with preserved

Gooseberries'. The inn, built in 1748, is still there and barely changed since Coleridge's visit.

Some of the Lake District's finest scenery – the Duddon Valley, Furness Fells, Great Gable and Scafell – are all within easy reach, and about 3 miles west of the town is **Swinside Circle**, a fine prehistoric stone circle, some 60 feet in diameter, containing 52 close-set stones and two outlying 'portal' or gateway stones.

The restored remains of **Duddon Iron Furnace** is a fine example of 18th century industry in this area; charcoal-fired blast furnaces such as this revolutionized the smelting process. It is situated on the scenic route between Broughton and Waberthwaite, 100 yards from Duddon bridge. Also in the Duddon Valley is the amazing **Duddon Mosses**, a conservation area brimming with wildlife and vegetation protected from human influence for the past 3000 years. Although these peat wetlands are hazardous to walk across, and this is prohibited due to the respect of the nature flourishing here, there is an English Nature boardwalk over Angerton Moss (part of a circular walk from Foxfield station, just outside of Broughton) which allows a safe passage across this mire. On higher, drier ground near Ulpha Fell, the remains of an old hunting lodge and packhorse Inn **Frith Hall** cuts an echoing remote image on the hilltop. The hall is a place of myth and legend seeped with tales of runaway marriages, smuggling and murder.

54 THE HIGH CROSS INN

Broughton-in-Furness

Stunning panoramic views from this 18th century Inn combine good food and accommodation in a relaxed environment.

🍴 🛏 *see page 172*

55 THE BLACK COCK INN

Broughton-in-Furness

This attractive pub stands in the heart of popular Broughton-in-Furness and provides wonderful food and drink as well as comfortable accommodation.

🍴 🛏 *see page 173*

56 THE MANOR ARMS

Broughton-In-Furness

Traditional family run pub located in the attractive Georgian Square of Broughton-In-Furness

🍴 🛏 *see page 173*

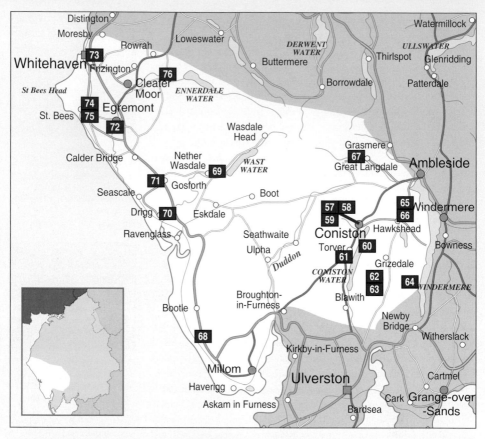

Coniston and Southwest Cumbria

This region is awash with literary connections from John Ruskin, the 19th-century author, artist and critic, who made his home at Brantwood on the shore of Coniston, to Arthur Ransome who used Coniston water as a setting for many of the adventures recounted in *Swallows and Amazons*. The desk defaced by a young and mischievous Wordsworth can still be seen in Hawkshead where he went to school, and Beatrix Potter, who, after holidaying at Near Sawrey as a child, later bought a house at Hill Top as well as many acres of farms which she bequeathed to the National Trust.

The enchanting scenery around Coniston Water and its environs is very much on the tourist trail, though for a more secluded trip you need only travel further west to Cumbria's 'Empty Quarter', a vast terrain of magnificent mountains and desolate fells beloved of climbers and walkers. England's highest mountain, Scafell Pike, rises here; the country's deepest lake, Wast Water, sinks to a depth of some 200 feet and is surrounded by sheer cliffs soaring up to 2,000 feet. The village of Wasdale Head claims to have the smallest church in England.

Bordering this untamed landscape is the narrow coastal strip stretching from Whitehaven down to Millom, which has its own identity as well as a quiet charm. The coastline is dominated by small 18th and 19th century iron-mining communities set between the romantic outline of the Lakeland fells and the grey-blue waters of the Irish Sea. The famous Ravenglass and Eskdale Railway carry many visitors from the coast up one of Cumbria's most picturesque valleys. There are also several genteel Victorian resorts along the coast, including the popular village of Seascale.

Tarn Hows, nr Coniston

47

CONISTON

Coniston village was once an important copper mining centre, and was also widely known for the beautiful decorative green slate, quarried locally, which is used on so many of the public buildings. The great bulk of the **Old Man of Coniston** overlooks the village; it was from this mountain, and some of the surrounding hills, that copper was extracted. At an impressive 2,631 feet, the Old Man of Coniston is a considerable climb, but many make the effort and the summit can be bustling with fell-walkers enjoying the glorious views.

Coniston Water, which holds strong connections with Beatrix Potter, John Ruskin, Arthur Ransome and Sir Donald Campbell, is the third largest and one of the most beautiful of the central Cumbrian lakes. From Coniston Boating Centre, you can hire boats (rowing or electric), kayaks, canoes and sailing dingys, as well as lessons for those who are new to watersports, so you can experience these beautiful waters at first hand. There are also picnic areas with great views for those who would prefer to sit and watch than get wet.

Beatrix Potter lived at Sawrey near Lake Windermere, but she owned the vast **Monk Coniston** estate at the head of Coniston Water. On her death she bequeathed it to the National Trust, a body she had helped to establish and to which she devoted much of her time and fortune. A few miles out of the village lies **Yew Valley Farm**, a delightful working farm set in 600 acres of spectacular farmland surrounded by Tarn Hows and Holme Fell. This farm was the location for part of the recent film "Miss Potter", about the much-loved author, and has a historic tea room decorated by Potter herself, as well as delightfully comfortable accommodation.

John Ruskin the 19th-century author, artist, critic, social commentator and one of the first conservationists came to Coniston in 1872, moving into a house he had never seen. Brantwood, on the eastern side of the lake, is open to the public and enjoys superb views across the water to the great crumpled hill of the **Old Man of Coniston**. From its summit there are even more extensive vistas over Scotland, the Isle of Man, and on a clear day as far as Snowdonia. He lies buried in Coniston churchyard and the **Ruskin Museum** nearby contains many of his studies, pictures, letters and photographs as well as his collection of geological specimens. Visitors can also see a pair of his socks, his certificate of matriculation from Oxford, and his funeral pall made of Ruskin lace embroidered with wild flowers. The lace was so called because Ruskin had encouraged the revival of flax hand-spinning in the area. Lace pieces made to his own designs and based on the sumptuous ruffs worn by sitters in portraits by Titian, Tintoretto and Veronese were attached to plain linen to make decorative cushions, table covers and bedspreads – many of these are on display. New additions to the museum include Campbell's boat Bluebirds K7's Orpheus Engine which is now on display, and due to be added to the "Bluebird wing" extension when it opens in late 2009. There are also guided walks, which take you around the area and give real insight into its history, and the famous figures who resided here. Although two miles in length, these walks are low-level and so not overly exerting. The museum is open daily in high season, and Wednesday to Sunday in winter months.

From the jetty at Coniston, a short ferry trip takes you to Ruskin's home, **Brantwood**, which occupies a beautiful setting on the eastern shores of Coniston Water. It was his home from 1872 until his death in 1900. When he arrived for the first time he described the house, which he had bought for £1,500 without ever seeing it, as 'a mere shed'. He spent the next 20 years extending the house, adding another 12 rooms, and laying out the gardens. The view from the Turret Room he had built was, Ruskin declared, 'the best in all England'. Visitors today can wander around rooms filled with Ruskin's watercolours, paintings by Turner (who was one of his heroes), see his study which is lined with wallpaper he designed himself, and watch a 20-minute video which provides a useful introduction to his life and works.

Coniston Water from Brantwood

Arthur Ransome's *Swallows and Amazons* has delighted generations with its tales of children's adventures set in and around the Lake District. As a child he spent his summer holidays near Nibthwaite at the southern end of the lake and recalled that he was always 'half-drowned in tears' when he had to leave. Later he bought a house overlooking Coniston Water and many locations in his books can be recognised today: **Peel Island**, for example, at the southern end of the lake, is the Wildcat Island of his books.

Sir Donald Campbell's associations with the lake were both glorious and tragic. In 1955 he broke the world water speed record here; 12 years later, when he was attempting to beat his own record, his boat, **Bluebird**, struck a log while travelling at 320 mph. In March 2001 his widow was present as the tailfin of the boat was at last hauled up to the surface. For 34

60 BRANTWOOD

Coniston

The home of John Ruskin from 1872 until his death in 1900, this beautifully situated house retains many of Ruskins personal belongings and is well worth a visit.

 see page 175

Steamship Gondola, *Coniston Water*

61 THE CHURCH HOUSE INN

Torver

This superb inn boasts a caravan and camper park as well as comfortable rooms.

🍴 🛏 see page 177

years the 15 feet rear section had lain on a bed of silt, 140 feet down and right in the middle of the lake. Sir Donald's body was later recovered and was buried on September 12th, 2001 in the village cemetery – an event that was comparatively little covered by the media, who were obviously concerned with the tragic events in the United States the day before.

Nowadays, boats on Coniston Water are restricted to a 10-mph limit – an ideal speed if you're travelling in the wonderful old steamship, the **Gondola**. So called because of its high prow, which enabled it to come in close to shore to pick up passengers, *Gondola* was commissioned by Sir James Ramsden, General Manager of the Furness Railway Company and first Mayor of Barrow, and was launched on Coniston Water in 1859. Abandoned after a storm in the 1960s, she was saved by a group of National Trust enthusiasts and restored and rebuilt by Vickers Shipbuilding. She was

relaunched in 1980. Up to 86 passengers can now travel in opulent comfort on her regular trips around the lake. Coniston Launch also offers lake cruises in its two timber launches, and at the boating centre craft of every kind are available to rent.

Just south of the village and beside the lake is **Coniston Hall**, the village's oldest building. Dating from the 16th century, it was the home of the Le Fleming family, the largest landowners in the area.

AROUND CONISTON

GRIZEDALE

3 miles SE of Coniston off the B5285

Grizedale is one of those special places which can develop and modernize, but still conserve the nature and history of the area. The Grizedale Arts is a perfect example of this; in their own words they "run a programme of events, projects, residencies and activity which seeks to develop the contemporary arts in new directions … and to make artists more useful in this complex and multiple-cultural environment". They endeavor to not just improve this region, but with projects like their ongoing "Happy Stacking" where they are presently working with the village of Nanling in China, create improved and sustainable lifestyles for many people with their art and innovation.

The village lies at the heart of the 9,000-acre **Grizedale Forest** which was acquired by the Forestry Commission in 1934 and is famous for its Sculpture. The Commission's original intention of cultivating the forest for its timber met with much resistance and, over the years, many pathways have been opened and a variety of recreational activities have been encouraged. The forest, too, is famously the home of some 80 tree sculptures commissioned since 1977. All are created from natural materials found in the forest, and made by some of Britain's best-known contemporary artists, including Andy Goldsworthy, as well as by artists from all over the world. The great beauty of these sculptures is their understated presence: there are no signposts pointing to the exhibits; visitors are left entirely on their own to discover these wonders — though there is a printed map obtainable from the **Grizedale Forest Visitor Centre**. The Centre vividly illustrates the story of the forest as well as showing how the combination of wildlife, re-creation and commercial timbering, work together. As well as information, you can receive a delicious meal from their restaurant, with large picture window facing out into the forest and outdoor terrace, or a snack from the chic "café in the forrest".

NEAR SAWREY

4 miles E of Coniston on the B5285

Though this little village will not be familiar to many visitors to the Lake District, its famous inhabitant, Beatrix Potter, almost certainly will be. After holidaying here in 1896, the authoress fell in love with the place and, with the royalties from her first book, *The Tale of Peter Rabbit*, she purchased **Hill Top** in 1905.

Following Beatrix Potter's death in 1943, the house and the land she had bought on the surrounding fells became the property of the National Trust. In accordance with Beatrix Potter's will, Hill Top has remained exactly as she would have known it. One of the most popular Lakeland attractions, Hill Top is full of Beatrix Potter memorabilia, including some of her original drawings. The house is very small, so it is best avoided at peak holiday times.

Tarn Hows, part of the 4,000-acre Monk Coniston estate bought and sold on to the National Trust, was created to resemble a Swiss lake and is very rich in flora and

62 THE EAGLES HEAD

Satterthwaite

Owners and head chef combine to make the Eagles Head a great place to enjoy real ales and top-notch cuisine.

see page 178

63 PEPPER HOUSE

Satterthwaite

A character-filled, traditional farmhouse, with endless views, nestled in an attractive valley and off the beaten track.

see page 177

64 GRAYTHWAITE FARM HOLIDAYS

Graythwaite

20 beautifully renovated holiday properties set in 6000 acres of stunning grounds surrounding the magnificent Lake Windermere.

see page 179

Hill Top, Near Sawrey

65 THE RED LION INN

Hawkshead

The historic 15th century coaching Inn accommodation, fantastic home cooked food and cask ales keep The Red Lion's vivacious atmosphere a pull for visitors and locals alike all year round.

 see page 180

66 THE QUEENS HEAD HOTEL

Hawkshead

Beautiful early 17th century hotel, sure to satisfy with the wonderful range on the locally sourced menu.

see page 181

fauna – it has been designated a Site of Special Scientific Interest.

HAWKSHEAD

3 miles E of Coniston on the B5285

There are more Beatrix Potter connections in the enchanting little village of Hawkshead. Her solicitor husband, William Heelis, worked from an office in the Main Street here, and this has now been transformed into **The Beatrix Potter Gallery** (National Trust). The gallery features an exhibition of her original drawings and illustrations alongside details of the author's life, as well as popular quizzes and goodie bags for children. New to the gallery is the Exhibition 'Because I Never Grew Up', celebrating 100 years since the publication of *Ginger and Pickles* and featuring original watercolours from the story. There is an admission discount for holders of tickets to Hill Top.

Situated at the head of **Esthwaite Water**, enjoying glorious views of Coniston Old Man and Helvellyn, Hawkshead has a history that goes back to Viking times. It's a delightful village of narrow cobbled lanes and white-washed houses, with a main square dominated by the Market House, or Shambles, and another square linked to it by little snickets and arched alleyways which invite exploration. The poet Norman Nicholson observed that 'The whole village could be fitted into the boundaries of a large agricultural show; yet it contains enough corners, angles, alleys and

entries to keep the eye happy for hours.' Cars are banned from the village, a large car park being provided on the outskirts.

Hawkshead was once an important market town serving the surrounding area; at that time most of the land here was owned by the monks of Furness Abbey. The only building in Hawkshead to survive from monastic times is the Courthouse, to the north of the village, part of a medieval manor house built by the monks. The village's main industry is now tourism; it holds many lovely guest house, shops, inns and tea rooms.

The **Church of St Michael & All Angels**, with its massive 15th-century tower, seems rather grand for the village but it too was built at a time when Hawkshead was a wealthy town. The church is the focal point of the annual Lake District Summer Music Festival and a popular venue for concerts and recitals. In the churchyard is a war memorial erected in 1919 and modelled on the ancient runic cross at Gosforth.

Some lovely walks lead from Hawkshead to **Roger Ground** and Esthwaite Water, possibly the least frequented of the Lakes, and also to the nearby hamlet of **Colthouse** where there's an early Quaker Meeting House built around 1690. Esthwaite Water was much loved by Wordsworth, as he shows in his poem The Prelude:

> *My morning walks were early;*
> *oft before the hours of school*
> *I travelled round our little lake, five miles*
> *Of pleasant wandering. Happy time!*

SEATHWAITE

5 miles W of Coniston via minor road off the A593

A mere 5 miles or so from Coniston as the crow flies, by road Seathwaite is nearly three times as far. It stands in one of the Lake District's most tranquil and least-known valleys, **Dunnerdale**. Wordsworth captured its natural beauty in a sequence of sonnets. In his poem *The Excursion*, he wrote about the Reverend Robert Walker, the curate of Seathwaite. Nicholas, or 'Wonderful Walker' as Wordsworth referred to him, served the church here for some 67 years though he also filled various other jobs such as farm labourer and nurse as well as spinning wool and making his own clothes. Fell-walkers and hikers who prefer to escape the masses will delight not only in the solitude of this glorious valley but also in the wide variety of plant, animal and birdlife that have made this haven their home.

HARDKNOTT PASS

5 miles W of Coniston off the A593

Surrounded by the fell of the same name, this pass is one of the most treacherous in the Lake District yet it was used by the Romans for the road between their forts at Ambleside (*Galava*) and Ravenglass (*Glannaventa*). Of the remains of Roman occupation, **Hardknott Fort** on a shoulder of the fell, overlooking the Esk Valley, is the most substantial and also provides some of the grandest views in the whole of the Lake District. The walls of the fort, known as

Hardknott Fort

Mediobogdum, still stand up to 2 metres high, and within them the foundations of the commander's house, headquarters building and granary can be seen.

BOOT

8 miles W of Coniston off the A595

Lying at the eastern end of the **Ravenglass and Eskdale Railway**, this is a wonderful place to visit whether arriving by train or car. A gentle walk from the station at Eskdale brings you to this delightful village with its pub, post office, museum, waterfall and nearby St Catherine's Church in its lovely secluded riverside setting. Perhaps because of the rugged walking country to the east, the village is well supplied – with both a campsite and bunkhouse available.

ESKDALE GREEN

10 miles W of Coniston off the A595

One of the few settlements in this beautiful and unspoilt valley, the village lies on the route of the

67 THE OLD DUNGEON GHYLL HOTEL

Great Langdale, nr Ambleside

Both the Highland Drove, World famous for the close-by climbing opportunities and hospitality.

see page 182

Ravenglass and Eskdale Railway. Further up the valley lies a group of buildings that make up **Eskdale Mill** where cereals have been ground since 1578; the original machinery for grinding oatmeal is in full working order and operated daily.

Overlooking Eskdale are the remains of **Hard Knott Roman Fort**, once one of the loneliest outposts of the Roman Empire, built between AD120 and AD138. From this high point there are breathtaking views of the region, which shouldn't be missed.

The **Gatehouse** in Eskdale is a sprawling and distinctive country house, with 60 acres of mature gardens and spectacular views. They offer bed & breakfast accommodation here, as well as a beautiful site to hold nuptials.

GREAT LANGDALE

9 miles N of Coniston on the B5343

One of the most dramatic of the Lake District waterfalls is **Dungeon Ghyll**, which tumbles 60 feet down the fellside. Nearby is the well known Old Dungeon Ghyll Hotel, which makes an excellent starting point for walks in this spectacularly scenic area where the famous peaks of Crinkle Crags, Bowfell and the Langdale Pikes provide some serious challenges for hikers and ramblers. The 'dungeon' is actually a natural cave.

RAVENGLASS

Lying as it does at the estuary of three rivers – the Esk, the Mite, and the Irt – as well as enjoying a sheltered position, it is not surprising that Ravenglass was an important port from prehistoric times. The Romans built a naval base here around AD 78 which served as a supply point for the military zone around Hadrian's Wall. They also constructed a fort, **Glannaventra**, on the cliffs above the town, which was home to around 1,000 soldiers. Little remains of Glannaventra except for the impressively preserved walls of the Bath House. Almost 12 feet high, these walls are believed to be the highest Roman remains in the country.

Today the estuary has silted up but there are still scores of small boats and the village is a charming resort, full of atmosphere. The layout has changed little since the 16th century; the main street is paved with sea pebbles and leads up from a shingle beach.

One of the town's major attractions is the 15-inch narrow-gauge **Ravenglass and Eskdale Railway** which runs for 7 miles up

Side Pike, Great Langdale

the lovely Mite and Esk River valleys. Better known as 'La'al Ratty', it was built in 1875 to transport ore and quarried stone from the Eskdale Valley, and opened the following year for passenger traffic. Since then the railway has survived several threats of extinction. The most serious occurred at the end of the 1950s when the closure of the Eskdale granite quarries wiped out the railway's freight traffic at a stroke. However, at the auction for the railway in 1960 a band of enthusiasts outbid the scrap dealers and formed a company to keep the little railway running.

Today, the company operates 12 locomotives, both steam and diesel, and 300,000 people a year come from all over the world to ride on what has been described as 'the most beautiful train journey in England'. The La'al Ratty is still the best way to explore Miterdale and Eskdale, and enchants both young and old alike. There are several

Ravenglass and Eskdale Railway, Ravenglass

stops along the journey, and at both termini there is a café and a souvenir shop. At the Ravenglass station there is also a museum which brings to life the history of this remarkable line and the important part it has played in the life of Eskdale.

A mile or so east of Ravenglass stands **Muncaster Castle**; voted number 1 in The Independent top

Muncaster Castle, Ravenglass

For many visitors to Munaster Castle the chief attraction is the World Owl Centre, where many endangered owl species are bred. Snowy owls have become great favourites on the back of the Harry Potter craze, and many visitors have enquired about keeping them as pets. The staff at the Centre have to point out that the snowy owl is a mighty predator with a 5-feet wingspan. Mighty as he is, he is not the mightiest of the owls at the Centre: that honour goes to the Eurasian eagle owl, whose full splendour can be seen at the daily demonstrations. Not all about size, more modestly sized breeds are well represented in their diverse range, including the Pigmy owl which is similar in size to a sparrow. Muncaster's latest attraction is the Meadow Vole Maze (these little creatures are the staple diet of barn owls, and visitors can find out what it's like to be a vole on the run from a hungry owl).

50 "Best Spring Days Out" in the UK. This historical building is recorded to have been the home of the Pennington family from as early as 1026. This beautiful castle holds many paintings and relics of bygone times, as well as a few ghosts (including the 16th century court jester Tom Fool). Apart from the many treasures, the stunning Great Hall, Salvin's octagonal library and the barrel ceiling in the drawing room, Muncaster is also famous for its gardens. The collection of species rhododendrons is one of the finest in Europe, gathered primarily from plant-hunting expeditions to Nepal in the 1920s, and there are also fine azaleas, hydrangeas and camellias as well as many unusual trees.

AROUND RAVENGLASS

WABERTHWAITE

4 miles S of Ravenglass on the A595

No visit to west Cumbria is complete without the inclusion of a trip to RG Woodall's shop. Found in the heart of this village, Richard Woodall is world famous for his sausages, in particular for the Waberthwaite Cumberland Sausage, and is the proud possessor of a Royal Warrant from the Queen.

Newbiggin Farm has a campsite perfectly situated for fell walker, beachcomber or sightseer, and is within four miles of Muncaster Castle.

BOOTLE

7 miles S of Ravenglass on the A595

This ancient village is particularly picturesque and quaint. The river Annas flows beside the main road and then dives under the village on its way to the sea. The village remains a lot quieter than many other locations in Lakeland, and its position sandwiched between the Cumbrian coast on one side and, on the other, the slopes of Black Combe and Bootle Fell, make it the perfect little slice of tranquility for visitors.

High up on **Bootle Fell**, to the southeast of the village, lies one of the best stone circles in Cumbria. Over the years, many of the 51 stones that make up the **Swinside Stone Circle** have fallen over. When it was originally constructed and all the stones were upright, it is likely, as they were also close together, that the circle was used as an enclosure.

SILECROFT

10 miles S of Ravenglass off the A595

Perhaps of all the villages in this coastal region of the National Park, Silecroft is the perfect example. Just a short walk from the heart of the village is the beach, which extends as far as the eye can see. On the horizon lies the distant outline of the Isle of Man. There is also a Site of Special Scientific Interest close by, a tract of coastal scrubland which provides the perfect habitat for the rare Natterjack toad.

MILLOM

13 miles S of Ravenglass on the A5093

This small and peaceful town stands at the mouth of the River Duddon with the imposing **Black Combe Fell** providing a dramatic backdrop. Originally called Holborn Hill, the present-day name was taken from nearby **Millom Castle** which is now a private, working farm. Like many neighbouring towns and villages in Furness, Millom was a small fishing village before it too grew with the development of the local iron industry. **Millom Folk Museum,** located in Millom railway station, tells the story of the town's growth and there is also a permanent memorial here to Norman Nicholson (1914-1987) who is generally regarded as the best writer on Lakeland life and customs since Wordsworth himself. Nicholson's book *Provincial Pleasures* records his affectionate memories of Millom, the town where he

spent all his life. Other displays include a full-scale reproduction of a drift and cage from nearby Hodbarrow mine.

South of Millom, at Haverigg, is the **RAF Millom Museum** situated in the former Officers Mess. Visitors to the site will find a fascinating collection of over 2,000 photographs of the wartime activities of the RAF in the area, various artefacts connected with the period and a number of items recovered from local crash sites. The museum also has a fine collection of aero engines including a Rolls Royce Merlin, a Westland Whirlwind helicopter, the cockpit section of a De Havilland Vampire jet trainer and an example of the HM14 or Flying Flea.

The Duddon Estuary is an important site for wildlife, and the RSPB site at **Hodbarrow** is home not only to birds but to many kinds of flora and fauna. **Hodbarrow Beacon**, which still stands, was built in 1879 as a lighthouse to

68 WAYSIDE LICENSED GUEST ACCOMMODATION AND WHISKY BARN

Whitbeck

Beautifully renovated farm house accommodation with four large en-suite rooms complete with Whisky Barn.

see page 183

Millom Church and Castle

69 THE SCREES INN

Nether Wasdale

The picturesque Screes Inn is the business with everything. Accommodation, great food and drink.

 see page 184

assist vessels taking iron ore from the mines to destinations in Europe.

SANTON BRIDGE

3 miles NE of Ravenglass off the A595

The churchyard of **Irton Church**, reached from Santon Bridge via an unclassified road, from the Holmebrook to Santon Bridge road, offers the visitor not only superb views of the Lakeland fells to the west but also the opportunity to see a beautiful Celtic Cross, in excellent condition, dating from the early 9th century. Though the original runic inscription has been eroded away over time, the fine, intricate carving can still be seen. The Bridge Inn here plays host each November to the 'World's Biggest Liar' competition (see Gosforth below).

WASDALE

6 miles NE of Ravenglass off the A595

To the northeast of Ravenglass runs Wasdale, the wildest of the Lake District valleys but easily accessible by road. The road leads to **Wast Water**, which is just 3 miles long but is the deepest lake in England. The southern shores are dominated by huge screes some 2,000 feet high that plunge abruptly into the lake; they provide an awesome backdrop to this tranquil stretch of water. A lake less like Windermere would be hard to find, as there are no motorboats ploughing their way up and down the lake. This is very much the country of walkers and climbers, and from here there are many

footpaths up to some of the best fells in Cumbria. From here you can find many walking tour groups and guides to help less experienced walkers find their way around the massive expanses of breath-taking scenery. And, with walkers feet in mind, there is the Wasdale Sock Company which, among their range of comfy socks, sells the famous Wasdale Walker sock.

Wasdale Head, just to the north of the lake, is a small, close-knit community with a far-famed Inn that has provided a welcome refuge for walkers and climbers since the mid-1800s who have been out discovering Wasdale and the lake. **Wasdale Church** is claimed to be the smallest in England, built in the 14th century, it is hidden away amidst a tiny copse of evergreen trees. Local legend suggests that the roof beams came from a Viking ship and it is certainly true that until late Victorian times, the church had only an earth floor and few seats.

As well as the deepest lake and the smallest church, Wasdale also boasts the highest mountain, **Scafell Pike** (3,205 feet) – and the world's biggest liars. This latter claim goes back to the mid-1800s when Will Ritson, 'a reet good fibber', was the publican at the inn. Will enthralled his patrons with tall stories of how he had crossed foxes with eagles to produce flying foxes and had grown turnips so large he could hollow them out to make a shed. In the same spirit, the 'World's Biggest Liar' Competition takes place every November, usually at the Bridge Inn at Santon Bridge, when contestants from all over the country vie in telling the most enormous porkies.

Sca Fell, about a mile away, is 'only' 3,162 feet, though getting from one to the other by a direct route isn't straightforward. The easiest routes are either via Lord's Rake on the Wasdale side or by descending and then re-ascending via Foxes Tarn on the Eskdale side.

A short drive outside of Wasdale is Woodhow farm, a traditional working farm in 158 acres of land, which is home to the **Cumbrian Goat Experience**. Here you can find many rare and native goat breeds (including cashmere goats – the fibre of their coats recognised as the height of comfort and luxury), enjoy their farm shop and even stay in one of their holiday cottages. It is said that goat milk is a healthy and tasty alternative to cow's milk, particularly for those with cow's milk intolerances.

Wastwater, Wasdale

HOLMROOK

2 miles N of Ravenglass on the A595

Situated on the banks of the River Irt, where it is possible to fish for both salmon and sea trout, this small village also lies on the Ravenglass and Eskdale Railway line. Though the village Church of St Paul is not of particular note, inside there is not only a 9th-century cross of Irish style but also memorials to the Lutwidges, the family of Lewis Carroll. **Carleton Hall**, a Grade II listed building, provides bed & breakfast accommodation, as well as a beautiful garden (including a 1000 year old oak tree) and a location only two miles from the Cumbria cycle way.

DRIGG

2 miles N of Ravenglass on the B5343

The main attractions here are the sand dunes and the fine views across to the Lakeland mountains and fells. There is an important nature reserve, **Drigg Dunes**, on the salt marshes that border the River Irt but – take note, adders are common here. The reserve is home to Europe's largest colony of black-headed gulls, as well as the endangered Natterjack toad and over 250 species of wildflower.

70 THE VICTORIA HOTEL

Drigg

A family run hotel with a great restaurant and bar.

🛏 🍴 see page 185

71 GOSFORTH HALL INN

Gosforth

This spectacular Inn boasts a truly magnificent four poster bed suite and gorgeous food in historical surroundings.

 see page 186

A major attraction in the appealing village of Gosforth is Gosforth Pottery, where Dick and Barbara Wright produce beautifully crafted work and also give pottery lessons. In their shop they sell not only hand-thrown pottery of their own and those of many other artists, but some beautiful paintings of the Lake District as well.

SEASCALE

4 miles N of Ravenglass on the B5343

One of the most popular seaside villages in Cumbria, Seascale enhanced its resort status in 2000 by restoring the **Victorian Wooden Jetty** to mark Millennium Year. Stretching out into the Irish Sea, it provides the starting point for many walks, including the Cumbrian Coastal Way which passes along the foreshore. This fine sandy beach enjoys views over to the Isle of Man and the Galloway Mountains of Scotland while, behind the village, the entire length of the western Lakeland hills presents an impressive panorama.

Once a popular Victorian holiday resort the village still retains some its Victorian charm in its buildings: the **Water Tower**, medieval in style and with a conical roof, and the old **Engine Shed** which is now a multi-purpose Sports Hall.

GOSFORTH

5 miles N of Ravenglass on the A595

On the edge of this picturesque village, in the graveyard of **St Mary's Church**, stands the tallest ancient cross in England. Fifteen feet high, the **Viking Cross** towers above the huddled gravestones in the peaceful churchyard. Carved from red sandstone and clearly influenced by both Christian and pagan traditions, the cross depicts the crucifixion, the deeds of Norse gods and Yggdrasil, the World Ash Tree that Norsemen believed supported the universe. The interior of the church also contains some interesting features. There's a **Chinese Bell**, finely decorated with Oriental imagery, which was captured in 1841 at Anunkry, a fort on the River Canton, some delightful carved faces on the chancel arch and a collection of ancient stones the most notable of which dates from Saxon times and depicts the Lamb of God trampling on the serpents of pagan faith.

CALDER BRIDGE

7 miles N of Ravenglass on the A595

From this small 19th-century settlement there is an attractive footpath to **Calder Abbey**. It was founded by monks of Savigny in 1134 but amalgamated with the Cistercians of Furness Abbey when it was ransacked by the Scots a few years later. After the Dissolution the monastery buildings lapsed slowly into the present-day romantic ruin. Part of the tower and west doorway remain, with some of the chancel and transept, but sadly these are unsafe and have to be viewed from the road. **Monk's Bridge**, the oldest packhorse bridge in Cumbria, was built across the River Calder for the monks. To the northeast of the village, the River Calder rises on Caw Fell.

EGREMONT

12 miles NW of Ravenglass on the A595

This pretty town is dominated by **Egremont Castle** with walls 20 feet high and an 80 feet tower. It stands high above the town, overlooking the lovely River Ehen to the south and the marketplace to the north. The castle was built between 1130 and 1140 by William de Meschines on the possible site of a former Danish fortification. The most complete part still standing is a Norman arch that once guarded the drawbridge entrance. Nearby is an unusual four-sided sundial and the stump of the old market cross dating from the early 13th century. The Castle grounds are now a park to be enjoyed by the townspeople, open from early morning to dusk.

In September every year the town celebrates its **Crab Fair**. Held each year on the third Saturday in September, the Fair dates back more than seven centuries – to 1267 in fact, when Henry III granted a Royal Charter for a three-day fair to be held on 'the even, the day and the morrow after the Nativity of St Mary the Virgin'. The celebrations include the 'Parade of the Apple Cart' when a wagon loaded with apples is driven along Main Street with men on the back throwing fruit into the crowds. Originally, the throng was pelted with crab apples – hence the name Crab Fair – but these are considered too tart for modern taste, so nowadays more palatable varieties are used. The festivities also feature a greasy pole competition (with a pole 30 feet high), a pipe-smoking contest, wrestling and hound-trailing. The highlight, however, is the **World Gurning Championship** in which contestants place their heads

"When I was a Lad", Egremont

through a braffin, or horse collar, and vie to produce the most grotesque expression. If you're toothless, you start with a great advantage!

WHITEHAVEN

The first impression of Whitehaven is of a handsome Georgian town, but it was already well established in the 12th century as a harbour used by the monks of nearby St Bees Priory. Whitehaven witnessed an astonishing growth between 1633 and 1693, where it developed from just six thatched cottages, to a sizeable, planned town with a population of more than 2,000. Its 'gridiron' pattern of streets, unusual in Cumbria, will be familiar to American visitors, and the town boasts some 250 listed buildings. Once the third-largest port in Britain (a trade industry halted by the shallow waters unsuitable for large iron

72 BLACKBECK HOTEL AND BREWERY

Egremont

A charming hotel with its own brewery that has gone from strength to strength since the current owners took charge.

 see page 187

73 THE RUM STORY

Whitehaven

Fascinating exhibition recounting Whitehaven's involvement in a trade that attracted pirates, smugglers, slavers and Nelson's navy.

    see page 188

steamships) much of the attractive harbour area – now full of pleasure craft and fishing smacks – and older parts of the town still remain largely unchanged. Whitehaven is now a lively town, with many events regularly being held, you get here a strong sense of community. The **Rosehill Theatre** is a great place to visit to catch a show, or the latest films, and the town holds a **market** every Thursday and Saturday (though Wednesday is considered a half day, with some shops closing early).

The harbour and its environs have been declared a Conservation Area, and here visitors will find **The Beacon**, where, through a series of innovative displays, the history of the town and its harbour are brought to life. Looking a bit like a small lighthouse, the museum deals with the history of the whole of Copeland (the district of Cumbria in which Whitehaven lies) with special emphasis on its mining and maritime past. The displays

reflect the many aspects of this harbour borough with a collection that includes paintings, locally-made pottery, ship models, navigational instruments, miners' lamps and surveying equipment. The Beilby 'Slavery' Goblet, part of the museum's collection, is one of the masterpieces of English glass-making and is probably the finest example of its kind in existence. Also here are the **Harbour Gallery**, with an ongoing arts programme, and the **Met Office Gallery**, where visitors can monitor, forecast and broadcast the weather. They can also learn about the 'American Connection' and John Paul Jones' attack on the town in 1778, or settle down in the cinema to watch vintage footage of Whitehaven in times past.

There's more history at **The Rum Story**, which tells the story of the town's connections with the Caribbean. The display is housed in the original 1785 shop, courtyards, cellars and bonded warehouses of the Jefferson family, the oldest surviving UK family of rum traders. Visitors can learn about the various processes involved in the making of rum, travel through realistic re-creations of far-off villages, and experience the sights, sounds and smells of life on board the trading ships, many of which participated in a trade then considered acceptable but nowadays, of course, abhorrent: the trade in human 'cargo', or slaves.

As well as the elegant Georgian buildings that give the town its air of distinction, there are two fine

Tall Ship, Whitehaven Harbour

parish churches that are worth a visit. Dating from 1753, **St James' Church** has Italian ceiling designs and a beautiful Memorial Chapel (dedicated to those who lost their lives in the two World Wars, and also the local people who were killed in mining accidents) while the younger **St Begh's Church**, which was built in the 1860s by EW Pugin, is striking with its sandstone walls. In the graveyard of the parish church of **St Nicholas** is buried Mildred Gale, the grandmother of George Washington.

Whitehaven is interesting in other ways. The grid pattern of streets dating back to the 17th century gives substance to its claim to be the first planned town in Britain. Many of the fine Georgian buildings in the centre have been restored and **Lowther Street** is a particularly impressive thoroughfare. Also of note is the **Harbour Pier** built by the canal engineer John Rennie and considered to be one of the finest in Britain. There is a fascinating walk and a nature trail around **Tom Hurd Rock**, above the town.

There are boat rides taken from Whitehaven, such as the Riptide boat tours, which offer a scenic 3 hour trip along the St Bees RSPB bird sanctuary – an ideal journey for bird enthusiasts (and even the possibility of seeing porpoises and dolphins, which can be found around the area). Another attraction is the free entry **Haig Mine Museum**; situated high on the cliffs above Whitehaven it tells

the history of the often perilous mines and the people who worked there. It features original winding engines which, thanks to a dedicated team of volunteers, are still in working order, many genuine and fascinating photographs of the mines at work, and a gift shop.

For cyclers, Whitehaven harbour is one of the starting points for the coast to coast (or C2C) cycle route, finishing in Tynemouth or Sunderland.

AROUND WHITEHAVEN

ST BEES

3 miles S of Whitehaven on the B5343

St Bees Head, a red sandstone bluff, forms one of the most dramatic natural features along the entire coast of northwest England. Some 4 miles long and 300 feet high, these towering, precipitous cliffs are formed of St Bees sandstone, the red rock that is so characteristic of Cumbria. Far out to sea, on the horizon, can be seen the grey shadow of the Isle of Man and, on a clear day, the shimmering outline of the Irish coast. The 190 mile coast to coast walk starts here, ending in Robin Hood's Bay on the east coast.

Long before the first lighthouse was built in 1822, there was a beacon on the headland to warn and guide passing ships away from the rocks. The present 99 feet high lighthouse dates from 1866-7, built after an earlier one was destroyed by fire.

St Bees Head is now an

74 QUEEN'S HOTEL

St Bees

Recently restored 17th century inn, specialising in hospitality and fine service

🍴 🛏️ see *page 189*

75 HARTLEY'S BEACH SHOP & TEA ROOM

St Bees

This sunny tea room specialises in delicious home made ice creams, perfect for the end of the famous coast to coast walk across the Pennines.

🍴 see *page 190*

important **Nature Reserve** and the cliffs are crowded with guillemots, razorbills, kittiwakes, gulls, gannets, and skuas. Bird watchers are well provided for with observation and information points all along the headland. There is a superb walk of about 8 miles along the coastal footpath around the headland from St Bees to Whitehaven. The route passes Saltam Bay and Saltam Pit, which dates from 1729 and was the world's first undersea mineshaft. The original lamp house for the pit has been restored and is now used by HM Coastguard.

St Bees itself, a short walk from the headland, is a small village which lies huddled in a deep, slanting bowl in the cliffs, fringed by a shingle beach. The village is a delightful place to explore, with its main street winding up the hillside between old farms and cottages. It derives its name from St Bega, daughter of an Irish king who, on the day she was meant to marry a Norse prince, was miraculously transported by an angel to the Cumbrian coast.

According to legend, on Midsummer Night's Eve, St Bega asked the pagan Lord Egremont for some land on which to found a nunnery. Cunningly, he promised her only as much land as was covered by snow the following morning. But on Midsummer's Day, 3 square miles of land were blanketed white with snow, and here she founded her priory. (Incidentally, this 'miracle' snowfall is a not an uncommon feature of a Cumbrian summer on the high fells.)

The Priory at St Bees grew in size and importance until it was destroyed by the Danes in the 10th century: the Benedictines later re-established the priory in 1129. **The Priory Church of St Mary and St Bega** is all that is now left, and

St Bees Priory Church

although it has been substantially altered there is still a magnificent Norman arch and a pre-Conquest, carved Beowulf Stone on a lintel between the church and the vicarage, showing St Michael killing a dragon. The most stunning feature of all is much more modern, a sumptuous Art Nouveau metalwork screen. In the south aisle is a small museum.

Close by the church are the charming Abbey Cottages and **St Bees School** with its handsome clock-tower. The original red sandstone quadrangle bears his coat-of-arms and the bridge he gave to the village is still in use. Among the school's most famous alumni is the actor and comedian Rowan Atkinson, creator of the ineffable Mr Bean. St Bees School was founded in 1583 by Edmund Grindal, Archbishop of Canterbury under Elizabeth I, and the son of a local farmer.

CLEATOR MOOR

3 miles SE of Whitehaven on the B5295

The name of this once-industrial town derives from the Norse words for cliff and hill pasture. Cleator developed rapidly in the 19th century because of the insatiable demand during the Industrial Revolution for coal and iron ore. As the Cumbrian poet Norman

Nicholson wrote:

From one shaft at Cleator Moor
They mined for coal and iron ore.
This harvest below ground could show
Black and red currants on one tree.

Cleator is surrounded by delightful countryside, and little evidence of the town's industrial past is visible. Near to Cleator, on the way to Egremont, is **Longlands Lake** and **Clints Quarry Nature Reserve**, a site of special scientific interest, both for botanical and geological resources. In this long abandoned limestone quarry you can find deep pools, and many delightful varieties of wild flower, including the illusive bee orchid, and beautiful deep purple pyramid orchid.

ENNERDALE BRIDGE

7 miles E of Whitehaven off the A5086

Wordsworth described Ennerdale's church as 'girt round with a bare ring of mossy wall' – and it still is. The bridge here crosses the River Ehen, which, a couple of miles upstream runs out from **Ennerdale Water**, one of the most secluded and inaccessible of all the Cumbrian lakes. The walks around this tranquil lake and through the quiet woodlands amply repay the slight effort of leaving the car at a distance.

76 THE SHEPHERDS ARMS HOTEL

Ennerdale Bridge

The Shepherds Arms Hotel is the ideal base to discover a wonderful part of the country.

see page 188

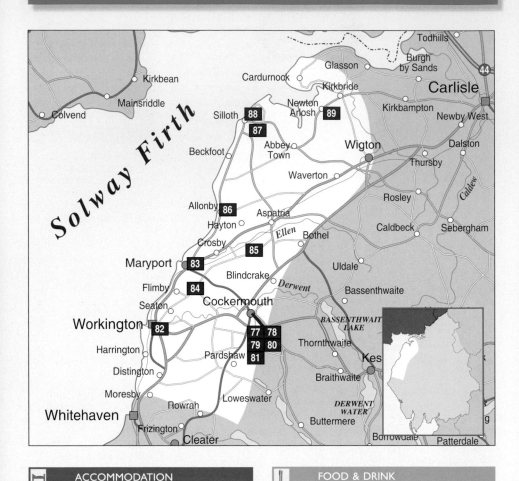

The North Cumbrian Coast

The North Cumbrian coast, from Workington in the south to the Solway Firth in the north, is one of the least-known parts of this beautiful county but it certainly has a lot to offer. It is an area rich in heritage, with a network of quiet country lanes, small villages, old ports, and seaside resorts. The

Cockermouth

coast's largest town, Workington, on the site of a Roman fort, was once a large port, prospering on coal, iron and shipping. It is now the peaceful location for several beautiful churches and interesting museums.

Further up the coast is Maryport, again a port originally built by the Romans. As well as being a quaint and picturesque place, Maryport is also home to a fascinating museum dedicated to the town's maritime past. This lovely harbour town is host to vibrant festivals every year.

A short distance inland lays Cockermouth on the edge of the Lake District National Park, a pretty market "gem town" with some elegant Georgian buildings, and individual arts & crafts and family-run businesses. However, most visitors will be more interested to see and hear about the town's most famous son, the poet William Wordsworth, who was born here in 1770.

The northernmost stretch of coastline, around the Solway Firth, is an area of tiny villages with fortified towers standing as mute witness to the border struggles of long ago. These villages were the haunt of smugglers, wildfowlers, and half-net fishermen. What is particularly special about this coastline is its rich birdlife. The north Cumbrian coast was also the setting for Sir Walter Scott's novel *Redgauntlet*, and the fortified farmhouse by the roadside beyond Port Carlisle is said to be the 'White Ladies' of the novel.

77 THE COCK AND BULL

Cockermouth

Well known for the homemade pies, so much so that they've won awards.

see page 191

78 ROOK GUEST HOUSE

Cockermouth

A charming 18th century property offering an ideal base for anyone wishing to explore all that Cockermouth has to offer.

see page 192

COCKERMOUTH

Cockermouth fully earns its designation as a 'gem town' recommended for preservation by the Department of the Environment. A market town since 1226, Cockermouth has been fortunate in keeping unspoilt its broad main street, lined with trees and handsome Georgian houses, and dominated by a statue to the Earl of Mayo, who was Cockermouth's MP for ten years from 1858. A pleasant way to familiarize you with this town, and its history, is the walk-through town trail, sign posted by cast iron numbered plaques created by the children of Cockermouth school. Leaflets detailing the trail are available from the tourist information centre.

It is speculated whether the two famous sons of Cockermouth ever met; Fletcher Christian and William Wordsworth both grew up here in the 1770's, and might well as young lads been friends, though they were both destined to become celebrated for very different reasons. Fletcher Christian, the elder of the two, would later lead the mutiny on the *Bounty*; the younger lad William Wordsworth, was born here in 1770 at Lowther House on Main Street, an imposing Georgian house now maintained by the National Trust. Now known as **Wordsworth House**, it was built in 1745 for the Sheriff of Cumberland and then purchased by the Earl of Lowther; he let it to his land agent, John Wordsworth, William's father. All five Wordsworth children were born here, William on 7th April 1770. Many of the building's original features survive, among them the staircase, fireplace, and fine plaster

Wordsworth House, Cockermouth

ceilings. A few of the poet's personal effects are still here and the delightful walled garden by the River Cocker has been returned to its Georgian splendour. The garden is referred to in *The Prelude*.

Wordsworth was only eight years old when his mother died and he was sent to school at Hawkshead, but later he fondly recalled walking at Cockermouth with his sister Dorothy, along the banks of the rivers Cocker and Derwent to the ruined castle on the hill. Built in 1134 by the Earl of Dunbar, **Cockermouth Castle** saw plenty of action against Scottish raiders (Robert the Bruce himself gave it a mauling in 1315), and again during the Wars of the Roses; in the course of the Civil War it was occupied by both sides in turn. Mary, Queen of Scots, took refuge at the castle in 1568 after her defeat at the Battle of Langside. Her fortunes were so low that she was grateful for the gift of 16 ells (about 20 yards) of rich crimson velvet from a wealthy merchant. Part of Cockermouth Castle is still lived in by the Egremont family; the remainder is usually only open to the public during the Cockermouth Festival in July.

Opposite the Castle entrance, **Castlegate House** is a fine Georgian house, built in 1739, which hosts a changing programme of monthly exhibitions of the work of Northern and Scottish artists - paintings, sculptures, ceramics and glass. To the rear of the house is a charming walled garden that is open from time to time during the summer.

Jennings Brewery offers visitors a 90-minute tour which ends with the option of sampling some of their ales – Cumberland Ale, Cocker Hoop or the intriguingly named Sneck Lifter. The last independent brewing company in Cumbria, Jennings have been brewing traditional beers since the 1820s. Today there are more than 100 Jennings pubs across the north of England. In addition to the tours, Jennings has a shop selling gifts and leisure wear, the latter boldly emblazoned with the names of its various brews.

More suitable for younger audiences is **Jordon's Jungle Fun House**, a perfect retreat on rainy days all year round, this indoor adventure play area has plenty to entertain your cheeky little monkeys. There is a café to sit and relax while they are playing, and with a soft play area for toddler's right next to it, you needn't worry about how to keep eye on very young ones.

A short walk from the Brewery is the **Kirkgate Centre**, which is housed in a converted Victorian primary school. Run by volunteers, the Centre offers a wide range of events and activities including live music, amateur and professional drama, films, dance, workshops, exhibitions of art and local history. Indeed, Cockermouth is a lively hive of arts and crafts activity, with its many galleries and individual art cafés.

The town really is brimming

79 THE BUSH

Cockermouth

A family friendly inn, offering homemade meals, a very hospitable host, occasional music nights and a friendly atmosphere.

see page 193

80 JUNIPERS RESTAURANT & CAFÉ BAR

Cockermouth

A tremendous meeting place for lovers of great food and great company.

see page 192

81 BEATFORDS COUNTRY TEA ROOMS

Lowther Went

A popular place to meet and enjoy a steaming hot chocolate and piece of homemade cake or cold drink and hot meal.

see page 194

with local gems such as **Bitter Beck Pottery**, the studio of Joan Hardie, who creates stunning pieces inspired by nature, and you can watch at work before purchasing a lovingly hand-crafted piece of your own. Or there is **JB Banks & Son**, an endearingly quaint family-run business providing a wide range of iron mongery, with nails and smaller items stored behind the mahogany counter in 172 original drawers (the oldest of which is dated 1870).

Just south of the town, the Lakeland Sheep & Wool Centre provides an introduction to life in the Cumbrian countryside with the help of a spectacular visual show, numerous breeds of sheep and a wide variety of exhibits. The Centre also hosts indoor sheepdog trials and sheep-shearing demonstrations.

AROUND COCKERMOUTH

BRIDEKIRK

2 miles N of Cockermouth off the A595

The village **Church** contains one of the finest pieces of Norman sculpture in the country, a carved font with a runic inscription and a mass of detailed embellishments. It dates from the 12th century and the runic inscription states that:

Richard he me wrought
And to this beauty eagerly me brought.

Richard himself is shown on one side with a chisel and mallet. Not only is this a superb example of early English craftsmanship but it is exceedingly rare to find a signed work. Ancient tombstones stand round the walls of this cruciform church and inside it has unusual reredos of fleur-de-lys patterned tiles.

BRIGHAM

2 miles W of Cockermouth off the A66

St Bridget's Church, which was probably founded as part of a nunnery, contains many interesting features, including the tunnel-vaulted west tower (which dates back to the 13th century), pre-Norman carved stones, a rare 'fish window' and a window dedicated to the Reverend John Wordsworth, son of William and vicar of Brigham for 40 years. Charles Christian, father of the *Bounty* mutineer Fletcher, was laid to rest here, and his tomb stone can still be seen in the graveyard.

EAGLESFIELD

2 miles SW of Cockermouth off the A5086

This small village was the birthplace of Robert Eaglesfield, who became confessor to Queen Philippa, Edward III's Queen. He was also the founder of Queen's College, Oxford, where he was buried in 1349. Even more famous is **John Dalton**, who was born here in 1766. The son of Quaker parents, Dalton was teaching at the village school by the time he was 12. Despite having had no formal education himself, he became one of the most brilliant scientists, naturalists, and mathematicians of his age and was the originator of the theory that all matter is composed of small indestructible particles called atoms. He was also the first to recognise the existence of colour blindness. He suffered from it himself, and in medical circles it is known as Daltonism.

A memorial to the remarkable John Dalton now marks the house where he lived in Eaglesfield.

WORKINGTON

The largest town on the Cumbrian coast, Workington stands at the mouth of the River Derwent and on the site of the Roman fort of **Gabrosentum**. Its prosperity was founded on the three great Cumbrian industries – coal, iron and shipping. As early as 1650 coal was being mined here and, by the end of the 18th century, Workington was a major port exporting coal as well as smelting iron ore. Many of the underground coal seams extended far out to sea In later years, Workington became famous for its fine quality steel, especially after Henry Bessemer developed his revolutionary steel-making process here in 1850. The seat of the Curwen family for over 600 years, **Workington Hall** has an interesting history. Originally built around a 14th-century pele tower, the hall was developed over the years with extensive alterations being made in the 18th century by the then-lord of the manor, John Christian Curwen. Now a stabilised ruin, it has several commemorative plaques which give a taste of the hall's history.

John Christian Curwen

travelled throughout Britain and Europe to research and develop a better and more profitable way of farming. His results were adopted worldwide and are still being used today.

There are numerous churches throughout the town; Workington's **Church of St John the Evangelist** is the grandest, built at enormous expense in 1823 to give thanks for the defeat of Napoleon at Waterloo. It is a copy of St Paul's, Covent Garden, and its walls were built with stones from the local Schoose and Hunday quarries. Though grand as it is the other churches, **St Michael** and **Our Lady & St Michael** are both quite special. St Michael's is the ancient parish church, sadly damaged in a fire in 1994, which has since undergone major rebuilding. Our Lady & St Michael has a breath-takingly ornate interior, including a dramatic high altar, gilt edged baptistery, and many stained glass windows.

The **Helena Thompson Museum**, situated on Park End Road, was given as a gift to the people of Workington by local philanthropist Helena Thompson, MBE, JP, on her death, after she had resided there for over seventy years. By her wishes it was opened as a museum in 1949; a fascinating place to visit with its displays telling the story of Workington's coal-mining, ship-building and iron and steel industries for which the town became internationally renowned. It also still contains some of Helena Thompson's own family heirlooms. The Georgian Room gives an

82 THE HALL PARK HOTEL

Workington

This quality hotel is located across the road from the well known Helena Thompson Museum.

⊨ see page 195

•

The most famous visitor to Workington was Mary, Queen of Scots, who sought refuge here when she fled from Scotland in 1568. She stayed for a few days, during which time she wrote the famous letter to her cousin Elizabeth I bemoaning her fate, 'for I am in a pitiable condition ... having nothing in the world but the clothes in which I escaped,' and asking the Queen 'to have compassion on my great misfortunes'. The letter is now in the British Museum.

•

insight into the variety of decorative styles which were popular between 1714 and 1830. One particularly interesting exhibit is the Clifton Dish, a locally-produced 18th-century piece of slipware pottery, while further displays demonstrate the links between this local industry and the famous Staffordshire pottery families. Fashion fans will be interested in the display of womens' and childrens' dresses from the 1700s to the early 1900s, together with accessories and jewellery. The building is also a host for several groups such as historical and arts & crafts. The museum is open 1.30 to 4.30 all year round (earlier opening time of 10:30am in summer months).

In recent years the centre of Workington has been transformed in a major redevelopment scheme. Among the many new features is an intriguing interactive mechanical clock that moves and chimes between 9am and 10pm.

Maryport Harbour

Workington is at the start of the C2C cycle route that runs to Sunderland and Newcastle. A short distance south of town is **Harrington Reservoir Nature Reserve**, a haven for wildlife with a rich variety of wild flowers, insects, butterflies, birds and animals. To the north, behind the ultra-modern Dunmail Park Shopping Centre, **Siddick Ponds** is another important wildlife site, with a wide variety of wildlife throughout the year, including butterflies, dragonflies and small mammals.

NORTH AND EAST OF WORKINGTON

MARYPORT

6 miles NE of Workington on the A596

Dramatically located on the Solway Firth, Maryport is a charming Cumbrian coastal town with a rich variety of attractions, and an intricate history.

The old part of the town is full of narrow streets and neoclassical, Georgian architecture that contrast with sudden, surprising views of the sea. Some of the first visitors to Maryport were the Romans, who built a clifftop fort here, **Alauna**, which is now part of the Hadrian's Wall World Heritage Site. The award-winning **Senhouse Roman Museum** tells the story of life in this outpost of the Empire. Housed in the striking Naval Reserve Battery, built in the 1880s, the museum holds the largest collection of Roman altars from a single site in Britain.

Modern Maryport dates from

the 18th century when another Senhouse, Humphrey, a local landowner, developed the harbour at what was then called Ellenfoot to export coal from his mines, and named the new port after his wife, Mary. Over the next century it became a busy port as well as a ship-building centre; boats had to be launched broadside because of the narrowness of the harbour channel. Today Maryport is as bustling as it ever was, with newly restored Georgian quaysides, clifftop paths, sandy beaches and a harbour with fishing boats.

The town's extensive maritime history is preserved in the vast array of objects, pictures and models on display at the **Maritime Museum** overlooking the harbour, sited on the first plot of land developed by the Senhouse family when they created the new town and the harbour. Housed in another of Maryport's more interesting and historic buildings, the former Queen's Head public house, the museum tells of the rise and fall of the harbour and docks. Other exhibits include a brass telescope from the *Cutty Sark* and the town's connections with the ill-fated liner, the *Titanic*, part of the White Star Line fleet founded by local man Thomas Henry Ismay, and with Fletcher Christian, instigator of the mutiny on the *Bounty*.

Close to the Maritime Museum in Maryport is the **Lake District Coast Aquarium** where a series of 45 spectacular living habitat re-creations introduce visitors to the profusion of marine life found in

Maritime Museum, Maryport

the Solway Firth – thornback rays (which can be touched), some small sharks, minuscule sea horses, colour-changing cuttlefish, spider crabs and the comically ugly tompot blenny among them. Open all year, the Aquarium also has a gift shop and a quayside café that enjoys superb views of the harbour and the Solway.

For those looking for more active attractions, Maryport has much to keep you gripped. The **Maryport Golf Club**, situated on

83 LAKE DISTRICT COAST AQUARIUM

Maryport

A fascinating collection of local fish, shellfish and invertebrates. A café, gift shop and amusements make this an ideal day out.

 see page 195

84 THE MINERS ARMS INN

Broughton Moor, nr Maryport

A 19th century Inn run by a friendly couple with live music, serving a delicious menu and fine ale.

see page 196

85 THE BEECHES CARAVAN PARK

Gilcrux

A scenic caravan park perfect for a hassle free family holiday exploring the Lakes.

see page 197

86 THE SHIP HOTEL

Allonby

A traditional and well-furnished hotel with views stretching across the Solway Firth.

see page 197

the Solway Firth, allows you to enjoy a game of golf on a course part traditional links and part parkland, while taking in the views of Criffel and South Scotland. **West Coast Karting** is one of the largest indoor go-karting tracks in the country. The new £3.3 million complex of **The Wave** is an entertainment, conferencing, historical centre situated on the harbour. Here you can find out information about the area in the interactive heritage visitors centre, take in a film or play in the theatre or buy locally made gifts from the shop.

Maryport is host to many festivals, which are well worth witnessing. An example is the Maryport Blues festival at the end of July, when the whole town comes alive with the best of blues.

DEARHAM

7 miles NE of Workington off the A594

This village has a very beautiful church with open countryside on three sides. The chancel of **Dearham Church** is 13th century, and the church has a fortress tower built for the protection of men and beasts during the Border raids. There are also some interesting relics within the church including the Adam Stone, dating from AD 900, which depicts the fall of man (with Adam and Eve hand in hand above a serpent), an ancient font carved with mythological beasts, a Kenneth Cross showing the legend of the 6th-century hermit brought up by seagulls, and a magnificent wheel-head cross carved with

Yggdrasil, the Norse Tree of the Universe.

GILCRUX

10 miles NE of Workington off the A596

From this village there are particularly good views across the Solway Firth to Scotland and it is well worth visiting for the 12th-century **Church of St Mary** which is believed to be the oldest building in the district. Standing on a walled mound and with a buttressed exterior, it has a thick-walled chancel. The village is remarkable for the number of its springs, at least five of which have never failed even in the driest summers.

ALLONBY

11 miles NE of Workington on the B5300

This traditional Solway village is backed by the Lake District fells and looks out across the Solway Firth to the Scottish hills. Popular with wind-surfers, the village has an attractive shingle and sand beach that received Seaside Awards in 1998 and 2005. The Allerdale Ramble and the Cumbrian Cycle Way both pass close by, and the village is also on the **Smuggler's Route** trail. Smuggling seems to have been a profitable occupation around here.

In the early 1800s, Allonby was a popular sea-bathing resort. The former seawater baths, built in 1835, the **Old Baths** are Grade II listed buildings, and stand in the old Market Square. In those days, the upper floor was in popular use as a ballroom for the local nobility; also in fashion was the drinking of sea water, in addition to bathing in it, as this was considered a health cure.

HOLME ST CUTHBERT

14 miles NE of Workington off the B5300

This inland hamlet is also known as Rowks because, in the Middle Ages, there was a chapel here dedicated to St Roche. The present church dates from 1845 but it contains an interesting torso of a medieval knight wearing chain mail. Found by schoolboys on a nearby farm, the hollowed-out centre of the torso was being used as a trough. It seems to be a 14th-century piece and could be a representation of Robert the Bruce's father, who died at Holm Cultram Abbey.

ASPATRIA

14 miles NE of Workington on the A596

Lying above the shallow Ellen Valley, Aspatria's main interest for most visitors lies in the elaborate **Memorial Fountain** to 'Watery Wilfred', Sir Wilfred Lawson MP (1829-1906), a lifelong crusader for the Temperance Movement and International Peace. According to one scribe, writing about Sir Wilfred Lawson, 'No man in his day made more people laugh at Temperance meetings.'

Also worth a visit is the much-restored **Norman Church** that is entered through a fine avenue of yew trees. Inside are several ancient relics including a 12th-century font with intricate carvings, a Viking hogback tombstone, and a grave cover with a pagan swastika-like engraving. Like many other churches in the area, the churchyard contains a holy well in which it is said St Kentigern baptised his converts.

BECKFOOT

16 miles NE of Workington on the B5300

At certain times and tides, the remains of a prehistoric forest can be seen on the sand beds here and, to the south of the village, is the site of a 2nd-century Roman fort known as **Bibra**. According to an inscribed stone found here, it was once occupied by an Auxiliary Cohort of 500 Pannonians (Spaniards) and surrounded by a large civilian settlement. The small stream flowing into the sea was used in World War I as a fresh water supply by German U-boats.

WIGTON

The pleasant market town of Wigton has adopted the title 'The Throstle Nest of all England' - throstle being the northern term for a thrush. The story is that a Wigton man returning home from the trenches of the Great War crested the hill and on seeing the familiar cluster of houses, churches, farms and the maze of streets, yards and alleys, exclaimed 'Awa' lads, it's the throstle's nest of England.'

For centuries Wigton has been the centre of the business and social life of the Solway coast and plain, its prosperity being based on the weaving of cotton and linen. It has enjoyed the benefits of a Royal Charter since 1262 and the market is still held on Tuesdays and Fridays.

Northeast of the hamlet of Holme St Cuthbert, and enveloped among low hills, is a lovely 30-acre lake known as Tarns Dub, which is a haven for birdlife. A couple of miles to the southwest, the headland of Dubmill Point is popular with sea anglers. When the tide is high and driven by a fresh westerly wind, the sea covers the road with lashing waves.

Wigton boasts a couple of interesting literary connections. Charles Dickens and Wilkie Collins stayed at The King's Arms Hotel in 1857, during the trip described in The Lazy Tour of Two Idle Apprentices, *and the author and broadcaster Melvyn Bragg (now Lord Bragg) was born here. The town, often disguised as Thurston, features in several of his novels, and sequences for the television dramatisation of* A Time to Dance *were set and filmed in Wigton. One mile south of Wigton are the scant remains of the Roman fort of Olenacum; most of its stones were removed to rebuild Wigton in the 18th and 19th centuries.*

87 TANGLEWOOD CARAVAN PARK

Causeway Head

Fully equipped mobile homes with all the mod cons you would expect to find in a self-catering property.

see page 198

Horse sales are held every April (riding horses and ponies) and October (Clydesdales, heavy horses and ponies). Today, most of the old town is a Conservation Area and, particularly along the **Main Street**, the upper storeys of the houses have survived in an almost unaltered state. On street corners, metal guards to prevent heavy horse-drawn wagons damaging the walls can also still be seen.

One feature of the town that should not be missed is the magnificent **Memorial Fountain** in the Market Place. It's gilded, floriate panels are set against Shap granite and surmounted with a golden cross. It was erected in 1872 by the philanthropist George Moore in memory of his wife, Eliza Flint Ray, with whom he fell in love when he was a penniless apprentice.

AROUND WIGTON

ABBEYTOWN

5 miles W of Wigton on the B5302

As its name suggests, Abbeytown grew up around the 12th-century **Abbey of Holm Cultram** on the River Waver and many of the town's buildings are constructed of stone taken from the Abbey when it fell into ruins. Founded by Cistercians in 1150, the Abbey bore the brunt of the constant feuds between the English and the Scots. In times of peace the community prospered and soon became one of the largest suppliers of wool in the North. The red sandstone **Church of St Mary** remained the parish church and was restored in 1883, a strange yet impressive building with the original nave shorn of its tower, transepts and chancel.

It has suffered further tragedy in a fire in June 2006 which destroyed the roof and historic papers, though the stained glass windows remained intact. The roof has since been replaced, though it remains closed to the public.

Near the church there are some lovely walks along the River Waver, which is especially rich in wildlife.

SILLOTH

11 miles NW of Wigton off the B5302

This charming old port and Victorian seaside resort is well worth exploring. With the coming of the railways in the 1850s, Silloth developed as a port and railhead for Carlisle. The Railway Company helped to develop the town and had grey granite shipped over in its own vessels from Ireland to build the handsome church which is such a prominent landmark. The town's name is derived from 'Sea Lath' – sea because of its position and lath being a grain store, used by monks from nearby Holm Cultram Abbey.

Visitors today will appreciate the invigorating but mild climate, the leisurely atmosphere, and the glorious sunsets over the sea that inspired Turner to record them for posterity. The town remains a delightful place to stroll, to admire the sunken rose garden and the pinewoods and 2 miles of promenades. Silloth's 18-hole championship golf course was the home course of Miss Cecil Leitch (1891-1978), the most celebrated lady player of her day. Another keen golfer was the great contralto Kathleen Ferrier. She lived for several years in Eden Street, Silloth, above the bank where her husband was the manager. A plaque on the wall records her stay here between 1936 and 1941.

One of the most popular attractions is the **Solway Coast Discovery Centre**, where Auld Michael the Monk and Oyk the Oystercatcher guide visitors through 10,000 years of Solway Coast history.

SKINBURNESS

11 miles NW of Wigton off the B5302

A lively market town, in the Middle Ages Skinburness was used by Edward I in 1299 as a base for his navy when attacking the Scots. A few years later a terrible storm destroyed the town; what survived became a small fishing hamlet. From nearby **Grune Point**, the start of the **Allerdale Ramble**, there are some tremendous views over the Solway Firth and the beautiful, desolate expanse of marshland and sandbank. Grune Point, which was once the site of a Roman fort, now forms part of a designated Site of Special Scientific Interest notable for the variety of its birdlife and marsh plants.

NEWTON ARLOSH

5 miles NW of Wigton on the B5307

Situated on the **Solway Marshes**, the village was first established by the monks of Holm Cultram Abbey in 1307 after the old port at Skinburness had been destroyed by

Sunset over the Solway, Silloth

the sea. The village's name means 'the new town on the marsh'. Work on the church did not begin until 1393, but the result is one of the most delightful examples of a Cumbrian fortified **Church**. In the Middle Ages there was no castle nearby to protect the local population from the border raids and so a pele tower was added to the church. As an additional defensive measure, the builders created what is believed to be narrowest church doorway in the country, barely 2 feet 7 inches across and a little over 5 feet high (It is said that the first partner through this tiny doorway at a wedding, as only one can fit through at a time, will be the boss!). The 12-inch arrow-slot east window is also the smallest in England. After the Reformation, the church became derelict but was finally restored in the 19th century. Inside there is a particularly fine eagle lectern carved out of bog oak.

88 SILLOTH CAFE

Silloth-on-Solway

A delightful café with a friendly host, offering homemade pies, cakes, scrumptious roast dinners and much more.

see page 199

89 JOINERS ARMS COUNTRY INN

Newton Arlosh

A handsomely decorated country Inn with fine atmosphere, dining, real ale and hospitality all rolled into one.

see page 199

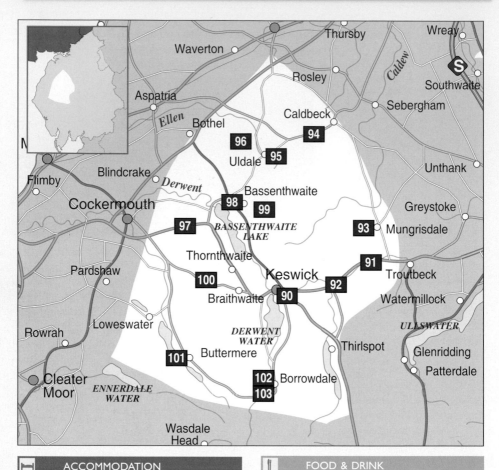

Keswick & The Northern Lakes

This part of the county is classic Lakeland; home to much of the wild and beautiful landscape which draws in so many visitors every year. The scenery is dominated by the rounded, heather-clad slopes of the Skiddaw range to the north of Keswick, and the untamed, craggy mountains of Borrowdale, to the south. Yet, despite this area's popularity, there are still many hidden places to discover and many opportunities to leave the beaten track.

The major town, Keswick, on the shores of Derwent Water, is a pleasant Lakeland town that has much to offer the visitor, with both the modern, in museums & galleries, and the historical, in churches and amazing historical locations. The lake too, is interesting as, not only is it in a near perfect setting, but it is unusual in having some islands – in this case four. It was the view over the lake, from Friar's Crag, that formed one of John Ruskin's early childhood memories.

It is the wonderful, dramatic scenery that makes this area of the Lake District so special. Not only are there several charming and isolated lakes within easy reach of Keswick, but Buttermere, considered by connoisseurs to be the best of all, lies only a few miles away. Not all the lakes, however, are what they first appear to be: Thirlmere, for example, is a 19th-century reservoir constructed to supply Manchester's growing thirst.

However, there is much more to this part of Cumbria than scenic appeal. The area is rich in history and there is frequent and significant evidence of Roman occupation. Castlerigg Stone Circle can be found here. The industrial heritage is also important, and many of the villages in the region relied on coal mining and mineral extraction for their livelihood.

The Lakeland Fells are home to Herdwick sheep, one of the country's hardiest breeds. Their coarse fleece cannot be dyed, but Herdwick sheep of various ages yield wool in a variety of subtle shades of grey and black which produces an unusual and very durable tweed-like weave used for carpet-making and insulation.

Derwent Water, nr Keswick

79

90 BRYSON'S OF KESWICK

Keswick

This family run bakery has been in business for over 60 years and a visit to Keswick is not complete without sampling the delicious cakes and pastries here.

¶ see page 200

KESWICK

"Above it rises Skiddaw,
majestic and famous,
and at its door is Derwentwater,
the lake beyond compare."

For generations, visitors to Keswick have been impressed by the town's stunningly beautiful setting, surrounded by the great fells of Blencathra, Saddleback, Helvellyn and Grizedale Pike.

Tourism, now the town's major industry, actually began in the mid-1700s and was given a huge boost, first by local clergyman Dr John Brown, and then by the Lakeland Poets in the early 1800s. By the 1780s the area was the most fashionable tourist destination in Europe, and the arrival of the railway in 1865 firmly established Keswick as the undisputed 'capital' of the Lake District with most of the area's notable attractions within easy reach. In a letter of 1752 Dr Brown wrote, *"The perfection of Keswick rests on three circumstances: beauty, horror and immensity."*

The grandeur of the lakeland scenery is of course the greatest draw but, among the man-made features, one not to be missed is the well-preserved **Castlerigg Stone Circle**. About a mile to the east of the town, the 38 standing stones, some of them 8 feet high, form a circle 100 feet in diameter. They are believed to have been put in place some 4,000 years ago and occupy a hauntingly beautiful position. Beautiful, but forbidding, as evoked by Keats in his poem *Hyperion*:

A dismal cirque of Druid stones,
upon a forlorn moor,
When the chill rain begins at shut of eve.
In dull November,
and their chancel vault,
The Heaven itself,
is blinded throughout night.

Keswick old town developed along the banks of the broad River Greta, with a wide main street leading up to the attractive **Moot Hall**. Built in 1813, the Hall has been at various times a buttermarket, courthouse and prison, Town Hall and now houses the Tourist Information Centre, with an art gallery above. A little further south, in **St John's Street**, the church of that name was built in the very same year as the Moot Hall and its elegant spire provides a point of reference from all around the town. In the churchyard is the grave of Sir Hugh Walpole, whose once hugely popular series of novels, *The Herries Chronicle* (1930-33), is set in this part of the Lake District.

In the riverside Fitz Park is the

Castlerigg Stone Circle

town's **Museum & Art Gallery** which is well worth a visit not just to see original manuscripts by Wordsworth and other Lakeland poets but also for the astonishing 'Rock, Bell and Steel Band' created by Joseph Richardson of Skiddaw in the 19th century. It's a kind of xylophone made of 60 stones (some a metre long), 60 steel bars and 40 bells. Four musicians are required to play this extraordinary instrument.

Surrounded by a loop of the River Greta to the northwest of the town is a museum which must be pencilled in on any visit to Keswick. This is the **Cumberland Pencil Museum**, which boasts the 6-feet long 'Largest Pencil in the World'. The 'lead' used in pencils (not lead at all but actually an allotrope of carbon) was accidentally discovered by a Borrowdale shepherd in the 16th century, and Keswick eventually became the world centre for the manufacture of lead pencils. The pencil mill here, established in 1832, is still operating – though the wadd, or lead, is now imported.

Other attractions in the town centre include the **Cars of the Stars Museum**, ideal for movie buffs since it contains such gems as Laurel and Hardy's Model T Ford, James Bond's Aston Martin, Chitty Chitty Bang Bang, Batman's Batmobile, Lady Penelope's pink Rolls-Royce FAB 1, the Mad Max car, and Mr Bean's Mini. There are film set displays and vehicles from series such as *The Saint*, *Knightrider*, *Bergerac* and *Postman Pat*, and Del Boy's 3-wheel Reliant from *Only*

Cars of the Stars Museum, Keswick

Fools and Horses is here, too. The bizarre **Puzzling Place** is an attraction based on optical illusion – where it is quite literally hard to believe your eyes. Experience the "anti-gravity room" where you'll swear balls can roll up hill, or the "ames room" using the same illusion as the "Lord of the Rings" film; making you visibly shrink to hobbit sized proportions, or grow to towering heights.

A short walk from the town centre, along Lake Road, leads visitors to the popular **Theatre by the Lake**, which hosts a year-round programme of plays, concerts, exhibitions, readings and talks. Close by is the pier from which there are regular departures for cruises around Derwentwater and ferries across the lake to Nichol End where you can hire just about every kind of water craft, including your own private cruise boat. One trip is to the National Trust's **Derwent Island House**, an

Keswick is host to several annual festivals, covering films, Cumbrian literature, jazz and beer. On the first Sunday in December a colourful 'Christmassy' Fayre is held in the Market Place In May the Keswick Mountain Festival is held; with a huge variety of events such as fell running, map reading and a triathlon, as well as less strenuous activities for all the family.

91 WHITE HORSE INN

Scales

Dating back to the 18th century, this inn still has all the same sociable character and charm.

 see page 201

92 THRELKELD MINING MUSEUM

Threlkeld, nr Keswick

A fascinating museum containing artefacts from the local mines and a unique collection of mining machinery.

 see page 200

Italianate house of the 1840s on a wooded island.

Another short walk will bring the visitor to **Friar's Crag**. This famous view of Derwent Water and its islands, now National Trust property, formed one of John Ruskin's early childhood memories, inspiring in him 'intense joy, mingled with awe'. Inscribed on his memorial here are these words: 'The first thing which I remember as an event in life was being taken by my nurse to the brow of Friar's Crag on Derwentwater.' The Crag is dedicated to the memory of Canon Rawnsley, the local vicar, who was one of the founder members of the National Trust, which he helped to set up in 1895.

AROUND KESWICK

THRELKELD

3 miles E of Keswick off the A66

From Keswick there's a delightful walk along the track bed of the old railway line to the charming village of Threlkeld, set in a plain at the foot of mighty **Blencathra**. The village is the ideal starting point for a number of mountain walks, including an ascent of Blencathra, one of the most exciting of all the Lake District mountains. Also known as Saddleback and a smaller sister of Skiddaw to the west, the steep sides ensure that it looks every inch a mountain. Threlkeld is famous for its annual sheepdog trials, though its economy was built upon the several mines in the area and the granite quarry to the south.

At **Threlkeld Quarry &**

Mining Museum visitors can browse through the collection of vintage excavators, old quarry machinery and other mining artefacts, wander through the locomotive shed and machine shop, or join the 45-minute tour through a re-created mine. The museum has interpretive displays of Lakeland geology and quarrying, and is used as a teaching facility by several university geology departments.

Threlkeld Mining Museum has perhaps the finest collection of small mining and quarrying artefacts – everything from wedges, chisels and drills to candles, clogs and kibbles (large iron buckets used to transport ore). The museum is open daily 10am – 5pm.

MATTERDALE END

8 miles E of Keswick on the A5091

This tiny hamlet lies at one end of Matterdale, a valley that is an essential stop on any Wordsworth trail – for it was here, on April 15th 1802, that he and his sister saw that immortal:

> *host of golden daffodils,*
> *Beside the lake, beneath the trees,*
> *Fluttering and dancing in the breeze.*

MUNGRISDALE

7 miles NE of Keswick off the A66

The village, still predominately a farming community, is quite popular with tourists, no doubt for its idyllic position overlooked by the imposing fells of Blencathra, Bowscale and Carrock and complemented by the Caldew and Glenderamakin becks.

The name of the village comes

from Mungo, the name by which St Kentigern was known by those close to him, and the village church, not surprisingly, is dedicated to him. Though **St Kentigern's Church** is believed to have been established here as early as AD 552, the present building dates from 1756 and contains a fine example of a 17th-century triple-decker pulpit. A memorial on the church wall reveals an intriguing connection with Wordsworth. The tablet commemorates Raisley Calvert whose son, also called Raisley, was 'nursed by Wordsworth'. The younger Raisley was a sculptor and friend of the poet, but fell ill of consumption (tuberculosis). Wordsworth spent many hours by his bedside in Penrith hospital but Raisley passed away in 1795, leaving in his will the huge sum of £900 to his friend. The bequest was timely and enabled the poet to complete, with his friend Coleridge, the seminal poems that were published in 1798 as the *Lyrical Ballads*.

CALDBECK
13 miles N of Keswick on the B5299

Caldbeck is perhaps the best-known village in the northern Lakes because of its associations with **John Peel**, the famous huntsman who died in 1854 after falling from his horse. He is buried in the churchyard here. His ornate tombstone is decorated with depictions of hunting horns and his favourite hound. Also buried here are John Peel's wife Mary and their four children.

A few paces from Peel's tomb lies 'The Fair Maid of Buttermere', whose grave bears her married name, Mary Harrison. With its picturesque church, village green, cricket pitch, pond and blacksmith's forge, Caldbeck has all the ingredients of a picture-postcard village.

There has been a **Church** here in Caldbeck since the 12th century, one of only eight in England to be dedicated to St Kentigern. The other seven are also to be found in the north of Cumbria, where Kentigern, a bishop in the Strathclyde area of Scotland who was also known as Mungo, spent his time in exile.

Some 200 years ago Caldbeck was an industrial village, with corn mills, woollen mills and a paper mill all powered by the fast-flowing 'cold stream' – the Caldbeck. **Priest's Mill**, built in 1702 by the Rector of Caldbeck, next to his church, was a stone-grinding corn mill, powered by a waterwheel which has now been restored to working order. The Priest's Mill buildings are also home to a gift shop, craft workshops and café.

HESKET NEWMARKET
13 miles N of Keswick off the B5305

Set around a well-kept village green, this pleasing little village used to have its own market, as the name suggests, and much earlier there was probably also a racecourse here, since that is what 'Hesket' meant in Old Scandinavian. It could well be the reason why the village's main street

93 THE MILL INN

Mungrisdale
A 17th century inn serving up sumptuous food, comfortable accommodation and wonderful service in equal measures.

see *page 202*

94 SWALEDALE WATCH

Whelpo, nr Caldbeck
Offering lovely B&B accommodation on a working sheep farm, surrounded by glorious, unspoilt countryside.

see *page 202*

95 PONDEROSA GUEST HOUSE

Uldale, nr Wigton

Remarkable guest house with friendly host, offering guests a stay they will want to repeat again. Self catering accommodation is also available in an adjacent cottage.

 see page 203

96 SNITTLEGARTH LODGES

Snittlegarth, nr Ireby

Superb self-catering lodges located in a peaceful and isolated setting. Open all year round.

see page 203

is so wide. Although the market is no longer held, Hesket hosts two important agricultural events each year: an Agricultural Show and Sheepdog Trials. There's also a vintage motor cycle rally in May.

Charles Dickens and Wilkie Collins stayed at Hesket Newmarket in the 1850s and wrote about it in their *Lazy Tour of Two Idle Apprentices*.

ULDALE

11 miles N of Keswick off the A591

To the northeast of Bassenthwaite Lake stretches the area known locally as the 'Land Back of Skidda', a crescent of fells and valleys constituting the most northerly part of the Lake District National Park. This peaceful region is well off the tourist track and offers visitors a delightful landscape of gently undulating bare-backed fells and valleys sheltering unspoilt villages such as Uldale. This village, a sheep farming area in the medieval ages due to the surrounding sheep-friendly hills and grasses, still retains its heritage. To this day haymaking still takes place on the village green, and dairy cows are very much part of the scenery.

Horace Walpole featured Uldale and its moorland surroundings in two of his *Herries Chronicle* novels, *Judith Paris* and *The Fortress*. This tranquil village has one additional claim to fame: it was the daughter of an Uldale farmer who eloped with and married the legendary huntsman, John Peel (see Caldbeck).

GREAT CROSTHWAITE

1½ miles NW of Keswick on the A66

In the churchyard of St Kentigern stands the grave of Robert Southey (1774-1843), one of the most distinguished of the Lake Poets.

BASSENTHWAITE LAKE

4 miles NW of Keswick on the A66

Only 70 feet deep and with borders rich in vegetation, Bassenthwaite Lake provides an ideal habitat for birds – more than 70 species have been recorded around the lake. Successful breeding is encouraged by the fact that no powerboats are allowed on the lake, and some areas are off limits to boats of any kind. Also, most of the shoreline is privately owned, with public access restricted mostly to the eastern shore where the Allerdale Ramble follows the lakeside for a couple of miles or so.

At the northern end of the lake, at Coalbeck Farm, **Trotters World of Animals** is home to many hundreds of animals – rare breeds, traditional farm favourites, endangered species, birds of prey and reptiles. In addition to the ring-tailed lemurs, wallabies, racoons and gibbons, there are rough-coated lemurs, lechwe antelope, red, fallow and sika deer and guanaco. Visitors to the 25-acre site can bottle-feed baby animals, cuddle bunnies, meet Monty the python, take a tractor trailer ride, watch the birds of prey demonstrations, find a quiet picnic spot or sample the fare on offer in Trotters Tea Room. And for the smaller children there's an indoor soft play climbing centre. Winner of the Good Britain Guide Cumbria Family Attraction of the Year, as a member of the National Association of Farms for Schools, Trotters can cater for school groups either for an informal day out or for a structured programme based on National Curriculum requirements.

Rising grandly above Bassenthwaite's eastern shore is **Skiddaw** which, ever since the Lake District was opened up to tourists by the arrival of the railway in the 19th century, has been one of the most popular peaks to climb. Although it rises to some 3,054 feet, the climb is both safe and manageable, if a little unattractive lower down, and typically takes around two hours. From the summit, on a clear day, there are spectacular views to Scotland in the north, the Isle of Man in the west, the Pennines to the east, and to the south the greater part of the Lake District.

Also on the eastern shore is the secluded, originally Norman, **Church of St Bridget & St Bega** which Tennyson had in mind when, in his poem *Morte d'Arthur*, he describes Sir Bedivere carrying the dead King Arthur:

> *to a chapel in the fields,*
> *A broken chancel with a broken cross,*
> *That stood on a dark strait of*
> *barren land.*

This, then, would make Bassenthwaite Lake the resting place of Excalibur but, as yet, no one has reported seeing a lady's arm, 'clothed in white samite, mystic, wonderful', rising from the waters and holding aloft the legendary sword.

Set back from the lakeside, **Mirehouse** is a 17th-century building which has been home to the Spedding family since 1688. This beautiful house, still a lived-in family home, is rich in history and makes for a delightful visit including live piano music. Literary visitors to the house included Tennyson, Thomas Carlyle, and Edward Fitzgerald, the poet and translator of *The Rubaiyat of Omar Khayyam*. As well as some manuscripts by these family friends, there is also a fine collection of furniture. Visitors are welcome to wander through the gardens and enjoy, among its attractions, an ancient wildflower meadow with 43 different species of plant, a sheltered bee garden and gentle lakeside walk. There are four woodland playgrounds for children to explore, as well as a heather maze which proves a delight for old and young alike. The gardens are open daily from the middle of March to

97 THE WHEATSHEAF

Embleton, nr Cockermouth
Popular inn just off the A66 in stunning surroundings.

see page 204

98 RAVENSTONE LODGE

Bassenthwaite
This lovely hotel is set amongst magnificent Cumbrian scenery.

see page 205

Mirehouse, Bassenthwaite Lake

99 LAKELAND COTTAGE HOLIDAYS

Melbecks, nr Bassenthwaite

60 self-catering properties available combining period charm with modern comforts.

see page 205

100 WHINLATTER FOREST PARK

Braithwaite

The forest provides many and varied opportunities for outdoor activities, amid exceptional scenery.

 see page 208

October but the house, because it is still a family home, is open only on Sunday and Wednesday afternoons during the season, and also on Friday afternoons during August.

BRAITHWAITE

3 miles W of Keswick on the B5292

This small village lies at the foot of the **Whinlatter Pass**, another of Cumbria's dramatic routes. The summit of this steep road, the B5292, is some 1,043 feet above sea level and, on the westerly descent, there are magnificent views over Bassenthwaite Lake.

The road runs through the **Whinlatter Forest Park**, the only Mountain Forest in England and one of the Forestry Commission's oldest woodlands. The park offers a wide range of activities for all ages and fitness levels, from waymarked trails to cycling, orienteering or just strolling along and admiring the views. Whinlatter Forest Park boasts a Visitor Centre, adventure playground, viewpoints, gift shop and a tearoom with a terrace overlooking the woodlands and valley, and it is the starting point for several trails suitable for the whole family.

Many of the record numbers who visit the centre come to see live footage of the Lake District ospreys, beamed to a special viewing facility, or to see the birds through high-powered telescopes at the Dodd Wood viewing point. **The Lake District Osprey Project** is a partnership of the Forestry Commission, the Lake District National Park Authority and the RSPB, whose aim is to protect the nesting ospreys and to encourage other ospreys to settle and breed in other suitable locations.

A new addition to the park is the **Go Ape!** High-wire adventure course, literally up in the forest canopy, this giant obstacle course (including the country's best zip lines) is great for a high adrenaline day in this beautiful location.

HIGH & LOW LORTON

8 miles W of Keswick on the B5292

Lorton began life as two smaller villages, though now they have grown together; Low lies in the vale of Lorton, a farming valley, while High is up near the end of the Whinlatter pass.

The ancient yew tree that Wordsworth wrote about in his poem *Yew Trees* is still there, behind the village hall of High Lorton. It was in the shade of its branches that the Quaker George Fox preached to a large gathering under the watchful eye of Cromwell's soldiers. In Low Lorton, set beside the River Cocker, is **Lorton Hall** (private) which is reputed to be home to the ghost of a woman who carries a lighted candle. Less spectral guests in the past have included King Malcolm III of Scotland, who stayed here with his queen while visiting the southern boundaries of his Kingdom of Strathclyde of which this area was a part.

LOWESWATER

10 miles W of Keswick off the B5289

Reached by narrow winding lanes,

Loweswater is one of the smaller lakes, framed in an enchanting fellside and forest setting. The name, appropriately, means 'leafy lake', and eons ago it was just part of a vast body of water that included what is now Crummock Water and Buttermere. Because it is so shallow, never more than 60 feet deep, Loweswater provides an ideal habitat for wildfowl, which also benefit from the fact that this is perhaps the least-visited lake in the whole of Cumbria. To the east of the lake lies the small village of the same name, while to the north stretches one of the quietest and least-known parts of the National Park, a landscape of low fells through which there are few roads or even paths.

CRUMMOCK WATER

8 miles SW of Keswick on the B5289

Fed by both Buttermere and Loweswater, this is by far the largest of the three lakes. In this less frequented part of western Cumbria, where there are few roads, the attractions of Crummock Water can usually be enjoyed in solitude. Best seen from the top of Rannerdale Knotts, to the east, the lake has a footpath running around it – though, in places, the going gets a little strenuous.

BUTTERMERE

8 miles SW of Keswick on the B5289

Half the size of its neighbour, Crummock Water, Buttermere is a beautiful lake set in a dramatic landscape. To many connoisseurs of the Lake District landscape, this is the most splendid of them all. The walk around Buttermere gives superb views of the eastern towers of **Fleetwith Pike** and the great fell wall made up of High Crag, High Stile and Red Pike.

In the early 1800s the village became involved in one of the great scandals of the age. Mary Robinson, the daughter of a local innkeeper, had been described as a maiden of surpassing beauty in J Budworth's book *A Fortnight's Ramble in the Lakes*. She became something of a local attraction, with people flocking to the inn to admire her beauty, among them Wordsworth and Coleridge. Another was a smooth-tongued gentleman who introduced himself as Alexander Augustus Colonel Hope, MP, brother of the Earl of Hopetoun. Mary fell for his charms and married him, only to discover that her husband was really John Hatfield, a bankrupt impostor and a bigamist to boot. Hatfield was tried at Carlisle for fraud, a capital offence in those days, and Coleridge supplemented his meagre income by reporting the sensational trial for the *Morning Post*. Hatfield was found guilty and was hanged at Carlisle gaol in 1802; Mary later married a local farmer and went on to live an uneventful and happy life.

The author, broadcaster and great supporter of Cumbria, Melvyn (Lord) Bragg, tells the story of Mary Robinson in his novel, *The Maid of Buttermere*.

Standing above the village is the small, picturesque **Church of**

101 DALEGARTH GUESTHOUSE AND CAMPSITE

Buttermere

A stunning guesthouse and luxury campsite nestled in one of the best fell walking areas in Cumbria.

see page 206

102 SEATOLLER FARM

Borrowdale

With a choice of B&B, self catering or camping, Seatoller is the ideal base for walking or simply just relaxing in the enchanting English Lake District.

see page 208

Buttermere

St James, where the special features of interest include an antique organ and a memorial to Alfred Wainwright, whose ashes were scattered on his favourite place, Haystacks, a fell near Buttermere.

BORROWDALE

Runs S from Keswick via the B5289

"The Mountains of Borrowdale are perhaps as fine as anything we have seen" wrote John Keats in 1818. Six miles long, this brooding, mysterious valley, steep and narrow with towering crags and deep woods, is generally regarded as the most beautiful in the Lake District. Just to the south of Derwent Water are the **Lodore Falls**, where the Watendlath Beck drops some 120 feet before reaching the lake. In woodland owned by the National Trust, lies the extraordinary **Bowder Stone** which provides an irresistible photo-opportunity for most visitors. A massive 50 feet square and weighing almost 2,000 tons, it stands precariously on one corner, apparently defying gravity. A wooden staircase on one side provides easy access to the top. South of Grange village, the valley narrows into the 'Jaws of Borrowdale'. Castle Crag, the western mandible of the Jaws, has on its summit the remains of the defensive ditches of a Romano-British fort.

From Seatoller, the B5289

slices through the spectacular **Honister Pass**, overlooked by the dramatic 1,000-feet-high Honister Crag. At the top of the pass, the 18th-century **Honister Slate Mine** has been re-opened and is once again producing the beautiful green slate that adorns so many Lakeland houses and is famous throughout the world. Buckingham Palace, The Ritz Hotel, New Scotland Yard and RAF Cranwell are among the prestigious buildings donned with this stone. Helmets and lights are provided for a guided tour through great caverns of the mine to show how a mixture of modern and traditional methods is still extracting the slate which was formed here some 400 million years ago. The monks of Furness Abbey are thought to have been the first to avail themselves of Honister Slate Mine's resources, about 500 years ago. After the tour, complimentary tea or coffee is served in the Bait Cabin beside a warm fire, and the complex also has an informative Visitor Centre (honoured as the friendliest in the North of England) and a gift shop selling the ornamental green slate.

THIRLMERE

4 miles S of Keswick off the A591

This attractive, tree-lined lake, one of the few in the Lakes that can be driven around as well as walked around, was created in the 1890s by the Manchester Corporation. More than 100 miles of pipes and tunnels still supply the city with water from Thirlmere. At first there was no public access to the lake shore, but today these have been opened up for recreational use with car parks, walking trails and picnic places.

The creation of the huge **Thirlmere Reservoir**, 5 miles long, flooded the two hamlets of **Armboth** and **Wythburn**. All that remains of these places today is Wythburn chapel towards the southern end.

103 ASHNESS FARM

Borrowdale

Very comfortable accommodation in the heart of the Borrowdale valley.

see page 207

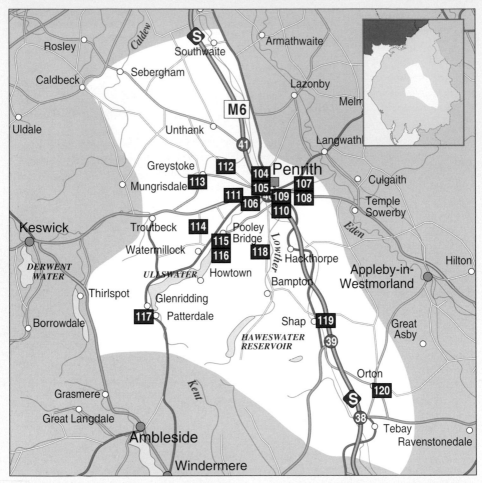

In and Around Penrith

Penrith is the most historic of Lakeland towns, no doubt for its position on the main west coast artery linking England and Scotland. Unfortunately much has been lost of this history from the landscape; today no visible remains of the forts built during Roman occupancy are here. Also most of the town's oldest buildings have also disappeared, victims of the incessant Border conflicts down the centuries.

The town of Penrith today is a busy place, its location close to the M6 and within easy reach not only of the Lakes but also the Border Country and the Yorkshire Dales making it a hub of this northwestern corner of England.

Only a few miles from the town, Ullswater, 8 miles long and the second longest lake in Cumbria, is also one of its most beautiful. The area around Penrith has some interesting old buildings, notably Shap Abbey and Brougham Castle, as well as two outstanding stately homes, Hutton-in-the-Forest where the Inglewood family have lived since 1605, and Dalemain, which has also been inhabited by the same family for more than 300 years. There is also the romantic, and slightly eerie, shell of Lowther Castle (the interior having been demolished in 1957, to be sold off), the grandeur of which has still survived and is due to become quite an attraction for the area through a project recently undertaken.

Brougham Castle

🍴 FOOD & DRINK

🏛 PLACES OF INTEREST

104 AGRICULTURAL HOTEL

Penrith

This stunning hotel has a wonderful history to go with the great accommodation and splendid service.

 see page 209

105 SCOTT'S FISH BAR & STEAKHOUSE GRILL

Penrith

Scott's Fish bar, serving fast food with a twist – it's all homemade.

 see page 210

PENRITH

This lively town has a charming mixture of narrow streets and wide-open spaces, such as **Great Dockray** and **Sandgate**, into which cattle were herded during Scottish raids. Later they became market places; a traditional market is still held here every Tuesday. There is also a new local farmers market which is held every third Tuesday of the month in market square.

A short walk from the town centre leads to **Penrith Castle**, built from attractive sandstone, which has a busy history. In 1399 William Strickland (the later Bishop of Carlisle and Archbishop of Canterbury) added to an earlier Pele tower, in defence of the raids which Penrith had become vulnerable to. The much-maligned Richard, Duke of Gloucester (later Richard III) strengthened the castle's defences and was responsible for keeping the peace along the border with Scotland. By the time of the Civil War, however, the castle was in a state of ruin; the townspeople helped themselves to the fallen stones to build their own houses. The castle ruins still stand to this day cutting an impressive sight within the town, high above a steep-sided moat, in the delightful castle park.

The town is dominated by **Beacon Hill Pike**, which stands amidst wooded slopes high above Penrith. The tower was built in 1719 and marks the place where, from 1296, beacons were lit to warn the townsfolk of an impending attack. The beacon was last lit during the Napoleonic wars in 1804 and was seen by the author Sir Walter Scott, who was visiting Cumberland at the time.

It is well worth the climb from the Beacon Edge, along the footpath to the summit, to enjoy a magnificent view of the Lakeland fells. It was on top of this hill, in 1767, that Thomas Nicholson, a murderer, was hanged. The gibbet was left on the summit and so, it is said, was Nicholson's ghost, seen in the form of a skeleton hanging from the noose.

Penrith has a splendid Georgian church in a very attractive churchyard, surrounded by a number of interesting buildings. The oldest part of **St Andrew's Church** dates from Norman times but the most recent part, the nave, was rebuilt between 1720 and 1722. Buried somewhere in the churchyard is Wordsworth's mother, but her grave is not marked, and there is a tablet on the wall recording the deaths of 2,260 citizens of Penrith in the plague of 1597.

Overlooking the churchyard is a splendid Tudor house, bearing the date 1563, which was at one time Dame Birkett's School. The school's most illustrious pupils were William Wordsworth, his sister Dorothy, and his future wife, Mary Hutchinson. The **Town Hall** is the result of a 1905 conversion of two former Adam-style houses, one of which was known as Wordsworth House, as it was the home of the poet's cousin, Captain John Wordsworth.

The red sandstone from which many of Penrith's Victorian houses were built was quarried along the escarpments of Beacon Edge, and one of the old quarries, at **Cowraik**, is now a local nature reserve. In addition to the interesting variety of wildlife established down the years, it is a Site of Special Scientific Interest for the geological interest of the quarry faces. The rocks are the remnants of sand dunes formed 250 million years ago when the Eden Valley was part of a dry, sandy desert that started just north of the Equator.

The **Penrith Agricultural Show**, held yearly on the fourth Saturday in July, has grown since its conception in 1834 when it was held in a field adjoining Croft House, so it is now held just out of Penrith town at the larger area of Brougham Hall Farm. It is not to be missed for its celebration of not just local agriculture and breeding, but for British food and farming in general. In addition to the livestock shows, there are a great range of rural crafts, trade stands and local entertainment to engage the whole family.

Penrith's most spectacular and dynamic visitor attraction, **Rheged Discovery Centre**, dedicates itself to 'a celebration of 2,000 years of Cumbria's history, mystery and magic – as never seen before'. Named after Cumbria's Celtic Kingdom, this extraordinary grass-covered building is also home to

Britain's only exhibition dedicated to mountains and mountain adventure. It also has a giant cinema screen, speciality shops, art and craft exhibitions, restaurants and a children's play area.

For those who are a fan of the quaint, a visit to the **Lilliput Lane Visitors Centre** housed in the charming thatched Honeysuckle cottage, in Skirsgill just outside of Penrith, is a perfect treat. Lilliput Lane miniature cottages, which are popular worldwide, was founded in 1982 and here you can see a huge range of cottages, including discontinued models and a special model of Dove Cottage – Wordsworth's house at Grassmere. Tours are also available, where you can see the intricate process of creating these miniature cottages at work.

The **Penrith and Eden Museum** is another attraction worth visiting on your trip to the town. Housed in the Robinson's school Elizabethan building which

106 RHEGED DISCOVERY CENTRE

Penrith

Penrith's most spectacular visitor attraction, **Rheged Discovery Centre**, dedicates itself to "a celebration of 2000 years of Cumbria's history, mystery and magic - as never seen before".

🏛 *see page 209*

Lilliput Lane Honeysuckle Cottage

107 BROUGHAM CASTLE

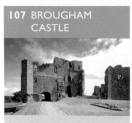

Brougham

Picturesque Brougham Castle was begun in the early 13th century by Robert de Vieuxpont, near the site of a Roman fort guarding the crossing of the River Eamont.

 see page 211

108 HORNBY HALL

Brougham

A gracious country house providing charming accommodation and first class cuisine within an enviable location.

 see page 211

109 THE BEEHIVE

Eamont Bridge

This 18th century inn offers all the best in hospitality as well as providing a menu, suitable for all- from pub classics to the very imaginative.

see page 212

dates from 1670, it provides exhibits exploring the history, geology and archaeology of the area, including prehistoric artefacts, and also a gallery of changing exhibitions of historic and contemporary arts interest.

AROUND PENRITH

BROUGHAM

1 mile SE of Penrith off the A66

About a mile southeast of Penrith, the substantial and imposing remains of **Brougham Castle** (English Heritage) stand on the foundations of a Roman fort. The castle was inherited in the 1640s by the redoubtable and immensely rich Lady Anne Clifford, whose patrimony as Countess of Pembroke, Dorset and Montgomery also included another five northern castles. She spent a fortune restoring them all in medieval style, though Brougham was Lady Anne's favourite castle and she died here in 1676 at the age of 86. The substantial ruins here, on the lovely site on the banks of the River Eamont, are open for the public to wander through. There are several rooms, including the one in which Lady Clifford slept, and died, and there is a passage which runs all the way around within the walls, from which you can get some lovely views.

From the castle there's a delightful riverside walk to **Eamont Bridge** and the circular **Mayburgh Henge**, which dates from prehistoric times. On the huge embankment, more than 100 yards across, stands a single, large stone about 10 feet high. Close to the village, on the banks of the River Eamont, is **Giant's Cave**, the supposed lair of a man-eating giant called Isir. This local tale is linked with the legend of Tarquin, a giant knight who imprisoned 64 men in

River Eamont, Brougham

his cave and was eventually killed by Sir Lancelot. A nearby prehistoric earthwork has been known as **King Arthur's Round Table** for many centuries.

Lady Anne also rebuilt the chapel that stands on a hill above the castle, next to **Brougham Hall**. Brougham Hall's colourful history goes back 500 years. The Hall today, set in its own park, is home to a number of shops, craft workshops, smokehouse, ornamental ironwork and a brewery. The chapel, dedicated to St Wilfred, contains a remarkable collection of items acquired by William Brougham, later the 2nd Baron Brougham and Vaux; notable among them are French and Flemish stalls from the 16th and 17th centuries. The old parish church of Brougham is the remotely located **St Ninian's**, also known as Ninekirks, which contains some family box pews that are screened so that they look almost like cages.

HUTTON-IN-THE-FOREST

6 miles N of Penrith on the B5305

The home of the Inglewood family since 1605, **Hutton-in-the-Forest Historic House** was originally a medieval stronghold and the **Pele Tower** still exists. Among the notable features are the 17th-century Gallery, the Hall dominated by a Cupid staircase, and a room decorated in the Arts and Crafts style. The splendid grounds include a beautiful Dutch walled garden built in the 1730s, topiary terraces that were originally laid out in the 17th century, and fine specimen trees and a 17th-century dovecote (built to accommodate an amazing 400 birds) that form part of the peaceful Woodland Walk. There are also three ponds, the largest and oldest middle pond dates to mid-eighteenth century.

STAINTON

2 miles W of Penrith off the A66 or A592

At Stainton **The Alpaca Centre** was set up in 1997 and has become a focal point for the development and expanding knowledge of the alpaca, fueling the increasingly popular farming of this strange and gentle creature in the UK. The Centre is a working farm: breeding, rearing and selling alpacas, and welcomes visits at any time of the year. Visitors can see the alpacas in their paddocks and browse through the goods in the Spirit of the Andes shop, mostly made from the exceptional alpaca fibre. Also at the centre are a tea room and a gallery with a collection of furniture and ornamental pieces in wood.

GREYSTOKE

5 miles W of Penrith on the B5288

Greystoke Castle is set in an estate of some three thousand acres. This huge expanse of land, offering dramatic views of the mountains of the Lake District and North Pennines, was traditionally used for sport, and now remains as active as ever. They offer exhilarating off-road 4x4 lessons and other pursuits such as falconry and fly fishing.

According to Edgar Rice Burroughs, the castle was the ancestral home of Tarzan, Lord of

110 THE CROWN HOTEL

Eamont Bridge

A welcoming former coaching inn set in the heart of the beautiful Eden Valley which has gained a fantastic reputation for top quality cuisine

see page 212

111 KINGS ARMS

Stainton

This well run inn has been in business since 1721 and the age adds to the excellent atmosphere.

see page 214

112 THE SUN INN

Newton Reigny

A popular choice for visitors and locals alike, with 5 comfortable bedrooms and a warm atmosphere. A quiz night is held every Wednesday.

see page 213

113 BOOT & SHOE

Greystoke

This 400 year old pub offers great food and warm, comfortable accommodation.

🍴 🛏 see page 214

the Apes. Tarzan's aristocratic credentials would have come as something of a surprise to the dignified Barons of Greystoke, whose effigies are preserved in **St Andrew's Church**. As imposing and spacious as a cathedral, St Andrew's boasts an east window with much 13th-century glass and, in the Lady Chapel, a figure of the Madonna and Child carved by a German prisoner-of-war. An ancient sanctuary stone, now concealed behind a grille, marks the point beyond which fugitives could claim sanctuary.

Greystoke village itself is a gem, its attractive houses grouped around a trimly maintained village green. Nearby are the stables where Gordon Richards trained his two Grand National winners, Lucius and Hello Dandy.

TIRRIL

2 miles SW of Penrith on the B5320

Like its neighbour, Yanwath, Tirril has connections with the Quaker Movement. At Tirril there is an old

Dalemain House and Gardens

Quaker Meeting House (now in private ownership), while **Yanwath Hall**, reputed to be the finest manorial hall in England, was the birthplace of the Quaker Thomas Wilkinson. Modern Yanwath also boasts an interesting gallery, located in a cottage garden setting.

DALEMAIN

3 miles SW of Penrith off the A592

Dalemain House is one of the area's most popular attractions – an impressive house with a medieval and Tudor core fronted by an imposing Georgian façade. The house has been home to the same family since 1679 – Sir Edward Hasell bought the property in that year – and over the years they have accumulated fine collections of china, furniture and family portraits. The grand drawing rooms boast some very fine oak panelling and in the Chinese Room is some beautifully preserved 18th-century Chinese wallpaper and a rococo chimneypiece by Nathaniel Hedges in Chinese Chippendale style; visitors also have access to the Nursery (furnished with toys from all ages) and Housekeeper's Room. Other interesting features include "Mrs Mouse's" house built into the back stairs. Also a homemade meal can be enjoyed here in the medieval tea room, during the summer and winter (with a welcoming open log fire for the colder season).

The Norman pele tower at Dalemain House displays the regimental collection of the Westmorland and Cumberland Yeomanry, a troop of mounted

Ullswater

infantry usually led by the Hasell family itself.

The 16th-century Great Barn contains an interesting assortment of agricultural bygones. The extensive grounds include a walled orchard with ancient apple trees, a medieval herb garden, a Tudor-walled knot garden with a fine early Roman fountain, a Tudor gazebo, a wild garden alongside Dacre Beck, a deer park, Fell Pony Museum and woodland and riverside walks.

DACRE

4 miles SW of Penrith off the A66

There is much of historic interest in this largely unspoilt village, surrounded by farmland and green hills. The **Church of St Andrew** occupies a site of a 7th century Saxon monastery, though the building here now is largely rebuilt from 1810. The church is renowned for its unusual four weather-beaten carvings of bears in the churchyard. The bears are shown, respectively, sleeping, being attacked by a cat, shaking off the cat and eating the cat.

POOLEY BRIDGE

5 miles SW of Penrith on the B5320

The charming village of Pooley Bridge stands at the northern tip of **Ullswater**, and there are regular cruise departures from here during the season, stopping at Glenridding and Howton. Rowing and powered boats are available for hire, and since Ullswater is in effect a public highway, private boats can also be launched. A speed limit of 10mph applies over the whole of the 8-mile-long serpentine lake. Also, the greater part of the shoreline is privately owned and landing is not permitted.

Wordsworth noted the curious fact that the lake creates a sextuple

114 THE HORSE AND FARRIER

Dacre

A traditional pub with a wide variety of delicious food in idyllic Cumbrian surroundings.

see page 215

115 POOLEY BRIDGE INN

Pooley Bridge, Lake Ullswater

Delightful family-run Inn, with traditional bar with fire-place, delicious locally sourced menu, and accommodation with en-suite.

see page 216

116 PARK FOOT

Pooley Bridge

The very best in camping, caravan and self-catering accommodation in superb location overlooking Ullswater.

see page 217

About 4 miles southwest of Watermillock, there are a series of waterfalls which tumble down through a wooded gorge and then into Ullswater. The name of the largest fall is Aira Force (70 feet high) and the second largest is High Force. They can easily be reached on foot through the woodlands of Gowbarrow Estate, which is owned by the National Trust. This famous waterfall, which can be viewed from stone bridges at top and bottom.

117 THE WHITE LION INN

Patterdale

A warm welcome is extended to all from the White Lion Inn offering comfy accommodation and quality food in the breathtaking land of the famous Kirkstone Pass.

see page 217

echo, a natural phenomenon that the Duke of Portland exploited in the mid-1700s by keeping a boat on the lake equipped 'with brass guns, for the purpose of exciting echoes'. In Wordsworth's opinion Ullswater provides *"the happiest combination of beauty and grandeur, which any of the Lakes affords"* – a view with which most visitors concur.

The oldest building in Pooley Bridge is part of **Holly House**, which dates back to 1691, while the Bridge of the village's name dates from 1763 when the elegant structure over the River Eamont was built at a cost of £400. At that time a regular fresh fish market was held in the village square. Before Bridge was added, the name Pooley meant 'pool by the hill' and was derived from the pond which existed behind **Dunmallard**, the cone-shaped hill on the other side of the River Eamont. Above the village, on the summit of Dunmallard, are the remains of an Iron Age fort and, of course, splendid views southwards over Ullswater. This is a very popular area for camping, with several spots located in the countryside around the village.

WATERMILLOCK

7 miles SW of Penrith on the A592

This small village, perfectly situated on the shores of Ullswater, is hidden amongst the woodland which occupies much of the lake's western shores. It is quite a popular spot for visitors, due to its lake-side position, and so many of the buildings have been converted into accommodation, for example several farm buildings and the traditional coaching Inn Brackenrigg.

GLENRIDDING

14 miles SW of Penrith on the A592

A popular base for walkers about to tackle the daunting challenge of **Helvellyn** (3,115 feet) via Striding Edge, Glenridding is the largest and busiest of Ullswater's lakeside villages. Lake cruises depart from here, rowing boats are available for hire and there's plenty of room for waterside picnics.

PATTERDALE

15 miles SW of Penrith on the A592

It is this village's magnificent setting that makes it such a popular tourist destination. Close to the head of Ullswater and with a series of fells framing the views, the scenery is indeed splendid. On the north side of the village is **St Patrick's Well**, which was thought to have healing properties. The medieval chapel dedicated to the saint was rebuilt in the 1850s.

ASKHAM

3 miles S of Penrith off the A6

Askham is a pleasant village set around two greens. In the centre of the village is one of its most interesting shops, the **Toy Works** (open Wednesday to Sunday), which combines a traditional toy shop with a toymaker's workshop. Special services include advice on restoring rocking horses and a repair service 'for ailing and worn old teddy bears'. This pretty village has many features, both aestheticly pleasing and historic, in its whitewashed cottages (one dating as far back as 1724) and two traditional pubs (the 18th century **Punch Bowl**, and 17th century **Queen's Head**) which have both retained original features. Also there is **Askham Hall** (private), an Elizabethan mansion converted from a 14th century pele tower.

Askham Fell, which rises to the west, is dotted with prehistoric monuments including one known as the Copt (or Cop) Stone, said to mark the burial site of a Celtic chieftain.

LOWTHER

4 miles S of Penrith off the A6

Lowther Castle, the ancestral owners of whom were the illustrious Earls of Lonsdale, is now only a shell, most of it having been demolished in 1957. Even in this state of emptiness it is still an imposing and grand place: after one visit Queen Victoria is reputed to have said that she would not return to the castle as it was too grand for her. Presently plans have been set in motion by the Lowther Castle & Gardens trust, to enhance the romantic beauty of the castle and its neglected gardens, for the benefit of the public. The future of this project will give access to the castle, areas to play and learn within the grounds, as well as a shop and restaurant, providing much useful revenue to the local area through visitors. A scholar of Wordsworth (whose father was the Steward at Lowther) visited the

gardens in August 2008 and remarked "...it is ironic that despite years of neglect, the site now better evokes the romantic ideal that inspired its construction than at any time in its history..." and this project is staying true to this sentiment – enhancing rather than synthetically restoring this historical monument.

In the walled garden in the grounds is situated the **Lakeland Bird of Prey Centre** (open daily April - Oct), whose aim is to conserve birds of prey through education, breeding and caring for injured or orphaned birds before releasing them back into the wild. Over 150 birds, including eagles, hawks, falcons and owls from all around the world, are housed here,

118 THE QUEENS HEAD INN

Askham

With a warm friendly atmosphere and set in the picturesque village of Askham The Queen's Head Inn is a popular place among locals and tourists and full of character.

🍴 🛏 *see page 218*

Lowther Bird of Prey Centre

Lowther Horse Driving Trials

and there is an opportunity to see some of them in all their natural glory when they are flown (weather permitting) three times a day.

Lowther village itself was built in the 1680s by Sir John Lowther, who moved his tenants here to improve the view from the new house he was building. He also built **St Michael's Church** where several generations of the Lowthers are buried in a series of magnificent tombs beginning with a medieval style alabaster monument to Sir Richard, who died in 1608. Fashions in funerary sculpture continue through the obligatory skull of the late 17th century to the grandiose representation of the 1st Viscount Lonsdale, who sits nonchalantly with his viscount's coronet. Later monuments show a moustachioed Henry, Earl of Lonsdale, in military garb, and a charming Pre-Raphaelite plaque to Emily, wife of the 3rd Earl, who is depicted with her favourite dog at her feet.

CLIFTON

3 miles S of Penrith on the A6

One of the last battles to be fought on English soil took place at nearby **Clifton Moor** in December 1745. The Rebels' Tree on the outskirts of the village, from which the surviving Highlanders were hanged, can still be seen; a sorry sight with its gaunt, dead branches, it remains a place of pilgrimage for the Scots.

To the southeast of the village is **Wetheriggs Country Pottery**, which was founded in 1855. Visitors can try their hand at the often messy business of throwing a pot, or they can paint a pot, paint on glass and make a candle, and also take a conducted tour of the steam-powered pottery, the only one of its kind in the UK, the engine for which was restored by none other than Fred Dibnah, the steeplejack who found fame as a broadcaster. The pottery was designated an Industrial Monument in 1973, and has a tearoom, several shops and a pond that is home to three types of newt. It remains a place of artisans; overflowing with a delightful atmosphere of creativity with not only the art of ceramics, but also with creators of natural skincare products, an art studio, traditional wooden workshop, glassblowing, gift and jewellery design, stationary design and even in the food which is a craft of homemade and regional specialties.

BAMPTON

8 miles S of Penrith off the A6

The village of Bampton, in a picturesque hamlet overlooked by cliffs, has become quite the star over the years as the backdrop for several films. The 1998 film *"The Land Girls"* staring Catherine McCormack (who also featured in *"Braveheart"*) and the 1987 cult classic *"Withnail & I"* staring Richard E Grant and Paul McGann, both used Bampton and the surrounding areas quite prominently in filming. As a backdrop for your visit it can prove a perfect location, not just for the spectacular surroundings, but also for the hospitality. Here, rather unusually, you can even stay in the **village store & post office**, which offers bed & breakfast accommodation – where you can get a great welcome and plate of local home cooked food.

A couple of miles south of Bampton, **Haweswater** is the most easterly of the lakes. It is actually a reservoir, created in the late 1930s to supply the growing needs of industrial Manchester. Beneath the water lies the village of **Mardale** and several dairy farms for which Haweswater Valley was once famous. By 1940 Haweswater had reached its present extent of 4 miles, and Manchester Corporation set about planting its shores with conifers. Today the area is managed as a nature reserve and walkers have a good chance of seeing woodpeckers and sparrowhawks, buzzards and peregrine falcons, and with luck may even catch sight of golden eagles gliding on the thermals rising above Riggindale. An observation is manned throughout the breeding season if the eagles are nesting.

SHAP

10 miles S of Penrith on the A6

This small village on the once congested A6 enjoys some grand views of the hills. In coaching days Shap was an important staging post

Above Haweswater runs the High Street, actually a Roman road, which is now one of the most popular fell walks in the Lake District. It overlooks the remote and lovely Blea Tarn and the lonely valley of Martindale, a cul-de-sac valley to the south of Ullswater, where England's last remaining herd of wild red deer can often be seen.

119 THE GREYHOUND HOTEL

Shap

Historic hostelry in superb countryside location offering excellent food and real ales, plus en suite rooms.

🍴 🛏 see *page 219*

Haweswater

Shap Abbey

for the coaches before they tackled the daunting climb up **Shap Fell** to its summit some 850 feet above sea level.

Shap Abbey, constructed in the local Shap granite which has been used in many well-known buildings including St Pancras Station and the Albert Memorial in London, stands about a mile to the west of the village, just inside the National Park. It is well worth seeking it out to see the imposing remains of the only abbey founded in Westmorland. It was also the only one in the Lake District Mountains, the last abbey to be consecrated in England (around 1199) and the last to be dissolved, in 1540. But the mighty west tower and some of the walls remain, and they enjoy a lovely setting – secluded, tranquil and timeless.

From the Abbey there's a pleasant walk of well under a mile to **Keld**, a tiny village of just 17 houses. So quiet today, in medieval times Keld was a busy little place servicing the monks of Shap Abbey nearby. It was the monks of Shap Abbey who built the village's oldest building, the early 16th-century **Keld Chapel** (National Trust). After the closure of the Abbey, the chapel fell on hard times and for 200 years was used as a dwelling house – that's when the incongruous chimney was added. In 1860 it was 'serving as a cow-house' but was saved from this ignominious role in 1918 by the

Keld Chapel, nr Shap

National Trust. A service is held in the tiny chapel once a year in August; at other times, a notice on the chapel door tells you where you can obtain the key.

ORTON

15 miles S of Penrith on the B6260

By far the best approach to Orton is along the B6290 from Appleby to Tebay. This scenic route climbs up onto the moors, passing **Thunder Stone**, some mighty limestone bluffs and the pavements of **Great Asby Scar**. As motorists descend the side of Orton Scar, grand views open up of the Howgills and the Lune Gorge with the Shap Fells looming on the horizon.

A village now (*"one of the prettiest in Westmorland"* according to one writer), for centuries Orton was a market town of some consequence. There are reminders of Orton's former importance in the noble church tower, completed in 1504, in the attractive proportions of **Petty Hall**, an Elizabethan house at the lower end of the village (a private residence) and the grandeur of **Orton Hall**, built in 1662 and now converted into holiday apartments.

The village church, in common with many in the Eden Valley, has a massive 16th-century tower built for defensive purposes and, presumably, was one place that the villagers sought shelter. Its features include an ancient oak parish chest and a stained glass window by Beatrice Whistler, wife of the American artist James McNeill Whistler. Orton was the birthplace of George Whitehead (1636-1723) who, along with George Fox, was one of the founders of the Quaker Movement.

TEBAY

17 miles S of Penrith, by Exit 38 of the M6

At one time a sheep-farming area and a railway settlement, this long rambling village now owes its importance to the arrival of the M6 motorway, Cumbria's main thoroughfare. The village was the home of Mary Baynes, the **Witch of Tebay**, who died in 1811 at the age of 90. She is said to have foretold the coming of fiery horseless carriages speeding across Loups Fell where, today, the London-to-Glasgow railway line runs. Greatly feared by the people of Tebay, she is said to have withered and died at the same time as some eggs on which she had placed a curse were fried in boiling fat.

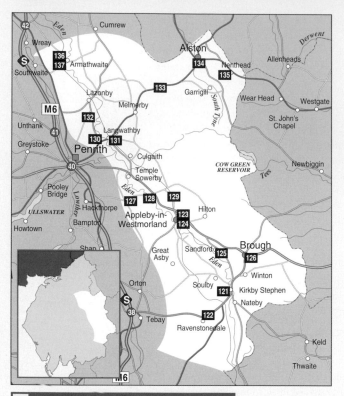

The Eden Valley & East Cumbria

The River Eden is entirely Cumbrian and is one of the few large rivers in England that flows northwards. The source of the river is on the high limestone fells above Mallerstang Common, near the North Yorkshire border, and it runs to the outskirts of Carlisle where it turns sharply east and flows into the Solway Firth. For much of its course, the river is accompanied by the famous Settle-Carlisle Railway, a spectacularly scenic route saved from extinction in the 1960s by the efforts of local enthusiasts.

Carved through boulder clay and red sandstone and sandwiched between the Lakeland fells and the northern Pennines, the Eden Valley is green and fertile – in every sense another Eden. Though not usually the first stop for tourists, many bypassing it for the more well-known areas in Cumbria, this region, beside the winding banks of the Eden River, holds some beautiful scenery and friendly villages rich in history and tradition.

The valley was vulnerable to Scottish raids in medieval times and the number of pele towers and castles in the area are testament to a turbulent and often violent past.

This, too, is farming country and many of the ancient towns and villages have a market place. Appleby-in-Westmorland, the old county town of Westmorland, had an important market and also an annual horse fair that continues today and has gained a large following. Outside of the village of Little Salkeld, 6 miles north east from Penrith, the amazing prehistoric site of Long Meg and her daughters (seconded only by Stonehenge in size) makes for a dramatic sight.

An attractive man-made feature of the valley is the collection of specially commissioned stone sculptures known as Eden Benchmarks dotted along its length. Each created by a different sculptor, they have been located beside public paths and, since they also function as seats, provide the perfect setting in which to enjoy the valley's unspoilt scenery. There are 10 of them in all, beginning with Mary Bourne's *Water Cut*, an intriguing limestone sculpture, shaped rather like a tombstone riven from top to bottom by a serpentine space representing the river. It stands on Lady Anne's Way, a public path along the eastern ridge of the Mallerstang Fells.

Eden Valley and The Pennines

105

Pennines , nr Kirkby Stephen

121 THE BLACK BULL
HOTEL

Kirkby Stephen

A hearty pub full of good
food and soul with quality
guest accommodation also
provided.

 see page 221

KIRKBY STEPHEN

Surrounded by spectacular scenery, the old market town of Kirkby Stephen lies at the head of the beautiful Eden Valley. To say that Kirkby Stephen is one of the most outstanding villages in Cumbria, and indeed England, would not be an overstatement, as in the last two years alone they have received four awards to this effect: *Calor Village of the Year for England 2009, Northern England Village of the Year 2009, Cumbria Village of the Year 2008* and *Cumbria in Bloom Best Large Village/Small Country Town 2008.*

Although essentially part of the Eden Valley, Kirkby Stephen has a strong Yorkshire Dales feel about it. Indeed, the church, with its long, elegant nave, has been called the "Cathedral of the Dales".

Dating from Saxon times, rebuilt in 1220 and with a 16th-century tower, the **Parish Church** is one of the finest in the eastern fells, dominating the northern end of the town from its elevated position. Until the last century the **Trupp Stone** in the churchyard received money from local people every Easter Monday in payment of church tithes and, at 8 o'clock, the curfew is sounded by the **Taggy Bell**, once regarded by local children as a demon. The splendid pulpit, given by the town in memory of a much-loved vicar, is made of Shap granite and Italian marble. The most remarkable feature, however, is the 10th-century **Loki Stone**, one of only two such carvings in Europe to have survived. Loki was a Norse God; presumably the Viking settlers brought their belief in Loki to Kirkby Stephen.

Between the church and the market square stand the cloisters, which served for a long time as a butter market. The **Market Square** is surrounded by an ancient collar of cobblestones which marked out an area used for bull-baiting – a 'sport' that ceased here in 1820 after a disaster when a bull broke loose. The market, still held every Monday, has existed since 1351 and has always been a commercial focus for the surrounding countryside.

Close to Kirkby Stephen are three spectacular railway viaducts. Merrygill, with 9 arches, and Podgill, 11 arches, were on the long-forgotten Stainmore Railway that linked Darlington with Tebay and Penrith. Smardale Gill viaduct, 90 feet high with 14 arches, is on the gloriously scenic Seattle-Carlisle line. All three viaducts are in the care of the Northern Viaduct Trust.

Surrounded by such spectacular scenery, it is only natural that Kirkby Stephen be a lively centre for walkers. In April 2009 they became the first town in Cumbria to be awarded **Walkers are Welcome** status, due to their efforts in, not just welcoming walkers, but improving the trails, signposting, and information available. This is one of many examples of the sense of community spirit in Kirkby Stephen, this award (and any of the many others they have achieved) being only possible through a cooperative and active community.

Walking is not the only sporting attraction on offer, there is also cycling, horse riding and even paragliding. Also fishing is quite abundant from the rivers (the Kirkby Stephen & District Angling Association is based here and always welcomes new members) the most common catch being that of the wild brown trout. In the interest of conservation it is advised that catches are thrown back, so as not to have a negative impact on the wildlife.

AROUND KIRKBY STEPHEN

NATEBY

2 miles S of Kirkby Stephen on the B6269

Now a quiet hamlet of houses standing alongside a beck, for centuries Nateby was dominated by **Hartley Castle**. Believed to have been built in the 13th century, the castle was the home of Sir Andrew de Harcala, a renowned soldier during the reign of Edward II. He was executed for treason in 1325 and the castle passed to the hands of the Musgrave family, who demolished the building and used the stone to build their manor house at Edenhall near Penrith. Today there are self-catering cottages on the land, as well as a working sheep farm which spans from the River Eden in Kirkby Stephen to Nine Standards Rigg.

OUTHGILL

5 miles S of Kirkby Stephen on the B6259

Outhgill is a small village, situated in the remote Mallerstang Dale. It has a scattered pattern, from its Norse roots, of a series of small hamlets and isolated houses, with no identifiable centre. The residence of James Faraday, father of scientist and pioneer of the electricity generation Michael, who was employed as a blacksmith in the village, is in the same place

Pendragon Castle Ruins, Outhgill

To the south to the village of Outhgill is Wild Boar Fell, a brooding, flat-topped peak where the last wild boar in England was reputedly killed, while tucked down in the valley are the romantic ruins of Lammerside and Pendragon Castles.

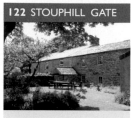

122 STOUPHILL GATE

Ravenstonedale

B&B and holiday cottage located in a glorious setting in a traditional Cumbrian farmhouse.

see page 221

today, and has been named Faraday Cottage in his memory.

This remote village has close links with the Clifford family of Skipton Castle, North Yorkshire. The village **Church of St Mary**, first built in 1311, was repaired by Lady Anne Clifford, and there is a plaque on the door commemorating this fact.

Pendragon Castle, about a mile north of the village, is shrouded in legend but there are claims that it was the fortress of Uther Pendragon, father of King Arthur. If so, nothing remains of that 6th-century wooden castle. The present structure dates from the 1100s and was built by Hugh de Morville, one of the four knights who murdered Thomas à Becket, to guard the narrow pass of **Mallerstang**. Twice it was burned by the Scots and twice restored, on the latter occasion by the formidable Lady Anne Clifford in 1660. Another mile or so downstream, **Lammerside Castle** dates from the 12th century, though only the remains of the keep survive. They can be found along a bridle path between Pendragon and Wharton Hall.

RAVENSTONEDALE
5 miles SW of Kirkby Stephen on the A685

Known locally as Rissendale, this pretty village of stone-built cottages clustered along the banks of **Scandal Beck** lies on the edge of the Howgill Fells. The parish **Church of St Oswald** dates to 1738 and is especially interesting. An earlier church, built on the

same site, had a separate bell tower that rested on pillars; at its centre hung a refuge bell. Anyone guilty of a capital offence who managed to escape to Ravenstonedale and sound the bell was free from arrest by the King's officials. This custom was finally abolished during the reign of James I.

Ravenstonedale's Church of St Oswald is one of the few Georgian churches in Cumbria. The present church, surrounded by yew trees, is well worth a visit. It features bow pews facing one another, a three-decker pulpit complete with a sounding board and, at the back of the third deck, a seat for the parson's wife. The window at the east end of the Church of St Oswald commemorates the last woman in England to be put to death for her Protestant faith.

There is a pleasant walk from the village of Ravenstonedale, through Smardale valley (also part of the coast to coast trail), including the Smardale nature reserve – habitat of the rare Scotch Argus butterfly. This walk takes you past some stunning scenery including an impressive viaduct from the former Tebay-Darlington railway line – its six arches stand 55 feet high and are spread out over 330 feet in length. Also of interest are some unusual large lime kilns, the product of which was transported on the railway to industrial centres.

CROSBY GARRETT
4 miles W of Kirkby Stephen off the A685

Local legend has it that the Devil, seeing all the stones lying ready to build **Crosby Garrett Church**, carried them in his leather apron to the top of a nearby hill. He reasoned that, as people grew old, they would be unable to climb the hill and attend church and thus would come to him rather than go to Heaven. Such tales apart, the church itself is said to be of Anglo-Saxon origin though the visible fabric is 12th century. Inside there are some superb carvings, particularly near the font. The church is also famous for its hagioscope, cut through the wall to allow people in the north aisle to see the altar. Near the church gates is a tithe barn, built in the 18th century to store farm produce given to the church as a religious tax. There are many other historic houses in the village, many with 17th century dates on their lintels. To the west of the village a splendid viaduct on the Carlisle-Settle Railway dominates the landscape.

WINTON

3 miles N of Kirkby Stephen off the A685

This is a quiet and picturesque hamlet whose name, in old English, means 'pasture farmland'. It is built on a spring line and, like many other Cumbrian villages of medieval origin, once followed the runrig, or two-field system of agriculture. The evidence is still visible in long, thin fields to the north of the village.

In the centre of the village is the manor house, built in 1726, which was formerly a boys' school where, apparently, the boys were treated like prisoners and not allowed to return home until the end of their eductaion in case they told of their lie at the school. The oldest building is **Winton Hall**, built of stone and dated 1665, but looking older with its stone buttresses and mullion windows with iron bars.

Those taking a walk on **Winton Fell** are likely to see red grouse lifting off from the large tracts of heather on the fellside. Indeed, the wildlife is much more prolific around this area where the limestone provides more plentiful food than on the fells around the lakes.

APPLEBY-IN-WESTMORLAND

The old county town of Westmorland, Appleby is one of the most delightful small towns in England. The town's uniquely attractive main street, **Boroughgate**, has been described as the finest in England. A broad, tree-lined avenue, its sides are lined with a pleasing variety of buildings, some dating back to the 17th century. At either end, High Cross and Low Cross mark the original boundaries of the market. At its foot stands the 16th-century **Moot Hall**; at its head rises the great Norman Keep of **Appleby Castle** which is protected by one of the most impressive curtain walls in northern England. Now in private hands, the Castle is not currently open to the public.

During the mid-1600s the remarkable Lady Anne Clifford, who has been mentioned several

123 THE MIDLAND HOTEL

Appleby-In-Westmorland

The Midland Hotel is an 18th century Railway Inn offering good pub food, great real ales and guest room accommodation.

see page 222

124 TUFTON ARMS HOTEL

Appleby-In-Westmorland

Second to none, absolutely outstanding and friendly family-run hotel, offering excellent cuisine and quality ensuite rooms.

see page 223

Moot Hall, Appleby-in-Westmorland

the week leading to the second Wednesday in June. More than 300 years later, the **Gypsy Horse Fair** is still thriving, with hundreds flooding into the little town (population 2,700) with caravans and horse-drawn carts. The trade, principally in horses, and the trotting races provide a picturesque and colourful spectacle.

AROUND APPLEBY-IN-WESTMORLAND

GREAT ORMSIDE

2 miles SE of Appleby-in-Westmorland off the B6260

times previously for her restorations of estates and churches, lived in Appleby Castle - and had quite an impact on Appleby which is still visible today. As well as churches and chapels in the area which benefited from her munificence, in 1651 she founded the almshouses known as the Hospital of St Anne, for '12 sisters and a Mother'. Set around a cobbled square, the picturesque cottages and minuscule chapel still serve their original function, maintained by the trust endowed by Lady Anne; visitors are welcome.

Lady Anne died in 1676 and was buried with her mother, Margaret Countess of Cumberland, in **St Lawrence's Church**. The church is well worth visiting to see their magnificent tombs and also the historic organ, purchased from Carlisle Cathedral in 1684, which is said to be oldest still in use in Britain.

Just a few years after Lady Anne's death, James II granted the town the right to hold a Fair during

This was once an important fort guarded by a pele tower, and the ancient **Church of St James**, which dates from the 11th century, occupies a site on the steep-sided defence mound. A silver gilt and enamel bowl from the 8th century has been found here and is regarded as one of the most important pieces of Anglo-Saxon metalware to survive. A particularly beautiful piece, richly decorated with vine scrolls, birds and animals, it is now on permanent display in the Yorkshire Museum in York.

Great Ormside is a pretty village, right on the banks of the Eden River, with much open countryside and farmlands around to admire. Nearby is the interesting two storey underground house (private), built by Philip and Helen Reddy into the wall of an old quarry, with the aim of being an environmentally friendly and resourceful home.

From the village a path leads

across fields to the village of **Little Ormside**, with its large cedar tree said to have been brought back from Lebanon as a sapling by General Whitehead. On the voyage home he grew it in his hat, and shared with it his daily ration of one pint of water.

WARCOP

5 miles SE of Appleby-in-Westmorland on the B6259

The largest village in this part of the Eden Valley, Warcop grew up as a crossing point of the river. The bridge, the oldest to cross the river, dates from the 16th century and the red sandstone buildings surrounding the village green, with its central maypole, make this a charming place to visit.

The red sandstone **Church of St Columba** is built outside Warcop on the site of a Roman camp. An interesting building in its own right, it is particularly famous for the rush-bearing ceremony which takes place in late June each year. The ceremony re-creates the practice of placing clean rushes on the earthen floor of churches, before churches began lying flagging on the floor instead. Warcop is surrounded by Ministry of Defence tank-firing ranges from which the public are understandably excluded, but on the hills above the village are stones, cairns and the remains of what is claimed to be a **Druid Temple**.

BROUGH

8 miles SE of Appleby-in-Westmorland on the A66/A685

This small town, standing at the point where the **Stainmore Pass** opens into the Vale of Eden, is, in fact, two settlements: **Church Brough** and **Market Brough**. Church Brough is a group of neat houses and cottages clustered around a little market square in which a maypole stands on the site of the former market cross. **Brough Castle**, built within the ramparts of the Roman camp of *Verterae*, was constructed to protect the Roman road over Stainmore Pass. Many times Scottish raiders laid siege to Brough Castle and fierce battles were fought. Another fortification restored by the remarkable Lady Anne Clifford, the castle, with its tall keep 60 feet high is well worth visiting, if only for the superb panorama of the surrounding fells seen from the battlements.

Market Brough is also an ancient settlement and was particularly important in the 18th and 19th centuries when it became a major coaching town on the stagecoach routes between England and Scotland. It was on the junction of several routes and boasted more than 10 inns. The width and breadth of its High Street also indicates its importance as a market town. Brough was granted a charter in 1330 enabling it to hold a weekly market as well as four cattle markets and an annual fair. A custom celebrated in Brough is the Twelfth Night Holly Burning, a unique festival with pagan origins.

The distinctive, low hills that lie to the west of Brough are drumlins – heaps of material deposited by

127 THE CROWN INN

Morland, nr Appleby-In-Westmorland

Warm and friendly pub, offering great food and drink in stunning location.

🍴 see page 226

128 EDEN VALE INN

Bolton Village, nr Appleby-In-Westmorland

The Eden Vale Inn is a great destination for discerning dishes.

🍴 🛏 see page 227

Ice Age glaciers. In this area many drumlins are marked by broad, grassy ridges, remains of ancient lynchets or ploughing strips.

NORTH STAINMORE

10 miles SE of Appleby-in-Westmorland on the A66

The village lies on the Stainmore Pass which carries the old Roman road, now the A66, through a remote area of the North Pennines which David Bellamy has described as 'England's last wilderness'. Near Stainmore summit are the foundations of **Maiden Castle**, a Roman fort built to guard the pass against marauders. A few yards over the Cumbrian border, into County Durham, is the stump of the ancient **Rey Cross** which was erected before AD 946 and which, until 1092, marked the boundary between England and Scotland. It is thought to be the site of the battle at which the last Viking King of York and North England, Eric Bloodaxe, was killed following his expulsion from the city.

GREAT ASBY

4 miles SW of Appleby-in-Westmorland off the B6260

This pretty village, a popular stop for walkers, is set in a wooded hollow, its houses separated by **Hoff Beck**. Alongside the beck is **St Helen's Well**, and nearby are the splendid almshouses of St Helen's, built between 1811 and 1820. Across a footbridge is **Asby Hall** (in private hands), built in 1670. It was once the home of the Musgrave family of Edenhall,

whose crest and coat of arms can still be seen above the door. Also of interest in the village is the **Old Rectory** (private) which has a pele tower.

MAULDS MEABURN

5 miles SW of Appleby-in-Westmorland off the B6260

This charming village in the Lyvennet Valley has a large green through which the river flows, crossed by footbridges and stepping stones. As well as a fine collection of 17th and 18th-century cottages, there is also an early 17th-century Hall.

TEMPLE SOWERBY

7 miles NW of Appleby-in-Westmorland on the A66

Temple Sowerby prides itself on the title 'Queen of Westmorland villages', an accolade justified by its lovely setting in the Eden valley. (Here's a bonus: the average rainfall here is half that recorded in the Lake District National Park to the west.) To the north, the massive bulk of **Cross Fell**, the highest point in the Pennines, swells skywards to provide a spectacular backdrop. The village of Temple Sowerby, picturesquely grouped around a sloping green and an 18th-century red sandstone church, takes its name from the medieval Knights Templar who owned the manor of Sowerby until their Order was suppressed in 1308.

By the side of the road in the village is an old Roman mile stone juts 4½ feet out of the ground (now in a fenced off area), which indicated the important fort located at Kirkby Thore parish one mile away – though now the stone is eroded and the engravings can't be seen.

From Temple Sowerby there are delightful walks through the Eden valley or, if you prefer a gentle stroll; it's only a mile to the National Trust gardens at **Acorn Bank** where **Crowdundle Beck** splashes beneath an elegant 18th-century bridge. The 16th-century manor house is now a Sue Ryder Home and not open to the public, but visitors are welcome to explore the attractive gardens planted with a collection of some 250 medicinal and culinary herbs. A circular woodland walk runs along the beck to a watermill that was first mentioned on the site as far back as the 14th century. The 'Acorn Bank' itself is a stretch of ancient oak wood sloping down to the beck.

BRAMPTON

2 miles N of Appleby-in-Westmorland off the A66

This village, along with the surrounding area, was said to be haunted by the ghost of Elizabeth Sleddall, the wife of a 17th-century owner of nearby Crackenthorpe Hall. Elizabeth died believing that she had been cheated out of her share of the estate, so to shame the false inheritors her spirit was seen being driven around the countryside in a coach drawn by four black horses. Her ghost became so troublesome that the local people exhumed her body and reburied the remains under a larger boulder. Her ghost, while no longer troubling the local people, is said still to visit the Hall.

DUFTON

3 miles N of Appleby in-Westmorland off the A66

Behind this delightful hamlet lies **Dufton Gill**, a beautiful, secluded wooded valley through which runs a footpath. Also from Dufton there is a track carrying the Pennine Way up to High Cup Nick, a great horseshoe precipice at the edge of the northern Pennine escarpment that was formed by a glacial lake during the Ice Age. Dufton was once a lead-mining centre under the management of the London Lead Company, who built cottages, a school and a library and supplied pipes for a reliable water supply.

LONG MARTON

3 miles N of Appleby-in-Westmorland off the A66

Visitors to this village can experience two very different forms of architecture, both of them equally impressive. The Norman village **church**, with its carvings of knights and monsters over the doorway, is remarkably unspoilt, while nearby the Settle-Carlisle Railway sweeps across a grand viaduct.

NORTH AND EAST OF PENRITH

EDENHALL

3 miles NE of Penrith off the A686

An old tradition asserts that in the

129 THE NEW INN COUNTRY PUB

Brampton, nr Appleby-In-Westmorland

Historical property offering tremendous food, local tipples and accommodation.

see page 228

130 EDENHALL COUNTRY HOTEL & RESTAURANT

Greystoke

Enjoying a beautiful location and offering outstanding AA Rosette cuisine and recently refurbished en suite rooms.

see page 227

131 BRIEF ENCOUNTER

Langwathby, nr Penrith

Beautifully quaint café-restaurant in a restored station building on the Settle-Carlisle line.

see page 229

8th century the monks of Jarrow, fleeing from Viking invaders with the body of St Cuthbert, stopped here briefly. As a result the village church is dedicated to the saint. Part of the **Church of St Cuthbert** appears to be pre-Norman but most of the structure dates from the 1100s.

Close to the church is the **Plague Cross** which stands where there was once a basin filled with vinegar. This acted as a disinfectant into which plague victims put their money to pay for food from the people of Penrith. The plague of the 16th century killed a quarter of the village's inhabitants.

Edenhall is particularly famous for the story of the 'Luck of Eden Hall', a priceless glass cup, which, according to legend, was stolen from some fairies dancing round the garden wall by a butler in the service of the Musgrave family back in the 15th century. Despite the fairies' entreaties, the butler refused to return the 6-inch high glass to them. As he departed with the precious goblet, the fairies laid a curse upon it: 'If ever this cup shall break or fall, Farewell the luck of Eden Hall.' On inspection, the glass was identified as a 13th-century chalice of enamelled and gilded glass that is thought to have come from Syria and may well have been brought back by a Crusader. It was a treasured heirloom of the Musgraves for many generations and is now in the Victoria & Albert Museum in London. The goblet is still intact, but Eden Hall has long since disappeared.

LANGWATHBY

4 miles NE of Penrith on the A686

Located on the opposite bank of the River Eden from Edenhall, Langwathby's name means 'the settlement by the long ford' and, though there are two prehistoric pathways crossing here, the name of the village and of its neighbouring settlements suggests a Viking past. Langwathby has a huge village green that still hosts maypole dancing on the third Saturday in May. The green is medieval in origin and would once have been surrounded by wood and mud houses, perhaps to protect cattle but also for defence against border raids. After the Civil War and the growth in prosperity in the late 17th century, these wattle-and-daub cottages were replaced by stone buildings.

West of the village of Langwathby Hall Farm, **Eden Ostrich World** offers the chance to see these splendid birds in a

Eden Ostrich World

farm setting in the heart of the Eden Valley. The farm is also home to rare-breed sheep, cattle and pigs, donkeys, deer, wallabies, alpacas and many other creatures from around the world. There is sheep milking here (the product of which is said to be higher in minerals and nutrients such as calcium and zinc than other types of milk) daily from February to mid October. There is also a giant maze, a tea room, gift shop, picnic areas and adventure play areas.

LITTLE SALKELD

6 miles NE of Penrith off the A686

A lane from the village leads to **Long Meg and her Daughters**, a most impressive prehistoric site and second only to Stonehenge in size. Local legend claims that Long Meg was a witch who, with her daughters, was turned to stone for profaning the Sabbath, as they danced wildly on the moor. The circle is supposedly endowed with magic so that it is impossible to count the same number of stones twice.

There are more than 60 stones in the Circle (actually an oval), which is approximately 300 feet across. The tallest, Long Meg, is a 15 feet column of Penrith sandstone, the corners of which face the four points of the compass. Cup and ring symbols and spirals are carved on this stone, which is over 3,500 years old. The circle is now known to belong to the Bronze Age, but no one is certain of its purpose. It may have been used for rituals connected

with the changing seasons, since the midwinter sun sets in alignment with the centre of the circle and Long Meg herself. The brooding majesty of the site was perfectly evoked by Wordsworth:

A weight of awe, not easy to be borne,
Fell suddenly upon my spirit – cast
From the dread bosom of the unknown past,
When first I saw that family forlorn.

In 1725 an attempt was made by Colonel Samuel Lacy of Salkeld Hall to use the stones for mileposts. However, as work began, a great storm blew up and the workmen fled in terror, believing that the Druids were angry at the desecration of their temple.

It was the same Colonel Lacy who gave his name to the **Lacy Caves**, a mile or so downstream from Little Salkeld. The Colonel had the five chambers carved out of the soft red sandstone, possibly as a copy of St Constantine's Caves further down the river at Wetheral, as at that time it was fashionable to have romantic ruins and grottoes on large estates. Colonel Lacy is said to have employed a man to live in his caves, acting the part of a hermit.

GREAT SALKELD

6 miles NE of Penrith on the B6412

The River Eden formed the boundary between the two old counties of Westmorland and Cumberland, so while Little Salkeld was in Westmorland, its larger namesake stood in Cumberland. The village is a picturesque collection of 18th-century cottages and farmhouses built in red

132 THE HIGHLAND DRIVE INN

Great Salkeld, nr Penrith

Both the Highland Drove, and its partner business The Cross Keys at Carleton, are a top quality destination for lovers of fine food, real ales, and a very warm welcome.

🍴 🛏 *see page 230*

Church of St Oswald, Kirkoswald

sandstone which are typical of this area. Great Salkeld is best known for the impressive **Church** with its massive, battlemented pele tower built in the 14th century and complete with a dungeon. The Norman doorway in the porch is less than a yard wide and its arch has three rows of deeply cut zigzags with five heads, one with a crown. The Dub just outside of the village, which now provides a habitat for the rare Great Crested newt, was once used as a watering hole for the animals of drovers, stopping off at public house The Highland Drove.

KIRKOSWALD

8 miles NE of Penrith on the B6413

The village derives its name from the **Church of St Oswald**: Oswald was the King of Northumbria who, according to legend, toured the pagan north with St Aidan in the 7th century. The church is unusual in having a detached bell tower standing on top of a grassy hill some 200 yards from the main building (this is in a valley, so the bells could not be heard by the villagers). Raven Beck runs through this village, the power of which was once utilized by several mills including paper and corn.

This once thriving market town still retains its small cobbled market place and some very fine Georgian buildings. There's also a striking ruined 12th-century **Castle**, (formerly the home of the Featherstonehaugh family) which, although not open to the public, can be seen from the road and footpath. The whole site once covered 3 acres, with the courtyard surrounded by a massive wall and a main gate with a drawbridge over the moat. Today there still exists a wide moat, as well as the great turreted tower which rises 65 feet above the remains of the vaulted dungeons.

One of Kirkoswald's most splendid buildings is the **College**, its name recalling the days when St Oswald's was a collegiate church. The two-storey house with its sloping-ended roof was originally built as a pele tower and converted into the college for priests in the 1520s. The manor house opposite has a particularly attractive entrance front in sandstone, which was added in 1696.

Just to the northwest of Kirkoswald are the **Nunnery Walks**, which start at a Georgian house built on the site a Benedictine Nunnery dating back to the time of William Rufus. Narrow footpaths have been cut into the sandstone cliffs along the deep gorge of Croglin Beck, passing through beautiful woodland to reveal exciting waterfalls.

MELMERBY

9 miles NE of Penrith on the A686

Melmerby nestles at the foot of **Hartside Pass**, its spacious village green dissected by three becks. Even today, every householder in Melmerby has grazing rights on the green. Horses are grazed more commonly now, but in the past it would have been more usual to see flocks of geese – indeed, there was once a cottage industry here making pillows and mattresses from goose feathers. During the Appleby Horse fair in June, gypsies camp on the green. Overlooking the 13-acre village green is **Melmerby Hall**, a defensive tower that was extended in the 17th and 18th centuries. This building is now a grade II listed manor, and the grounds include an archery lawn, Victorian castle folly (now a childrens' play area) and walled vegetable gardens. It is available to rent as holiday accommodation. The village church, with its tower, is a Victorian building, but the first known rector of the church on the site came here in 1332. Among its many assets, Melmerby also boasts its very own fell – Melmerby Fell.

From Melmerby the main road climbs out of the Eden Valley to the east and the landscape changes suddenly. The road passes Fiend's Fell, close to the highest point in the Pennine Chain, the summit of Cross Fell. Early Christians erected a cross on the highest point of the

Lazonby, nr Penrith

fell to protect travellers from the demons who haunted the moors. Today, a cairn marks the spot where the cross once stood.

ALSTON

18 miles NE of Penrith on the A689/A686

For a few weeks in 1999 the small town of Alston, 1,000 feet up in the Pennines, became transformed into Bruntmarsh, the fishing village in which the fictional Oliver Twist spent his early years. To re-create the squalid conditions of the poor in early 19th-century England, production designers 'dressed down' the town, so much so that

133 HARTSIDE TOP CAFE

Hartside, nr Alston

A warm and friendly café serving up quality hot and cold lunches and snacks alongside unbeatably stunning mountain views hits the spot every time.

see page 231

134 THE CUMBERLAND INN

Alston

A convivial spot to meet for a drink, a fine choice for a meal and a comfortable base for leisure and business visitors.

see page 232

anxious visitors noticing the soot-blackened buildings enquired whether there had been a major fire.

One of the many strengths of Alan Bleasdale's re-working of the Dickens classic was the authenticity of the locations. Alston proved to be ideal, since the town centre has changed little since the late 1700s and there are many buildings even older than this.

The town has a cobbled main street and, from the picturesque **Market Cross**, narrow lanes radiating out with courtyards enclosing old houses. Many of the older buildings still have the outside staircase leading to the first floor – a relic from the days when animals were kept below while the family's living accommodation was upstairs. This ancient part of Alston is known as **The Butts**, a title acquired by the need of the townspeople to be proficient in archery during the times of the border raids.

The tall spire of **St Augustine's Church** is a well-known local landmark and its churchyard contains a number of interesting epitaphs, as well as affording wonderful views of the South Tyne Valley. Also, in the village centre, is a restored waterwheel, designed by John Smeaton (architect of the

Alston Market Cross

Eddystone lighthouse in Plymouth) in 1767.

Considering its small population, Alston supports an astonishing diversity of shops and pubs. It is renowned for its delicious locally made cheeses, such as the Cumberland mustard and Alston Cheese varieties. In addition, the town is home to a wide variety of craftspeople, ranging from blacksmiths to candlemakers, wood-turners to potters, and also boasts an outstanding art and crafts centre in the **Gossipgate Gallery**. Housed in a converted congregational church built 200 years ago and with its original gaslights still intact, this gallery is the premier centre in the North Pennines for contemporary art and craft. A programme of exhibitions runs non-stop from February to December, and in the gallery shop a huge range of artefacts is for sale, including original watercolours and prints, jewellery, glass, ceramics, sculpture and striking turned wooden bowls made from native woods.

Another popular attraction in Alston is the **South Tynedale Railway**. This narrow-gauge (2 feet) steam railway runs regular services during the summer months and at the northern terminus of the 2½-mile long track travellers can join a stretch of the Pennine Way that runs alongside the River South Tyne. The trains also operate for a special Christmas service on a few dates in the festive season. In between the station and the A686, is the **HUB Exhibition** of historic vehicles, a wealth of local images and the stories that bring them alive.

Alston Moor, to the south of the town, was once the centre of an extremely important lead mining region, one of the richest in Britain. Lead and silver were probably mined on the moor by the Romans, but the industry reached its peak in the early 19th century when vast quantities of iron, silver, copper and zinc were extracted by the London Lead Company.

Nenthead Mines Heritage Centre is a 200-acre site high in the hills that tells the story of the

lead and zinc mining industry. One of the main visitor attractions is 'The Power of Water', an impressive interactive area that looks at the technology used, including three working water wheels that drive model machinery. Another is the Brewery Shaft with its 328 feet drop and amazing virtual stone feature.

ARMATHWAITE

10 miles N of Penrith off the A6

Set on the western bank of the River Eden, the village has a particularly fine sandstone bridge from which there is a lovely view of **Armathwaite Castle** (private), the home of the Skelton family, one of whose forebears was Poet Laureate to Henry VIII. **Armathwaite Hall** has existed here in some form or another since the 11th century, although the building there now is much later with extensive remodeling having been done in 1880s. It now provides a location for a luxury hotel and spa, set in 400 acres of deer park and woodland.

Worth seeking out in **Coombs Wood** to the south is one of the Eden Benchmarks. Entitled *Vista* and created by Graeme Mitchison, this remarkable sculpture seems to make the Lazenby Sandstone flow into liquid shapes. North of Armathwaite, the River Eden approaches Carlisle and the Solway Firth; these lower stretches of the river are surveyed in the next chapter.

135 NENTHEAD MINES HERITAGE CENTRE

Nenthead

The 200-acre centre at Nenthead, in the North Pennines, is in an Area of Outstanding Natural Beauty and offers a unique insight into the lives of the miners who transformed these fells.

 see page 232

136 THE FOX AND PHEASANT INN

Armathwaite

Outstanding accommodation on the banks of the river Eden.

 see page 233

137 THE DUKES HEAD INN

Armathwaite

A homely country Inn providing fine country cuisine and accommodation in the friendliest environment in town.

 see page 234

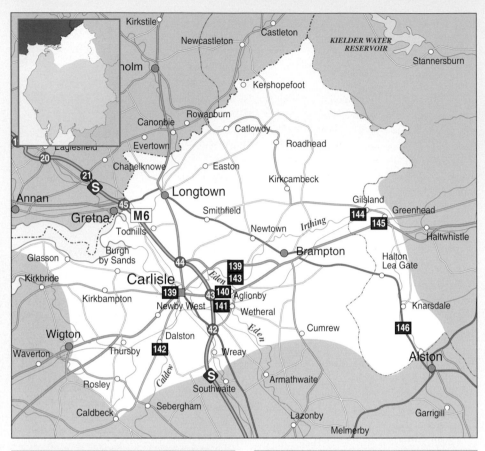

Carlisle and The Scottish Borders

For more than 350 years the area around Carlisle was known as the Debatable Lands, a lawless region where the feared Border Reivers sacked and plundered at will. Every winter, when their own food stocks were almost depleted, armed gangs from across the border would ride southwards to seize the cattle and sheep of their more prosperous neighbours. Stealing and murdering, they wreaked havoc in this area and almost every village would have had a fortified structure, usually a pele tower, where the inhabitants and their animals could hide safely. Anyone who wishes to find out if their family was involved, from some of the 77 names on record, should go to Carlisle's Tullie House Museum.

This is, too, the country of Hadrian's Wall, the most important monument built in Britain by the Romans; many stretches of the wall are still visible, and Birdoswald and other centres give an excellent insight into Roman border life. The wall was built as a great military barrier across the narrowest part of Britain, from the mouth of the River Tyne, in the east, to Bowness-on-Solway, in the west.

There are many ways of exploring the Wall (including the bus number AD 122!), and for those with the energy to walk from end to end the newly opened Hadrian's Wall National Trail passes some of the country's greatest archaeological monuments.

Beyond the history, this region of Cumbria holds some delightful villages, woodlands and parks which are well worth exploring. In the Gelt Woods, south of Brampton, is an impressive quarry where marks from the tools used to extract the stones used for part of Hadrian's Wall can be seen. The Talkin Tarn provides an extensive 120 acres of parkland in which a whole host of sports can be enjoyed, including canoeing, windsurfing, orienteering, cycling, fishing, and of course walking.

Lanercost Priory, nr Brampton

CARLISLE

Carlisle's castle, cathedral, many
other historic buildings, parks,
thriving traditional market,
shopping centres and leisure
facilities all combine to endow
Carlisle with the true feel of a
major city. Carlisle is the largest
settlement in Cumbria, with a
population of around 130,000, and
is also its county town. Yet despite
its size it is an enchanting and
lovely town; according to a survey,
if you are born in Carlisle you are
more likely to stay here than the
inhabitants of any other place in
England.

Originally the citizens of
Carlisle were granted charter to
hold an annual fair in August in
1352 by Edward III. Carlisle great
fair has now become something
akin to a mini-Edinburgh festival,
with entertainment being held daily
on the bandstand and the focus

being on the exceptional food
market. Part local Cumbrian stalls,
and part exciting continental stalls,
this food market offers a real
spread of delicious varieties to
excite all of your senses – as well as
beautiful handmade fare on the
craft stands.

The squat outline of **Carlisle
Castle** (English Heritage)
dominates the skyline of this
fascinating city. There has been a
castle at Carlisle since 1092 when
William Rufus first built a palisaded
fort. The Norman Castle was
originally built of wood, but,
during the Scottish occupation in
the 12th century, King David I laid
out a new castle with stones taken
from Hadrian's Wall. The 12th-
century keep can still be seen,
enclosed by massive inner and
outer walls. Entry is through a
great 14th-century gatehouse,
complete with portcullis, and with a
maze of vaulted passages,
chambers, staircases,
towers and dismal
dungeons. Children,
especially, enjoy the
legendary 'licking stones'
from which parched
Jacobite prisoners tried to
find enough moisture to
stay alive. Archaeologists
working outside the castle
walls unearthed the
remains of three Roman
forts, and many of the
finds are on display in a
special exhibition at the
castle. Carlisle Castle is
everything a real castle
should be and is still the

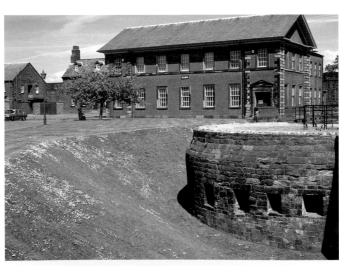

Carlisle Castle Courtyard

headquarters of the King's Own Royal Border Regiment, whose **Regimental Museum** is located within the castle walls. Two floors of displays include uniforms, weapons, medals, pictures, photographs and archives, and outside is a 25-Pounder Field Gun of 1940 and a Ferret Scout Car. There is also a gift shop with many souvenirs and books on the rich history of the castle and Carlisle.

Although an appointment is usually necessary, a visit to the **Prior's Tower** is a must. On the first floor of this 15th-century pele tower is a wonderful 45-panel ceiling incorporating the popinjay crest and arms of the Prior Senhouse. Today the tower also houses an interesting collection of Angela Bevan dolls – each one a lovingly handmade representation of the kings and queens of England, including ones of the present Royal family. The 16th-century Prior's gatehouse leads to a narrow lane called Paternoster which is named after the prayer the monks would recite during their offices.

Like many great medieval cities, Carlisle was surrounded by walls. Guided walks and tours are available and the best view is to be found in a little street called **West Walls** at the bottom of Sally Port Steps, near the **Tithe Barn**. The walls date from around the 11th century and they remained virtually intact until the 1800s. It is unusual to find a Tithe Barn within a city wall, but this exception was probably made because of the

Skating in Old Town Square, Carlisle

Border raids. The barn dates from the 15th century and was used to collect and store taxes, or tithes, destined for the Priory.

The award-winning **Tullie House Museum & Art Gallery**, in the centre of the city close to the cathedral, is certainly another place not to be missed. Through skilful and interpretive techniques the fascinating, and often dark, history of the Debatable Lands, as this border region was called, is told. One of the Museum's centrepieces is its story of the Border Reivers who occupied the lands from the 14th to the 17th century. These lawless, unruly people raged interfamily warfare with each other, destroying or threatening the lives of the local people with their bloodthirsty raids. Their treacherous deeds have also added such words as 'bereave' and 'blackmail' to the English language.

The city of Carlisle dates back far beyond those desperate days,

123

•

Located on the northwestern edge of the city of Carlisle, Kingmoor Nature Reserve occupies an area of moorland given to the city in 1352 by Edward III. Citizens enjoyed the right to graze sheep on the moors and to cut peat for fuel. A half-mile circular path wanders through the woodland with gentle gradients of 1 in 20 making it fully accessible to wheelchairs and pushchairs, and with seats every 100 yards or so providing plenty of resting places. Another path links the reserve to Kingmoor Sidings, which since the old railway sheds closed has been colonised by a wide variety of wildlife. In 1913 Kingmoor became one of the first bird sanctuaries in England, and today provides a peaceful retreat away from the bustle of the city centre.

•

however, and Tullie House also has an extensive collection of Roman remains from both the city and the Cumbrian section of Hadrian's Wall. The Art Gallery features contemporary arts and crafts, and the spectacular underground Millennium Gallery has a stunning collection of local minerals, archaeological finds of wood and leather, artist-made glass and interactive exhibits. Old Tullie House showcases paintings and drawings by renowned Pre-Raphaelite artists, as well as other artworks and a selection of fine English porcelain.

A short walk from the Museum leads to the **Linton Visitor Centre** in Shaddongate which provides an insight into the city's industrial heritage. Standing next to a 280 feet high chimney built in 1836 as part of what was once one of the largest cotton mills in Britain, the Centre has displays of hand-weaving on original looms, informative displays and a selection of world-famous fabrics and designer knitwear for sale.

The **Guildhall Museum**, a branch of Tullie House, is housed in an unspoilt medieval building constructed by Richard of Redeness in 1407. Originally a town house, the Grade 1 listed building provides an ideal setting for illustrating the history of both the Guilds and the City. Several rooms are devoted to creating the atmosphere of trade Guilds such as the shoemakers, the butchers, the weavers and the glovers. There is a splendid early 19th-century banner of the Weavers

Guild and an impressive collection of 17th and 18th century Guild silver, as well as other items relating to the history of Carlisle, including medieval stocks and a magnificent ironbound Muniment Chest dating from the 14th century. Conducted tours of this remarkable Guildhall are available.

Not far from the Guildhall Museum is the **Citadel**, which is often mistaken for the Castle. In fact, this intimidating fortress with its well-preserved circular tower was built in 1543 on the orders of Henry VIII to strengthen the city's defences. Though much of it was demolished in the early 1800s to improve access to the city centre what remains is very impressive, and public are allowed access to the West Tower. Across the road from the Citadel is the railway station. So elegant was its interior – and much of it remains – that Carlisle was known as the 'top hat' station. It is still an important centre of communications; InterCity trains from Glasgow and London now link with lines to Dumfries, Tyneside, West Cumbria and Yorkshire, and it is, of course, the northern terminus of the famous **Settle-Carlisle Railway** line.

Carlisle Cathedral is now one of the smallest cathedrals in England, partly because stones from the cathedral were taken by puritans for their own building – yet it retains many interesting features, including an exquisite east window that is considered to be one of the finest in Europe. Below the beautifully painted wooden ceiling of the choir, with its gold star shimmering against deep blue, are the carved, canopied choir-stalls with their medieval misericords. These wonderful carved beasts and birds include two dragons joined by the ears, a fox killing a goose, pelicans feeding their young, and a mermaid with a looking glass.

Carlisle Cathedral is one of the few where visitors can enjoy refreshments actually within the precincts, in this case in the Prior's Kitchen Restaurant situated in the Fratry Undercroft. Seated beneath superb fan vaulting, customers have a good choice of home-made soups, cakes and pastries, as well as morning coffee, lunches and afternoon teas.

Just outside Carlisle, and near the Eden Golf course, is **Rickerby Park** – some 100 acres of parkland dedicated to the fallen of the Great War (1914-1918) with an impressive memorial cenotaph at its centre. This park, open for public enjoyment, every year is transformed from a tranquil haven to a lively centre of activity when it is host to the Cumberland County Show in the summer. The show, once held at Bitts Park near Carlisle Castle but since 1991 has been moved to the larger location of Rickerby Park, is a glorious display of agriculture and farming, with shows and awards for the most impressive Cumbria has to offer, which has been run by the Cumberland Agricultural society for over 170 years. In addition to this there are huge marquees and outdoor events for crafts, food, horticulture & gardens, and games, rides and activities for younger audiences (aimed partly at spreading the knowledge of agriculture and farming's massive significance).

AROUND CARLISLE

WREAY

5 miles S of Carlisle off the A6

This little village is known for its extraordinary **Church of St Mary**, designed by a local woman, Sarah Losh, in memory of her sister and her parents. It was built in 1835 and incorporates many Italian Romanesque features. The church is full of beautiful touches, including the carvings, mostly by Sarah herself, on the font. The village has what is known locally as the "Twelve Men", a self-appointed body who still meet every year in the local public house to discuss the welfare of Wreay village.

About a mile North East of the village is **Wreay Woods nature reserve**, sadly now much decreased in size due to trees having been felled over many years to make way for more farmland, it is now protected by Cumbria Wildlife Trust. The ancient woodland, which makes for a lovely peaceful walk, is home to much wildlife and plant life including wild garlic and the magnificent Kingfisher bird.

DALSTON

4 miles SW of Carlisle on the B5299

Lying on the banks of the **River Caldew** (which provides a pleasant 2-mile circular walk from the

139 NO. 10

Carlisle

One of the finest eateries in the area providing an unbeatable service.

see page 235

140 THE WATERLOO

Aglionby, nr Carlisle

A traditional Inn with fine home cooking, entertainment and a tranquil beer garden to relax in.

see page 235

141 WILLOWBECK LODGE

Scotby, nr Carlisle

Superb lodge standing in acres of beautiful scenery, oozing class and style.

see page 236

125

142 COUNTRY KITCHEN

Dalston

A good old country tea room serving a wide range of home cooked delights, breakfasts and main meals and light lunches in a cosy, comfortable atmosphere in the heart of Dalston.

❚❚ see page 237

•

Dalston holds a delightful annual village festival in August which, among the many activities and events going on, hosts a rather unusual scarecrow competition – which proves very popular and gets a little competitive!

•

village), Dalston became a thriving centre of the cotton industry in the late 18th century, thanks to George Hodgson of Manchester, who used the river as a source of power for the flax mill and four cotton mills that were established here. The local economy was sustained still further by the creation of a forge and two corn mills.

At the eastern end of the village square stands **St Michael's Church**, believed to date back to Norman times, which can be approached via a memorial lychgate. One of the few red-brick buildings to be found in the village is the **Victorian Chapel**, which stands somewhat hidden between several Georgian houses along the village green.

BURGH BY SANDS

5 miles W of Carlisle off the B5307

On 7th July 1307, the body of King Edward I was laid out in the village church: he was already a dying man when he left Carlisle to march against his old enemy, Robert the Bruce. A monument to Edward was erected on the marshes and a later monument still marks the spot. At the time of the king's death, the **Church of St Michael** was already well over a century old and is possibly the earliest surviving example of a fortified church. Dating from 1181 and constructed entirely of stones from a fort on the Roman wall, the church was designed for protection against Border raids, which is why its tower has walls seven feet thick. The tower can only be entered through a strong iron grille.

PORT CARLISLE

12 miles W of Carlisle off the B5307

At one time sailing boats could make their way by canal from Port Carlisle to the heart of the city of Carlisle. Boats were towed there, a journey that took about 1 hour 40 minutes, enabling Carlisle to be reached within a day by sea from Liverpool. The canal was later replaced by the Bowness railway, the viaduct for which altered the deep-water channels, causing Port Carlisle to silt up. Although now dismantled, the railway's old course can still be traced and stretches of it form part of the Cumbrian Cycle Way.

BOWNESS-ON-SOLWAY

14 miles W of Carlisle off the B5307

Hadrian's Wall continues along the Solway coast (now classed a Coast Area of Outstanding Natural Beauty) to Bowness, and many of the sandstone cottages around here contain stones from the Wall. Some of these stones can easily be identified, such as the small inscribed altar let into a barn near the King's Arms. The Roman fort of **Maia** once covered a 7-acre site, but today there is only a plaque explaining where it used to be. Bowness is sometimes said to be the end of the Wall, but in fact the Wall just turned a corner here and continued south along the coast for another 40 miles. Due to this position, the walk now has been defined as "National trail", many walkers visit Bowness as a starting or ending point following Hadrian's Wall.

One local story tells that, in 1626, some Scotsmen crossed the Solway and stole the Bowness church bells. The thieves were spotted, chased and forced to lighten their boats by throwing the bells overboard. Later, the men of Bowness crossed the Firth and, in retaliation, seized the bells of Middlebie, Dumfries – every new vicar for which still requesting the return of these bells, a request which is always refused.

Two miles south of the village lies **Glasson Moss National Nature Reserve**, a lowland raised mire extending to 93 hectares. Many species of sphagnum moss are to be found here, and the birdlife includes red grouse, curlew, sparrowhawk and snipe.

LONGTOWN

9 miles N of Carlisle on the A7

Until 1750 Longtown was a small hamlet of mud dwellings. Dr Robert Graham, an 18th-century clergyman, proposed the building of the Esk bridge (over the River Esk) which was completed in 1756, and it was this venture that led to Longtown's establishment as a bustling border town. These days it has some fine individual buildings and broad, tree-lined terraces of colour-washed houses.

On the outskirts of Longtown is **Arthuret Church**. The earliest records of the church date from 1150 and it was originally served by the monks of Jedburgh. But it is thought that the earliest church here may have been founded by St Kentigern in the 6th century;

recent research has led some to believe that it has strong connections with King Arthur. The present church, dedicated to **St Michael and All Angels**, was built in 1609, financed by a general collection throughout the realm which James I ordered after a report that the people of Arthuret Church were without faith or religion. The people that he referred to, of course, were the infamous Reivers, ungoverned by either English or Scottish laws.

Just outside of Longtown is Oakbank Country Park; 60 acres of parkland with four lakes from which you can fish for trout, carp and salmon. There is also a bird sanctuary in the grounds.

BEWCASTLE

14 miles NE of Carlisle off the B6318

Roman legionaries assigned to the fort at what is now Bewcastle must certainly have felt that they had drawn the short straw. The fort stood all on its own, about 9 miles north of Hadrian's Wall, guarding a

Bewcastle Castle Ruins

143 CROSBY LODGE COUNTRY HOUSE HOTEL & RESTAURANT

Crosby-on-Eden

Crosby Lodge ranks among the top county house hotels in the region, with outstanding service, food and accommodation.

 see page 238

139 NO.10 AT EDEN GOLF CLUB

Crosby-on-Eden

One of the finet eateries in the area providing an unbeatable service.

 see page 235

crossing over the Kirk Beck. The site covered around 6 acres and most of it is now occupied by the ruins of a **Norman Castle**. Most of the south wall is still standing but little else remains and the castle is best admired for its setting rather than its architecture. It is now located on private land, but permission to view the ruins from a nearby path can be obtained, along with a leaflet containing information on the buildings history. An impressive survival in the village churchyard is the **Bewcastle Cross**, erected around AD670 and one of the oldest and finest stone crosses in Europe.

CROSBY-ON-EDEN

4 miles NE of Carlisle off the A689

The tiny hamlet of **High Crosby** stands on the hillside overlooking the River Eden; the small village of **Low Crosby** sits beside the river, clustered around a Victorian sandstone church. Inside the church there's a modern square pulpit, intricately carved with pomegranates, wheat and vines. Apparently, it was carved from one half of a tree felled nearby; the other half was used to create a second pulpit which was installed in the newly-built Liverpool Cathedral. Also, unusually, are the 16 side windows with segmental arches with lacy tracery pelmets of stone – the tracery heads themselves featuring, rather than the stained glass, cut clear glass in the shape of stars.

WETHERAL

4 miles E of Carlisle off the A69

Wetheral stands above the **River Eden**, over which runs an impressive railway viaduct, carrying the **Tyne Valley Line**, which was built by Francis Giles in 1830. Wetheral **Parish Church** lies below the village beside the river and contains a poignant sculpture by Joseph Nollekens of the dying Lady Mary Howard clasping her dead baby.

Wetheral is built around a triangular village green, in one corner of which stands Wetheral Cross. It makes for a very pleasant visit – with much of the houses made out of local stone, and the surrounding woodlands and countryside ideal for a leisurely walk. *Flight of Fancy*, another of the **Eden Benchmarks** (sculpted in St Bee's sandstone by Tim Shutter), has scenic views beside the river and is a nice place to take a rest and enjoy the tranquil atmosphere.

St Constantine was the local patron and the church is dedicated to the Holy Trinity, St Constantine and St Mary. Constantine is said to have lived in caves in what are now National Trust woodlands alongside the river, a location known as **Constantine's Caves**. (The caves were also used later by the nearby Priory to conceal their valuables during the Reiver raids.)

WARWICK

4 miles E of Carlisle on the A69

Warwick, beside the River Eden, is home to two rather grand houses.

The existing Warwick Hall, a neo-Georgian piece of architecture, was built on a previous house which burnt down in 1936. Part of the building is available for luxury self-catering accommodation. Holme Eden Hall, built in the style of an early Tudor mansion in 1937, is a very impressive property once the home of Benedictine nuns as an enclosed convent. Unfortunately the building was nearly lost to dry rot, but through recent renovations the property is due to be converted into luxury apartments.

The stone church of St Leonard dating mostly back to 1870, has surviving Norman features such as the arch dating 1130 and Norman apse with two small windows.

BRAMPTON

Nestling in the heart of the lovely Irthing Valley, Brampton is a delightful little town where the Wednesday market has been held since 1252, authorised by a charter granted by Henry III. Overlooking the Market Place is the town's most striking building, the octagonal **Moot Hall** topped by a handsome clock tower. There has been a Moot Hall here since 1648, though the present Hall was built in 1817 by Lord Carlisle. The iron stocks at the foot of a double flight of external stairs were last used in 1836. The hall now houses the information centre.

To the east of the town towering above Brampton is a rather high tree-covered **motte**,

about 135 feet high, at the top of which is a statue of the 7th earl of Carlisle erected in 1870. **St Martin's Church** in Brampton, famed for being the only church designed by Pre-Raphaelite Phillip Webb, contains a stunning array of stained glass windows, described by Sir Nikolaus Pevsner 'a remarkable building'…'the windows glowing with gem-stone colours'. The influence of nearby Hadrian's Wall is present here in a statue of the Roman Emperor Hadrian, stood on a plinth near the church in the towns centre.

South of Brampton are **Gelt Woods**, lying in a deep sandstone ravine carved by the fast-flowing River Gelt. By the River Gelt is an inscribed rock called **Written Rock** which is thought to have been carved by a Roman standard-bearer in AD 207. Access is discouraged however, as the path can be dangerous. A hidden gem in Gelt woods is a **quarry**, alongside the river Gelt, from which some of the stone for Hadrian's Wall was sourced. The grand and imposing quarry walls serve as a real testament to the incredible size of Hadrian's Wall, and the chisel marks can still be seen running across it in a herringbone type pattern. Here also is an RSBP nature reserve, protecting the many varieties of birds that find their habitat here, and ancient beech and oak trees, as well as over 200

The area around Brampton had good reason to be grateful to the Dacres of Naworth, who as Wardens of the Northern Marches protected it against marauding Scots. However, the townspeople of Brampton in Victorian times must have had mixed feelings about a later descendant, Rosalind, wife of the 9th Earl of Carlisle. An enthusiastic supporter of total abstinence, she contrived to get most of the small town's 40 public houses and drinking rooms closed.

Hadrian's Wall, Hare Hill

species of flowering plants and wild flowers.

AROUND BRAMPTON

TALKIN

2 miles S of Brampton off the B6413

Talkin Tarn, now the focus of a 120-acre country park, has been a popular place for watersports for over 100 years. Glacial in origin, the Tarn was formed some 10,000 years ago and is continually replenished by underground springs. Modern-day visitors can sail, windsurf, canoe or hire a rowing boat. Talkin Tarn Rowing Club has been rowing on the tarn for 130 years, and holds its annual regatta in July. Fishing licences are available, there's a nature trail and an orienteering course, a play area for children under 8, a tea room and a gift shop; guided walks with a warden are also available for organised groups. There is a 1.3 mile path around the tarn suitable for wheelchair users. The park is a peaceful place but, according to legend, beneath the surface of the lake there is a submerged village destroyed by a wrathful god, the ruins of which can still be seen below the water's surface in a certain light.

LOW ROW

3 miles E of Brampton off the A69

Within easy reach of the town is **Hadrian's Wall**, just 3 miles to the north. If you've ever wondered where the Wall's missing masonry went to, look no further than the fabric of **Lanercost Priory** (English Heritage). An impressive red sandstone ruin set in secluded woodland, the priory was founded in 1166 by Robert de Vaux. Lanercost is well preserved, and its scale is a reminder that it was a grand complex in its heyday. However, the Priory suffered greatly in the border raids of the 13th and 14th centuries. One such raid is known to have been led by William Wallace, an early campaigner for Scottish independence. When the Priory was closed in 1536, the sandstone blocks were recycled once again for houses in the town. But much of the Priory's great north aisle remains intact, set in a romantic and hauntingly beautiful position in the valley of the River Irthing. The Priory is well

Lanercost Priory, Low Row

signposted and lies only 3 miles off the A69 (leave at Brampton).

Also most impressive is **Naworth Castle**, built around 1335 in its present form by Lord Dacre as an important border stronghold. The castle passed through the female line to the Howard family after the last Lord Dacre was killed as a child – improbably as it might seem, by falling off his rocking horse. Now owned by the Howard family, Earls of Carlisle, the Castle is private but there are good views from the minor road off the A69 that passes in front of it – the scene is particularly attractive in spring when the lawns are ablaze with daffodils. Pre-booked parties are welcome all year round and the Castle has become a popular venue for weddings and corporate events.

Naworth Castle's supreme glory is the Great Hall, hung with French tapestries and guarded by four unique heraldic beasts holding aloft their family pennants. The Long Gallery extends for 116 feet and was used as a guardroom. It now houses an interesting collection of paintings, many brought together by the 9th Earl, George Howard. He entertained many pre-Raphaelite painters here, but the only surviving example of their work is Burne-Jones's *Battle of Flodden* – the rest were destroyed by a fire in 1844. In the courtyard there are some intriguing medieval latrines!

GILSLAND

7 miles E of Brampton on the B6318

Located in one of the most picturesque settings along the whole length of Hadrian's Wall and overlooking the River Irthing, **Birdoswald Roman Fort** (English Heritage) is one of the best-preserved edifices along the Wall and unique in that all the components of the Roman frontier system can be found here. Set high on a plateau with magnificent views over the surrounding countryside, the early turf wall, built in AD 122, can be seen along with the fort. Originally, Birdoswald Roman Fort would have covered 5 acres and may have been the base for up to 500 cavalry and 1,000 foot soldiers. A few hundred yards to the east is the mile-castle of Harrow Scar. There is now a visitor's centre here, with tea shop selling local home-made produce, and a family picnic area so visitors can relax here and learn the amazing history of this ancient fort.

Gilsland village is well known for its sulphur spring; there was once a convalescent home for miners and shipyard workers here. Now a hotel, it is owned by the Co-Operative Society and people still drink the waters as a cure for arthritis and rheumatism. Near the spring on the hotel grounds is the **Popping Stone**, traditionally the place where a man 'popped the question' to his lover. It was here that Sir Walter Scott successfully 'popped' to Charlotte Carpenter, daughter of a French refugee, after just three weeks' courtship. In spite of his family's early disquiet, the two were happily married for 30 years and had four children.

144 HOUSE OF MEG TEA ROOMS

Gilsland

With an historic background, this tearoom is full of character and offers scrumptious light bites, cakes and beverages.

see page 239

145 GREENHEAD HOTEL & HOSTEL

Greenhead, nr Brampton

Outstanding premises located in the dramatic countryside of Hadrians Wall.

see page 240

146 KIRKSTYLE INN

Slaggyford, nr Brampton

The Kirkstyle Inn is an oasis and treasure for lovers of fine food.

see page 239

Accommodation, Food & Drink and Places of Interest

The establishments featured in this section includes hotels, inns, guest houses, bed & breakfasts, restaurants, cafes, tea and coffee shops, tourist attractions and places to visit. Each establishment has an entry number which can be used to identify its location at the beginning of the relevant chapter or its position in this section. In addition full details of all these establishments and many others can be found on the Travel Publishing website - www.findsomewhere.co.uk. This website has a comprehensive database covering the whole of Britain and Ireland.

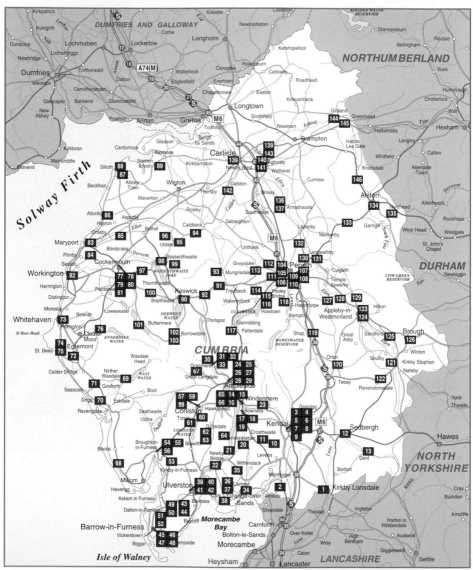

1 THE SNOOTY FOX HOTEL

Main Street, Kirkby Lonsdale,
Cumbria LA6 2AH
Tel: 01524 271308
e-mail: snootyfoxhotel@talktalk.net
website: www.thesnootyfoxhotel.co.uk

Situated in the heart of the picturesque old market town of Kirkby Lonsdale, **The Snooty Fox Hotel** is a traditional 17th Century coaching inn, full of charm and character. Visitors to this delightful inn are guaranteed to receive a

warm and friendly welcome from attentive hosts Glen and Lynn Massam who took over in June 2007.

The charming premises have long won acclaim for fine food, beer, wine and accommodation, all of which have been enhanced even further since Glen and Lynn have been at the helm. Whether stopping by for a drink and a snack, stopping longer for an excellent meal or staying for a short break, the greeting is genuine. Excellence continues in the elegant

restaurant where diners are treated to the most exciting, imaginative menu. The food is prepared from fresh local, seasonal ingredients and Glen and Lynn aim to provide guests with some of the region's finest produce thus sourcing it from the finest suppliers in Cumbria, Lancashire and North Yorkshire.

In addition to the cuisine, Glen and Lynn offer first class accommodation which is just as pleasing and consists of nine charming en-suite bedrooms, all offering total comfort to complete the perfect stay.

2 HERON CORN MILL

Mill Lane, Beetham, nr Milnthorpe,
Cumbria LA7 7PQ
Tel: 01539 565027
website: www.heronmill.org

Heron Corn Mill on the banks of the River Bela in South Cumbria, close to the Lancashire border, is one of the few working mills in the area. There is documentary evidence to show that a mill existed on the site prior to 1096. In 1220 the Lord of the Manor gave the monks of St Marie's York, the right to grind their grain at this mill without multure (payment).

The mill passed through many hands till in 1927 it came into the hands of W & J Pye, millers of Lancaster. In 1955 they rationalised their business and closed the mill. For the next two decades the mill was unused and decaying. In 1973 Henry Cooke Ltd., leased the mill to the newly-formed Beetham Trust, to rescue the mill for the benefit of the public.

In 1975 the mill was opened by Princess Alexandra and has continued up till the present time to show the mechanics of a water driven corn mill to the public. It is a unique feature of South Lakeland's industrial heritage.

3   YE OLDE FLEECE INN

14 Highgate, Kendal,
Cumbria LA9 4SX
Tel: 01539 720163 Fax: 01539 732641

Ye Olde Fleece Inn lives up to its name with an olde worlde interior fit to make any guest feel like they have walked straight into the 18th century coaching inn it -once was. The main feature is the original wood panelled walls, beautifully hand carved, creating a mature yet cosy atmosphere for its guests – and it's not just the décor people keep coming for; Ye Olde Fleece Inn provides quality food and drink all year round.

The inn is situated in the historic town of Kendall which, just a few miles from the sea is the perfect setting for a holiday in the lake district with many of its major attractions such as Lake Windermere being a mere 9 miles away. Ye Olde Fleece Inn is nestled in the centre of this bustling town and a visit here will certainly not leave you disappointed.

Guests can choose from the very varied menu or the specials board – both of which are created by the professional chef employed throughout the week and cooked by tenant Michael Peart himself on the chef's day off. Local produce is used wherever possible and all the meat and vegetables are sourced from within the county itself so you are guaranteed a real taste of Cumbria. Food is available from 11am-4pm in the winter months and from 11am-9pm Mon-Thurs and 11am-6pm Fridays and Saturdays in the summer months.

Michael prides himself on running a ship shape establishment that allows both locals and tourists to mix freely whilst enjoying the comfortable and elegant surroundings whilst enjoying some fine food and drink. Michael has been here for 4 years starting out as manager and after falling in love with this stunning property, becoming a tenant in November 2008. He offers two real rotating ales for those that know their drink which are brewed in Cumbria's very own popular breweries.

On Fridays and Saturdays Ye Olde Fleece Inn steps up the tempo taking a dive into the 21st century by hosting Kendal's very own Disco from 8:30pm until midnight free of charge so you can put on your dancing shoes after taking your fill from the hearty selection available here. Children are welcome, all major credit cards accepted apart from Amex and Diners.

ACCOMMODATION, FOOD & DRINK AND PLACES TO VISIT

4 BURGUNDY'S WINE BAR

19 Lowther Street, Kendal,
Cumbria LA9 4DH
Tel: 01539 733803
e-mail: burgundys@tiscali.co.uk
website: www.burgundyswinebar.co.uk

Back in 1986, Michael and Yvonne Pennington took over a derelict 19th century building in the heart of Kendal and transformed it into the highly popular **Burgundy's Wine Bar.** The thing that strikes you immediately when you enter the bar is the relaxed, friendly atmosphere and Michael and Yvonne are proud of the fact that age, here, does not create any barriers. Whilst Burgundy's is in the centre of busy Kendal, the atmosphere is more akin to that of a friendly village pub!

It is, though, the range of drinks on offer that has a very special appeal to customers. There are always 4 real ales to enjoy with Yates Fever Pitch as the regular brew, along with other rotating ales from Cumbrian breweries. Unusual beers and whiskeys, including speciality beers from Germany and Belgium, add to the diversity of choice. And, naturally, there's an excellent selection of wines from around the world with a

special range of varieties from the area of France that the bar takes its name from. Jazz lovers should make a point of visiting Burgundy's on a Thursday when there's live jazz from 8.30pm.

6 HAMPERS TEA ROOMS

14 New Shambles, Kendal,
Cumbria LA9 4TS
Tel: 01539 726420

Opened in April 2009 by owners Tammie and Nicholas the **Hampers Tea Rooms** is set in the heart of Kendal in New Shambles. Offering a warm and friendly service, it is just a short walk from Kendal's main thoroughfare and traditional, home-cooked food is their specialty.

Serving hot meals as well as sandwiches, jacket potatoes, salads and soup they offer an extensive menu and there are plenty of mouth-watering puddings for customers to choose from. Growing ever-popular with locals and tourists, Hampers Tea Rooms is child friendly and seats 33 people inside and four outside. Their breakfasts and salads have proved extremely popular and among the delights on offer are Roast Turkey with Cranberry Sauce Salad and The Ultimate Plum Pudding, which is a famous, locally made plum pudding with rum butter, served with cream or custard. Locally made chutneys and mustards accompany some of the meals and there is a wide choice available for

customers to purchase too. If it is afternoon tea or a spot of lunch you are after a visit to this delightful, quaint tea room should not be missed.

Hampers Tea Rooms is open every weekday from 9.30am-4pm and each Saturday 9am-4pm.

136

5 DICKIE DOODLES

Yard 2, Stricklandgate, Kendal,
Cumbria LA9 4ND
Tel: 01539 738480
e-mail: dickie-doodles@hotmail.com
website: www.dickiedoodles.com

For lovers of great music and well kept ales, **Dickie Doodles** is the place to head for. Open every evening from 8 till late, it is home to a multitude of musical talent covering many areas of the modern music spectrum with performers ranging from talented amateurs to well-known professionals. Behind this successful venture is friendly owner Shaun Bainbridge. He took over the empty premises in 1999 and finally realised his dream, transforming the place into a live music venue that is open seven nights a week.

The week unfolds as follows:

> *Monday: Acoustic jamming*
>
> *Tuesday: Electric jamming*
>
> *Wednesday: Folk session (jamming)*
>
> *Thursday: New and up-and-coming bands*
>
> *Friday and Saturday: Professional rock bands*

Entrance (over 18's only) is free, and drinks (cash only) include a good choice of draught and bottled beers, lagers and cider. From August real ales will be available from Cumbrian breweries. There is certainly something here for everyone's taste. Snacks such as Chilli & chips/rice are available from 10pm Thurs/Fri/Sat.

Dickie Doodles also shows arts and crafts exhibitions showcasing the work of talented local artist amd makers. These change every two months so ring for details. Shaun is a blacksmith by trade and some of his forgework is also on display.

Stricklandgate is one of the busy narrow streets at the heart of old Kendal, and the yards (alleyways) are a distinctive feature of the town. In times past, these were a line of defence against the constant threat of marauding Scots and could be sealed off by closing the single small entrance, keeping families and their livestock safe inside. The Scottish threat has long since abated, and now tourists from around the world come in peace to Kendal throughout the year. For music lovers visiting this area, a visit to Dickie Doodles is a must!

137

7 SAWYERS ARMS

Stricklandgate, Kendal, Cumbria LA9 4RF
Tel: 01539 729737
e-mail: gillianwalber@btinternet.com

Sawyers Arms is situated in the heart of the popular town of Stricklandgate in Kendal. Stricklandgate is a fine spot for an afternoons browsing, with a well pedestrianised market place and range of quaint shops. Sawyers Arms sits in the centre of this pleasant town and is renowned locally and further afield for its hospitality, well kept ales and quality accommodation. This historic building dates back to the late 18th century, when it used to be a former coaching inn.

Sawyers Arms still today provides a restful night's sleep for weary travellers in one of the 8 en-suite bedrooms on offer. There is a good range of sizes to choose from to suit all needs, couples or families and the tariff includes a hearty full English breakfast in the guests' dining room which is guaranteed to keep even the most ambitious rambler going throughout the day. Unlike most bed and breakfast accommodation however, there is also the option of taking a smoking room – welcome news to some.

Gill and Norman Walber have been running Sawyers Arms for 3 years now, and their knack for creating a friendly and comfy environment has served them well over that time. Gill's local knowledge, born and bred in the area, ensures that this establishment is popular with not just locals but is constantly revisited by tourists and business men.

Open all day everyday this inn offers only food to its residents but prides itself on offering a good selection for its drinkers all year round. The most popular drink here is Carling Lager, but for those ale lovers Hartleys XB is regularly on tap with the occasional guest ale following from the Robinsons Brewery nearby. The bar also offers a wide range of spirits in a comforting wood panelled den, with large windows offering a pleasant view of the Stricklandgate roads.

Each week Gill and Norman take the atmosphere up a notch with a disco or live music on a Saturday evening from 9pm to get the musical juices flowing, and a weekly Sunday night quiz welcoming all from 9pm also, making this a perfect stop for a memorable insight into rural town life in Cumbria, or simply a quiet base for exploring the stunning countryside further afield.

9 DUKE OF CUMBERLAND

**I Appelby Road, Kendal,
Cumbria LA9 6ES
Tel: 01539 724054**

The Duke of Cumberland is situated where the A6 and the A685 meet, just yards from the centre of Kendal. The premises itself dates back to the mid 18th century when it was a former coaching and posting inn catering for weary travellers and locals for over 250 years. Today the Duke of Cumberland still opens its doors to both young and old providing quality food and drink every day.

Leaseholders Heather and Patrick took over this inn in May 2008, giving the Duke a new lease of life – locals say it really has a buzz about the place. Certainly it is a popular place to dine and unwind and is open Mon-Sat 11am-11pm and Sundays 12-11pm.

The bar offers up to 3 real ales to enjoy with Cumberland Ale and Bomberdier brews being the popular choices here. They also offer a wide selection of wines, spirits and soft drinks. Food is served from opening until late daily – the menu carefully selected by Patrick himself who has many years experience as a qualified chef. He oversees a hard working team in the kitchen so your dishes are guaranteed to be top notch every time. Guests have the option of choosing from the main menu displayed on the blackboard or the daily specials board which often include some of the tastiest seasonal produce around. Regular customers of the Duke of Cumberland rave over the homemade steak and ale pie and the Cumberland sausage dish – both heart warming creations sure to fill you up after a hike in

beautiful surrounding countryside. On Sundays a generous roast dinner is added to the menu with a choice of fine cuts of roasted beef, lamb or chicken served with vegetables and all the trimmings and comes highly recommended by all who try it.

Heather and Patrick also cater for up to 60 people in a separate function room at the Inn perfect for private or corporate events. There is also ample parking in two large car parks adjacent to the building adding convenience to this property's qualities. At the rear of the building is a stunning beer garden and patio area – the perfect place to enjoy a summer evening after a day wandering around the charming town of Kendal. All major credit cards are accepted and children are welcome all day.

8 CAFE 34

34 Stramongate, Kendal,
Cumbria LA9 4BN
Tel: 01539 726494

Café 34 is a small friendly family run diner in Kendal, situated in Stramongate. Its contemporary feel and relaxed atmosphere welcomes all, open Monday to Saturday 8.45am-4.30pm, both cash and credit cards accepted. Locals say what the property lacks in size it more than makes up for in hospitality, with owners Helen, Mike, daughter Charlotte and a hard working team of dedicated employees delivering quality food and drinks all year round.

Cafe 34 is licensed and also offers a wide range of hot and cold beverages. A range of snacks, paninis, salads, jacket potatoes and sandwiches with an impressive range of fillings is on offer including traditional Ploughman's lunch, or heart warming homemade soup of the day.

Locals say that Helen and Mike have made a real success of the business and rave over the wide range of tasty breakfasts available for any appetite. Cafe 34 also offers a range of fresh fish dishes created with the help of next doors fishmonger Nik, all cooked fresh to order. There really is something to suit everyone which is why this charming property is always full to the brim of satisfied customers.

11 CROSTHWAITE HOUSE

Crosthwaite, nr Kendal,
Cumbria LA8 8BP
Tel: 01539 568264
e-mail: bookings@crosthwaitehouse.co.uk
website: www.crosthwaitehouse.co.uk

Located in a superb and lush surrounding, **Crosthwaite House** is the perfect setting to relax, unwind and enjoy the spectacular views of the pleasant fells.

Robin and Marnie Dawson offer their visitors star quality accommodation, with splendid views, tremendous furnishings and luxurious space, in order to feel well at home. With 6 ensuite bedrooms available, as well as 2 cottages for self-catering- there is accommodation available to suit every taste.

The cottages are converted from 300 year old barns, Top Bank sleeps 2, Middle Bank sleeps 4 and they both share an exquisite garden. Located in the main house dining room, residents and non residents can enjoy traditional home cooking by Marnie on her Aga, using local produce, including fruit from the orchard.

At the end of a long day, guests can retire to the spectacular lounge and browse through the numerous books, including sites to see and recommended walks. Robin has a wealth of knowledge about the local areas and is more than happy to point you in the right direction, in order to make your stay memorable.

140

10 THE WHEATSHEAF

Brigsteer, Cumbria LA8 8AN
Tel: 01539 568254
e-mail: wheatsheaf@brigsteer.gb.com
website:
www.thewheatsheafbrigsteer.co.uk

Brigsteer is a tiny village in the shadow of Scout Scar, 3 miles from Kendal and 5 miles from Junction 36 of the M6, west of the A591 or north from the A590 via Levens. The building that houses **The Wheatsheaf** has been an integral part of the local community for almost 250 years. Before becoming licensed in the early part of the 19th century, the Wheatsheaf consisted of three cottages and a shoeing room for horses. It was once the starting point of the local hunts and the inside walls are adorned with pictures of the hunting days.

Now sympathetically modernised whilst retaining its traditional charm, it is owned and run by Lee Rowbotham and his family and is a great place to visit, whether it's for a drink, a snack or a full meal. It is even a brilliant base from which to explore the surrounding beauty that is the Lake District. For guests who choose to stay, there are 3 luxuriously appointed en suite rooms for Bed & Breakfast.

In a village that is centrally located yet peaceful and relaxing, the Wheatsheaf is the perfect place to unwind and enjoy the surroundings, or to explore the many and varied attractions, both scenic and historic, that the region has to offer. These include Lake Windermere, Kendal, Latterbarrow Wildlife Reserve, Whitbarrow, Levens Hall and the National Trust's Sizergh Castle.

Lee is very proud of what the Lake District has to offer, and this shines through in the menu, as  much of the menu as possible is sourced from local suppliers. The food available is classically British with a contemporary twist, using seasonal meat, game and poultry, daily delivered fresh fish and seafood for the à la carte menus. Examples of this delicious menu include roast chump of lamb with garlic mash, carved loin of Holker venison with confit potato and pan-roasted duck breast with a plum jus. The bar is open from 12 pm to 3 pm and from 6 pm to 11 pm, and food is served anywhere in the open plan ground floor from 12 pm to 2 pm and between 6 pm and 9 pm. The bar is well stocked and two locally brewed real ales are always available.

12 ELLIE'S BAKERY AND TEAROOM

57 Main Street, Sedburgh,
Cumbria LA10 5AB
Tel: 01539 621058

Ellie's Bakery and Tearoom assures a warm welcome to both locals and visitors alike – it's a place of peace and tranquillity where guests can relax with the local paper and sample some of the most wholesome home cooking in Sedburgh.

Mum Mel Missenden and children Kate, Harvey and Ellie run this small 26 seated tearoom with 4 more outdoor seats serving a variety of hot and cold snacks and beverages, breakfasts, lunches and cakes, 80% of which are baked in house by Mel who rises as 5am daily to ensure her culinary delights are fresh from the oven at opening time. The range of cakes is enough to baffle the sweetest of toothes and the lamb stew will truly melt in your mouth. Open from 8am-5pm Mon-Sat and 10-5pm on Sundays this is also the perfect place to breakfast offering continental, fried and vegetarian options.

Surprisingly upstairs there is a holistic centre where visitors can indulge in a range of aromatherapy, hot stone therapy, counselling, homoeopathy massage, reflexology and Reiki treatments offered by a group of local practioners one of whom is the marvellous Mel herself. Please book in advance for the holistic centre. Children and dogs are welcome at the bakery, cash and cheque only please.

13 STONE CLOSE TEA ROOM AND BED & BREAKFAST

Main Street, Dent, Sedbergh,
Cumbria LA10 5QL
Tel: 01539 625231
e-mail: stoneclose@btinternet.com
website: www.dentdale.com/stoneclose

Janet Browning and her lovely dog Maisie welcome visitors to **Stone Close Tea Room and Bed and Breakfast**, tucked away in the village of Dent in one of Cumbria's finest dales. The building started life in the 17th century as two separate cottages and retains many of the original features including beams, flagstones and cast iron ranges, which have fires lit during cold weather. A recent addition to the property is the treatment room, with stunning views across the Dale; this room is available to guests for quiet relaxation or for pre-booked treatments.

The tea room is open from 12 noon to 5 pm, Tuesday to Thursday & weekends, as well as some fridays and bank holiday Mondays, for a selection of delicious, imaginative dishes based almost entirely on organic produce. The tea room is large enough to seat 30 people and features food cooked on site by Janet.

Janet has three rooms for B & B guests, a twin on the ground floor and a twin and a double upstairs. The reasonable tariff includes a continental breakfast, or for just a small extra charge, a delicious full English can be catered for.

142

14 THE LAKES HOTEL

1 High Street, Windermere,
Cumbria LA23 1AF
Tel: 01539 442751 Fax: 01539 446026
e-mail: admin@lakes-hotel.com
website: www.lakes-hotel.com

The Lakes Hotel is a small family run hotel in the centre of Windermere, just a stones throw away from the rail and bus stations.

Occupying a handsome, mid-Victorian building, that was formally a bank, when built in 1860, the property is situated in a prime location. Close to the shops and a good variety of restaurants, The Lakes Hotel is the perfect base to explore this wonderful village in the Lake District.

Andrew and Marie Dobson offer 10 ensuite bedrooms, in a variety of sizes- double, twin and family rooms, with all rooms being decorated and furnished to a good standard.

The couple also own Lakes Supertours, which operates from the hotel and provides spectacular and informative Lake District tours including scenic and cultural attractions. Luxury high-topped mini-coaches, with ample legroom are on offer and each coach is driven by friendly, well-informed driver/guides. Itineries include the complete Beatrix Potter's Lakeland and Wordsworth and by coach and boat to Borrowdale, Buttermere and Ullswater. There are plenty of special offers available and all tours start from the hotel forecourt.

15 WINSTER HOUSE

Sunny Bank Road, Windermere,
Cumbria LA23 2EN
Tel: 01539 444723
e-mail: enquiries@winsterhouse.co.uk
website: www.winsterhouse.co.uk

Winster House offers you an ideal solution to holidaying away in the stunning Lake District allowing you privacy, luxury and space all in one. Three apartments are available; Little Winster, Bowness Studio and the Windermere suite - all of which have been carefully thought out to provide total comfort and relaxation. All apartments come with the option of a breakfast full of delicious local produce and each with their own cooking facilities, central heating, dining area, T.V, DVD, sofa and en suite. The Windermere suite is slightly larger with separate living room and bedroom whereas the other rooms have ingenious fold away beds that sacrifice no comfort for the extra space they provide. Each apartment also has its own south facing patio and garden area which is a real sun trap in the summer months, making Winster House a home from home from which to enjoy the surrounding beauty.

Set ideally between the villages of Windermere and Bowness, within walking distance of plenty of shops, restaurants and Lake Windermere itself, Jenny and John Whalley have created a quality establishment second to none.

16 WICKED WINDERMERE

4 High Street, Windermere,
Cumbria LA23 1AF
Tel: 015394 44954
website: www.wickedwindermere.co.uk

Located at the top of High Street in a lovely, traditional setting lies the superb restaurant **Wicked Windermere.** Offering elegant style and tremendous food, as well as a friendly but efficient and welcoming atmosphere, the staff here are keen to make your visit a memorable one.

Having been open for the last 2 years, Wicked Windermere is owned and personally run by Brian Wisdom. This business is certainly one to add to your list of favourites and has been recommended by people visiting, far and wide. The food on offer has also had 'rave' reviews in the local and national papers, magazines and cook books- meaning that upon your visit, you will be able to experience something truly special.

The atmosphere throughout this business is divine. The extremely stylish and beautifully clean-cut décor, combined with the traditional and historic façade, is fabulously inviting, creating a warm environment, which can be enjoyed by all. As well as this, the reputation for superb quality, traditional Cumbrian cuisine and the value that is on offer, really does make this place 'wicked'.

The menu available encompasses much local produce and the professional Chefs, which Brian employs, expertly transform traditional recipes in to dishes of mouth-watering works of art. There are several menus throughout the day, including the early bird menu and à la carte menu. Dishes such as smooth chicken liver parfait with home made pickles and fruit chutney; pan fried fillet of salmon topped with a herb crust and grilled chicken breast with a creamy leek sauce can be seen on the early bird menu; whilst king prawns cooked in tomato, cream and garlic sauce, slow braised lamb shank served on a smooth mint mashed potato, pan fried fillet steak and marinated grilled chicken kebab can be seen on the a la carte menu. There is also a tantalising dessert menu and an equally impressive wine list.

Brian previous to running this superb restaurant was a personal butler for 22 years on Princess cruises. Having rubbed shoulders with the stars, he is always happy to share his stories and has many fine photos displayed around the restaurant.

Open daily from 12-2pm and 6 9pm, with Sundays being open from 12-8pm, where better place is there to spend a lunchtime break or a relaxing diner? Wicked Windermere's will make your day.

17 BLENHEIM LODGE

Brantfell Road, Bowness-on-Windermere,
Cumbria LA23 3AE
Tel: 015394 43440
e-mail: enquiries@blenheim-lodge.com
website: www.blenheim-lodge

Built in 1868, with acres of beautiful National Park fields and woodlands on its doorstep, **Blenheim Lodge** is situated at the top of a hill in Bowness on Windermere, a PERFECT location away from 'the madding crowd', but only a 5-minute walk to the centre of Bowness village and Lake Windermere, where you can enjoy the amenities and attractions of this popular Lakeland village. Walkers may appreciate being close to the Dales Way, which is literally a minute's stroll from our front door!

Offering delicious breakfasts using quality handmade local produce, Blenheim Lodge has 11 double, twin, single and family bedrooms with en-suite/private facilities. All rooms have tea/coffee making facilities and flat screen TVs. Rooms are beautifully decorated in Laura Ashley colours and soft furnishings and many feature antique furniture, including 4-poster and Louis XV beds, and luxurious pocket sprung mattresses. Ten bedrooms at Blenheim Lodge offer gorgeous Lake Windermere views, and one bedroom offers tranquil countryside views, with that 'getting away from it all' feeling!

There are many activities and facilities in the surrounding areas for guests to enjoy, including fishing and golf. Indeed, our guests are welcome to take advantage of FREE country club membership and FREE fishing permits when staying with us. We also have a private car park.

Please contact us if you are celebrating a special occasion, or want to purchase a gift voucher. We are always happy and can arrange flowers, champagne, and luxury handmade chocolate truffles for special occasions. We can even arrange for you to enjoy a luxury yacht cruise with transport and 4-course dinner on board!

18 ST MARTIN'S COFFEE HOUSE

4 St Martin's Parade, Bowness-on-Windermere, Cumbria LA23 3DY
Tel: 015394 46404
e-mail: judychappell@hotmail.co.uk

Located in the heart of Bowness, close to the main car park and the lake in St Martin's Parade, **St Martin's Coffee House** is very much a family run enterprise with owner Judy Chappell supported by her mum Nora (who makes the preserves at home), and on occasion by her daughters Lucy, Amy, Ruth and Mary.

The smartly furnished and decorated dining area has both regular table seating and also comfortable armchairs, while there's further seating outside on the patio. The day begins with a good choice of breakfasts ranging from a heartily filled breakfast baguette to hot croissants, all served until 11.30am. Throughout the day, an inviting selection of hot food is served, including a home-made Dish of the Day, along with paninis, sandwiches, toasties, baguettes, salads and pizza. Children have their own choices. Bakery items include delicious home-made scones (six different varieties), cakes and biscuits, all made on the premises. Judy estimates that 75% of the ingredients used here come from local sources, including the ham and cheeses.

The coffee house is open daily from 10am to 5pm; there's good disabled access, and payment is by cash only.

19 ROYAL OAK INN

Brantfell Road, Bowness-on-Windermere,
Cumbria LA23 3EG
Tel: 015394 43970
e-mail: info@royaloak-windemere.co.uk
website: www.royaloak-windemere.co.uk

Situated in the heart of the popular town of Bowness-on-Windermere and just a stone's throw from the glorious Lake Windermere is the **Royal Oak Inn**. Angie, Steve and their family run this beautiful inn which dates back to the 19th century when it began life as a coaching inn. A warm and friendly atmosphere has been created for many years now with the help of licensee Dave who ensures things run smoothly. There is a real team spirit in this establishment and it's carried through to customers who receive quality service in every aspect.

Open all day, every day the Royal Oak offers at least 3 real ales, regulars including Cumberland Ale and Coniston Bluebird with great home cooked food available until 9:30pm. They serve a good selection of light bites, starters, sandwiches and burgers and a hearty choice of mains that include Cumberland pie, rack of lamb, and mushroom and pepper tagliatelle. There is also a children's menu and boards displaying a tempting selection of specials, steaks and desserts and entertainment is sometimes provided in the

evenings. And for convenience and comfort there are 8 double rooms (6 en suite) available all year round complete with breakfast. An ideal breakaway with many local attractions within walking distance.

HIDDEN PLACES GUIDES

Explore Britain and Ireland with *Hidden Places* guides - a fascinating series of national and local travel guides.

Packed with easy to read information on hundreds of places of interest as well as places to stay, eat and drink.

Available from both high street and internet booksellers

For more information on the full range of *Hidden Places* guides and other titles published by Travel Publishing visit our website on

www.travelpublishing.co.uk
or ask for our leaflet by phoning
01752 697280 or emailing
info@travelpublishing.co.uk

21 STOTT PARK BOBBIN MILL

Lowstott Park, Ulverston,
Cumbria LA12 8AX
Tel: 01539 531087
website: www.english-heritage.org.uk

This extensive working mill was begun in 1835 to produce the wooden bobbins vital to the Lancashire spinning and weaving industries. Although small compared to other mills, some 250 men and boys (some drafted in from workhouses) worked here in often arduous conditions to produce a quarter of a million bobbins a week. Guided tours are

included in the admission charge: the last tour begins ½ hour before closing. Please call for details of steam days.

20 THE HARE & HOUNDS

Bowland Bridge, Grange-over-Sands,
Cumbria LA11 6NN
Tel: 01539 568333
e-mail: blanchardjc@tiscali.co.uk
website: www.brilliantpub.co.uk/
harehoundscumbria

Surrounded by hundreds of acres of beautiful countryside, **The Hare & Hounds** is a 17th century establishment providing great food, well kept ales and comfortable accommodation. The property is believed to have monastic origins, but during its varied history has been a farmhouse, an alehouse, a posting inn and at one time, a mortuary! Standing on an old drover's road that ran between Kendal and Newby Bridge, the impressive stone built building exudes a warm and welcoming feel as you approach. Adorned with hanging baskets which are bursting with colour, the premises are attended to by leaseholder James Blanchard and his mother Muriel. Originally hailing from Yorkshire, James took the plunge in August 2008 and the premises have gone from strength to strength in their capable hands.

The interior of the pub doesn't disappoint, the long wooden bar is always clean and well stocked. The Hare & Hounds is open every day all day for ale; there are three available at any one time, two of which are Cumberland Ale and Sneck Lifter, plus one rotating guest ale. The Hare & Hounds also offers accommodation, at the moment there is one en suite double room available for hire on a B & B basis all year round, there are imminent plans however, for a further three rooms.

James is also the head chef and the cuisine here is spectacular; food is available daily from 12 noon to 9 pm and in order to avoid disappointment, it is recommended that reservations be made to eat on Thursdays, Fridays, Saturdays and Sundays. The extensive menu is made up of traditionally English dishes; the home made steak and ale pie and the ultimate fish and chips are both very popular. Other sumptuous sounding choices include the home made chicken, ham and leek pie, pan fried breast of duck with a spicy mango relish or orange sauce and the Hare & Hounds platter, which consists of fresh crevettes, smoked salmon, tuna and prawns! There is also a seafood board, which holds such tempting fare as salmon and prawn en croute, 1 kg fresh mussels in a garlic and white wine sauce, pan fried king scallops on a bed of creamy mash and seared tuna with a lemon spinach dressing and potato rosti. On Sundays, roast dinners are added to the menu and these are extremely popular with visitors and locals alike.

22 THE ANGLERS ARMS

**Haverthwaite nr Ulverston,
Cumbria LA12 8AJ
Tel: 01539 531216**

Ten real ales and great food served in a convivial atmosphere brings customers from near and far to **The Anglers Arms**, a traditional country pub which stands in the heart of Haverthwaite, 200 yards off the A590 and a short distance from Ulverston. New landlords Katrina, Graham and Sheena continue to ensure that the Anglers Arms is a thriving part of the community, extending a warm welcome to young and old (and their dogs!) all day every day.

All appetites are catered for with a wide range of light bites from rustic homemade soups to stilton and Guinness infused chicken liver pate served with salad and melba toast, or a choice of sumptuous main meals like the slow roasted lamb henry cooked with fresh rosemary, thyme and garlic in a red wine gravy, with a hearty roast also offered on Sundays. Food is served 12-2pm and 5:30-9pm weekdays and from 12-9pm on weekends. All major credit cards accepted except American Express. It is advised to book Fri/Sat/Sun though as Graham's invaluable experience as Head Chef of the Angler's Arms for over two years ensures a full house most nights. All dishes are cooked to order with local produce offering a variety of seasonal fish, game, pies and innovative vegetarian dishes such as the flavoursome mushroom stroganoff cooked in a red wine,

garlic, paprika and French cream sauce – and that's not including the specials board which offers a range of exotic treats or simply a good old chicken balti curry! A children's menu is also available.

It's not just the food they take seriously here though, with up to 10 real ales rotating in the summer months and up to 30 real ales during their annual beer festival in August from a range of local and national breweries, which can be enjoyed in the sunshine from the large outdoor seating area, complete with patio heaters.

The charming rural community of Haverthwaite is also home to the restored Lakeside & Haverthwaite Railway which sports steam-engine hauled services from just over the road. The Anglers Arms also offers live music on Saturday nights, providing a vibrant but cosy stop in the outstanding beauty of the surrounding Lake District National park.

23 WILF'S CAFE

Mill Yard, Back Lane, Staveley, nr Kendal,
Cumbria LA8 9LR
Tel: 01539 822329 Fax: 01539 822969
e-mail: food@wilfs-cafe.co.uk
website: www.wilfs-cafe.co.uk

Wilf's Cafe has been offering the general public mouth-watering snacks and meals since 1997 and is still going strong. Overlooking the River Kent in the village of Staveley, this traditional building, combined with its modern furnishings and eye-catching artwork adorning the walls, keeps the locals and visitors returning again and again.

Wilf, Charlotte, Chef Martin Lovett and their wonderful team, provide a spectacular atmosphere, as well as tantalising food for all of the family. The team produce an excellent range of meals, everything from mighty breakfasts, both vegetarian and non, hot spuds, with a great list of fillings, salads, sandwiches and Wilf's rarebits, as well as snacks of toasted t-cakes with jam, bacon or sausage butty, fresh croissants and garlic bread with cheese. There are also splendid puddings and cakes, including sticky toffee cake, caramel shortbread and a hot pudding, which is advertised on the specials board. To accompany the spectacular feast on offer, Wilf's also offer a wide range of fair-trade tea and coffees and cold drinks.

The aforementioned food can be enjoyed in a large space for 120, which is often full to the brim with laughter and friendly faces. The café is linked to its neighbour the Hawkshead Brewery and customers at the café can take a tour and sample the ales, as well as bring back a glass of their choice to accompany their meal.

If you don't wish to make the effort of eating in, Wilf's also provides a take away service, which is new for 2009. These meals can be supplied frozen or ready to go in the oven and are all cooked in the kitchen, using local products wherever possible. These dishes are in bulk and each main meal or dessert is enough for 8 adult portions. Dishes included in the takeaway service include favourites such as cottage pie, beef lasagne and lamb hot pot, as well as spinach and feta cheese pie, smoked mackerel dauphinoise and vegetable stroganoff crumble.

What's more, Wilf's offer speciality nights throughout the year- Moroccan, Thai, Spanish, with authentic dishes served in a set menu. Prices are £19.95, with a £5 deposit required upon booking.

24 LUIGI'S RESTAURANT

Osborne Villa, Kelsick Road, Ambleside,
Cumbria LA22 0BZ
Tel: 015394 33676
e-mail: booking@luigis-ambleside.co.uk
website: www.luigis-ambleside.co.uk

Since it was established some 20 years ago, **Luigi's Restaurant** has become something of an Ambleside institution. This family-owned restaurant uses recipes passed down from generation to generation and offers, freshly made, traditional Italian home cooked food. Michael Goddard, the present owner is self

taught, and he has worked his way up through the hospitality business and trained under the eponymous Luigi before taking over in 2004. The aim here, over the years, has remained unchanged; to serve good traditional Italian food and a fine selection of wines in a relaxed and friendly atmosphere.

As much of the food as possible is fresh, locally sourced and prepared to order. Naturally, some of the ingredients have to be obtained in Italy to ensure the authentic flavours are maintained. So, among the starters for example, you'll find an Affettato Misto - a selection of cold meats from Italy, along with typical Italian dishes such as Parma ham and melon. Or you could settle for the tasty home-made soup of the day. As a main dish, how about chicken breast or veal escallops in Marsala wine, or grilled sirloin steak with a tomato and garlic sauce? Naturally, there's a good choice of pasta dishes, ranging from a traditional lasagne or risotto to Cannelloni Spinaci - home-made pancake with spinach and ricotta cheese, topped with tomato and white sauces. The regular menu is supplemented by a specials board which changes about once a week. The restaurant is licensed for diners and Luigi's wine list presents an excellent choice of Italian wines, by the glass or bottle, along with beers, spirits and liqueurs.

The restaurant is on two floors with seating for 23 customers on each floor. Children are welcome and can have half portions of the dishes listed on the main menu. During the season, Luigi's is open from 6pm until late; out of season, it is closed on Monday and Tuesday. Booking is advisable at all times, and essential at the weekend. All major credit cards are accepted, apart from American Express and Diners; there is good disabled access to the ground floor.

25 THE OLD VICARAGE AT AMBLESIDE

Vicarage Road, Ambleside,
Cumbria LA22 9DH
Tel: 015394 33364
e-mail: info@oldvicarageambleside.co.uk
website: www.oldvicarageambleside.co.uk

Set in two acres of grounds and dating back to the Victorian age **The Old Vicarage at Ambleside** is an oasis in the heart of the village.

The superb and charming family-run guest house has 15 delightful en-suite rooms - all furnished to a high standard - and has a heated, indoor swimming pool, sauna, hot tub, sun lounge and roof terrace for guests.

Owned by Helen and Ian Burt, along with their daughter Liana for the past 20 years, visitors return again and again to enjoy the outstanding facilities, location and unbelievable hospitality. The Burt's offer a hearty, quality English breakfast. Surrounded by superb scenery it provides an ideal base to explore the surrounding area, including the fells and lakes and there are plenty of activities available in the area, including fishing, riding, climbing, golf and water sports. Just a stones throw away from Rothay Park; the child friendly guest house is tucked quietly away from traffic noise and welcomes dog owners.

26 STAMPERS RESTAURANT

The Old Stamp House, Church Street,
Ambleside, Cumbria LA22 0BU
Tel: 01539 432775
e-mail: stampers.restaurant@tiscali.co.uk
website: www.stampersrestaurant.co.uk

Described as *the* place to dine in Cumbria – **Stampers Restaurant** is truly fantastic. Set in the cellar of one of Ambleside's finest buildings is the town's favourite dining place. Owner Heather Tennant has been running the show here for a phenomenal 26 years and with a hard working team including Chef Geoff Jones and daughter Maria, Heather's sons Callum and Ewan to help her provide stellar service and cuisine to guests year and year out. They set out many years ago to promise customers 1st class service with 1st class food at realistic prices and according to our guests they have upheld their side very well.

Stampers itself is a beautiful and character filled place with its status as a grade II listed building. Today it retains its original wooden beams, stone floors and four feet thick stone walling! Despite this olde worlde feel Stampers feels bright and warm thanks to its tasteful décor. For over thirty years the building was Ambleside's Stamp House where the legendary William Wordsworth was once the distributor for the areas stamps. The history here is well recorded and seeps through the walls creating an interesting yet intimate vibe in which to dine.

There is a fantastic range of food available on various menus and specials boards, the à la carte menu being what really draws in the crowds. They have a massive variety of starters, pasta dishes, mains and desserts, the majority of which are made with locally sourced produce using specialist farmers and producers including meat raised on the fells, ice cream made in local town Kendal, cheese from a local farmers consortium in Appleby and traditionally smoked meats in Cartmel. All food is cooked to order which also allows all diner's special dietary requirements to be taken into account, including vegan and lacto-vegetarians. Some of the favourites on the menu include crispy fried brie starter, smoked chicken and prawn pasta, fresh swordfish served with ratatouille, vegetable strudel and 10oz sirloin steak. As you can see the menu here is not only mouth watering but innovative with attention to detail and it is those qualities that keep Stampers busy throughout the week, so its advised to book at all times.

Opening hours are Wednesday to Saturday from 6pm with last orders at around 10-10:30pm. Stampers also holds a fully licensed bar which has a healthy selection of wine, beers, spirits and liquers. Children welcome.

27 THE GIGGLING GOOSE CAFÉ AT THE OLD MILL

North Road, Ambleside,
Cumbria LA22 9DT
Tel: 01539 433370

The Giggling Goose Café is a real hidden treasure and once it's found it's never forgotten. Set in the idyllic surroundings of the charming community of Ambleside it can be found either side of North Street or through the delightful pastoral gardens at its rear which lie adjacent to the Beck off Ambleside's main thoroughfare.

Owners and creators of the Giggling Goose café Craig and Janine Hunter-Lowe have been open for 4 years now and have created a popular reputation within the local community and surrounding businesses for fine quality homemade food. The tremendous effort they put into delivering a hospitable and friendly service for good food has gone a long way as they are highly recommended by all in town.

Home cooking is really what this place is about, with the entire range of delicious cakes, scones and breads are all made daily on the premises. Craig and Janine also pride themselves on making their own jams, chutney, salad dressings, vinaigrettes, soups, stews and clotted cream ensuring that every mouthful taken here is a satisfying one. There are 30 indoor seats in a fresh country tearoom setting, with 50 more seats outside in the tumbling garden full of vibrant flowers and shady trees making for a relaxing stop indeed. There is a range of breakfast available from 10-11am including the house speciality of granola and natural yoghurt drizzled with berry coulis and a fresh fruit salad, and a lunch menu runs from 11:30am-3:30pm that offers a range of tempting doorstep sandwiches, warm salads like the grilled goats cheese salad served on toasted chilli plum jam bread with mixed baby salad leaf, cucumber, onion and tomato with homemade vinaigrette and balsamic syrup and a rustic farmhouse brunch platter. Hungryman soup of the day (it's a whole pint!) served with a choice of bread or half a doorstep sandwich is served all day along with a beautiful choice for those with a sweet tooth with an astounding 16 cakes in summer months when the Giggling Goose is open 7days a week from 10am-5pm. In the winter months they are open weekends and some weekdays.

They also offer a plentiful selection of hot chocolates, coffees, teas and soft drinks with a children's menu also available. Cash or debit/credit card only, well behaved dogs are welcome on leads.

153

28 STAGSHAW GARDEN

Ambleside, Cumbria LA22 0HE
Tel: 15394 46027
e-mail: stagshaw@nationaltrust.org.uk
website: www.nationaltrust.org.uk

This steep woodland garden, noted for its flowering shrubs, was created by the late Cubby Acland, Regional Agent for the National Trust. It contains a fine collection of shrubs, including rhododendrons, azaleas and camellias. Adjacent to the garden are Skelghyll Woods, which offer delightful walks and access to the fells beyond.

Photo by Stephen Robson

HIDDEN PLACES GUIDES

Explore Britain and Ireland with *Hidden Places* guides - a fascinating series of national and local travel guides.

Packed with easy to read information on hundreds of places of interest as well as places to stay, eat and drink.

Available from both high street and internet booksellers

For more information on the full range of *Hidden Places* guides and other titles published by Travel Publishing visit our website on

www.travelpublishing.co.uk
or ask for our leaflet by phoning
01752 697280 or emailing
info@travelpublishing.co.uk

29 QUAYSIDERS CLUB LIMITED

Barrans Road, Waterhead, Ambleside,
Cumbria LA22 0JH
Tel: 01539 433969 Fax: 01539 433988
e-mail: ian@quaysiders.co.uk
website: www.quaysiders.co.uk

Lake Windermere in the south eastern corner of the Lake District has long been one of Cumbria's most popular tourist hot spot and there is no better place to take advantage of all the area has to offer than **Quaysiders Club**. These quality premises stand across the road from the lake in Waterhead and are geared towards providing excellent facilities for all who visit. General manager Ian Davison has been here 22 years now and was joined by wife Veronica 10 years ago. Together they have built the complex up to a very high standard; there are 18 apartments and two hotel rooms available for hire.

All of the apartments are self catering, can sleep up to six and are taken on a weekly basis during the busy season; shorter breaks can be provided during off season. The two hotel rooms are en suite, one will sleep two people and the other will sleep 3 in extremely comfortable style.

The extensive facilities include a small indoor swimming pool with Jacuzzi, sauna, laundry room, a courtyard BBQ and WiFi throughout. The website is excellent and provides full information about the complex; there are even virtual tours to be taken around the premises!

30 LANCRIGG COUNTRY HOUSE & THE GREEN VALLEY RESTAURANT

Easedale, Grasmere, Cumbria, LA22 9QN
Tel: 01539 435317
e-mail: 00.info@lancrigg.co.uk
website: www.lancrigg.co.uk

Set in 30 acres of beautiful gardens and woodland, with views of peaceful Easedale, the elegant **Lancrigg Country House Hotel** is an ideal place to come for a tranquil escape in the Lake District. This hotel has been renovated from a 17th century farmhouse, and has provided a meeting place for The Lake Poets, Charles Dickens and Wilkie Collins. It is easy to see how writers of such great words would wish to stay here; the solitude and breathtaking views are timelessly inspiring.

Within the hotel you can stay in one of 11 light and spacious individually decorated and furnished rooms all with en-suites, the personal touches, such as whirlpool baths and finest organic teas, are sure to make you feel at home.

In addition there are 3 cottages nestled in the woods, a 5-minute walk from the main hotel, if you wish to have complete calm away from the hustle and bustle. These are all open all year round, so whatever the weather you can come and enjoy all the Lancrigg Country House Hotel has to offer.

Also on offer to further enhance your relaxation and wellbeing there are Health Creation Breaks, where you get a day membership at the award winning Langdale leisure centre, where you can get a Shiatsu massage, Swedish massage, Therapeutic healing, Reiki or Personalised nutritional consultation.

It is impossible to talk about the hotel without mentioning the **Green Valley certified Organic Vegetarian Restaurant**. They cater for Vegetarian, Vegan, Gluten-, wheat-, dairy- and sugar-free diets, example dishes are Cajun spiced aubergine, corn cakes & guacamole served with refried beans, tomato salsa & coriander mojo, and Tofu burger topped with pesto, char grilled vegetables & mayonnaise served with paprika wedges, tomato sauce & salad. With food this fresh colourful and tasty it is an unmissable treat for anyone. The aim of this restaurant is to serve delicious vegetarian organic food, to give you a feeling of well-being and rejuvenation which will complete your trip to the Lancrigg Country House. As the food is fresh and organic, there will sometimes be variations to the menu available, but the utmost will always be done not to compromise the integrity of the taste in these instances. Dinner is served between 6:30-8:30pm but the restaurant is open from 8:30am for breakfasts, morning coffee, light lunches and afternoon teas. There is an advantage to booking for non-residents. The restaurant is licensed, welcomes children and dogs, and accommodation includes dinner, bed and breakfast.

31 | DALE LODGE HOTEL

Grasmere, Cumbria LA22 9SW
Tel: 01539 435300
Fax No: 01539 435570
e-mail: enquiries@dalelodgehotel.co.uk
website: www.dalelodgehotel.co.uk

Dale Lodge Hotel has established itself as one of the very best hotels in the region, with a big reputation and a large following for both accommodation and food. The beautifully refurbished Georgian building dates back to 1840, standing in 3 acres of beautiful grounds. This stunning setting and scenery combined with quality service and hospitality make it a perfect base from which to explore the many local attractions, or simply relaxing and feeling the stress melt away.

It's also an unbeatable venue for weddings or other celebrations, with 16 spectacular en suite bedrooms, each decorated in its own individual style. Four of the rooms are situated in the new Mews building, oozing luxury with their own hot tub and terrace, complete with in-room lounge, king size bed, and skylight which allows guests to gaze at the stars from the comfort of their bed.

Owners Brian and Gillian Roberts, son Alex and Head Chef James Goodall have created an exciting selection of dishes for Tweedies Bar and the Lodge Restaurant. The food is a fusion of traditional pub fare and contemporary European cuisine, ranging from classics such as homemade steak and ale pie with golden puff pastry, seasonal vegetables and chunky chips, to hearty Cumbrian dishes with an expert twist like slow roasted crispy pork belly served with cider fondant potato, broccoli puree, caramelised apple, black pudding and a Dijon mustard sauce, or the cracked black pepper and honey duck breast, pressed confit thigh with sage and apricots served with potato galette, parsnip puree and buttered spinach in a Madeira sauce. A large range of stunning seafood dishes is available, complete with a children's menu and choice of appetisers which can be cooked to order as main meals if the fancy takes you. The sumptuous food, intimate setting and first class service create a special evening for all. The bar also offers a range of real ales catering for most tastes from Cornwall to Shetland and a fine range of traditional Cumbrian brews, with a distinguished wine cellar also offering wine of the month. Food is served from 12-3pm/6-9pm Mon-Sat and from 12-4pm/6:30-9pm on Sundays.

This outstanding luxury hotel and eatery really does surpass even the highest of expectations, inviting guests to truly unwind, take in the scenery and indulge themselves in what has to be some of the finest food and drink in the Lake District.

32 GREEN'S CAFÉ AND BISTRO

College Street, Grasmere,
Cumbria   LA22 9SZ
Tel: 01539 435790
e-mail: stealys@tiscali.co.uk

'Owned and well run by Karen and Rob, **Green's Café and Bistro** is a wonderful little eatery set in the heart of Grasmere, described by Wordsworth in 1799 as 'the loveliest spot that man hath ever found'.

This Bistro exudes a warm atmosphere making it a pleasant place to sit and eat.

The excellent menu is derived from the freshest of ingredients, sourced where possible from local suppliers and fair-trade and cooked to order. The menu proudly states that they will do their best to cater for those with special dietary needs, especially Coeliacs, Vegans and Small Children. They always have gluten free bread and cakes, a selection of gluten free hot meals and gluten free puddings, as well as dairy free and Vegan Cakes and hot meals. The menu is varied with five or six daily specials, hot meals, sandwiches, paninis and baked potatoes.

Green's Bake all of their own cakes so they can tell you exactly what is in them. All their delicious cakes are available to take away as well as their puddings. Green's is open Friday to Wednesday from 9:45 to 5:30pm.

33   OAK BANK HOTEL

Broadgate, Grasmere Village, Cumbria
Tel: 015394 35217
Fax: 015394 35685
e-mail: info@lakedistricthotel.co.uk
website: www.lakedistricthotel.co.uk

An impressive one hundred and thirty seven year old Lakeland Victorian building in the heart of the picturesque village of Grasmere, **Oak Bank Hotel** is the perfect place to stay for a relaxing break, romantic weekend, or Lakeland holiday. Commissioned as a private residence in 1872, it has been a hotel since the 1920s, and has been run at the finest quality by owners Simon and Glynis since April 2007.

The accommodation ranges through the 14 high-quality rooms, from the very reasonably priced to the highest standard in luxury, to ensure the needs of all guests are catered for. The light and spacious top range rooms are the Acorn Suite with a separate lounge area and a Jacuzzi, situated on the ground floor and the Iris Room with a four-poster bed and a balcony looking out over the gardens, river and fells. Choose dinner, bed and breakfast so you can really relax and soak in the hotels atmosphere and explore the surrounding countryside during your stay.

The restaurant is an elegant and intimate affair, seating just 30, which adds to the cosy atmosphere. There is a conservatory in-keeping with the hotels Victorian style, which looks out over the garden and, for the winter, wonderfully welcome open fires. The real heart however is in the fine food, which is lovingly prepared, seasonal and sourced where possible from within the county. The four course dinner menu changes daily, so you are assured of always being served the freshest and best produce, at the height of its seasonal abundance and is served between 6:30pm and 8:00pm.

Examples from the menu are Ballontine of Organic Salmon with Perigord truffle dressing, fromage blanc, pickled cucumber and sorrel; Oven Roasted Goosnargh Corn Fed Chicken, with grilled polenta, crispy lardons, braised shallots and sage infused liquor; and Oak Bank's Sticky Toffee Pudding, with caramel toffee sauce and vanilla ice-cream.

There is also an excellent range of fine wines to complement your meal perfectly. A very popular Sunday lunch is available between 12:30 and 2:30pm on Sundays, and all week you can get morning coffees, light bites, snacks and afternoon teas. This really is the finest quality pampering food, and at very reasonable prices.

There is off-road parking for guests, so you can completely unwind during your stay, without the concerns of parking and car safety.

34 BLACKROCK HOLIDAY FLATS

Morecambe Bank, Grange-over-sands,
Cumbria LA11 6DX
Tel: 01539 534107/532836

Located in an enviable position overlooking the stunning Morecambe bay are the **Blackrock Holiday Flats**. Ideally situated in the heart of Grange-over-Sands where the shops, gardens and promenade are a mere stroll away. The three self-contained units, each sleeping two, are equipped with everything needed for an independent, go-as-you-please self-catering stay. Standing in a private cul-de-sac, Dolphin Cottage commands striking views of Morecambe bay from the lounge/dining room and the bedroom and also has its own private car park.

Situated on the first floor, Blackrock flat no 1 also benefits from superb views and is accessed via a path by the side of the garages and up a few steps. One garage is exclusively for the use of this flat. Located partly below flat no 1 is Blackrock flat no 2 which also has its own garage. The lounge and bedroom are in open plan layout utilising maximum space. All the flats are cosy and comfortable and available all year round thus attracting many repeat visitors. Bookings are weekly in season with shorter breaks available outside peak periods. The flats are ideal for older clients due to facilities and easy flat access to the rear walkways along the bay. Grange-over-Sands is a very pleasant place for a holiday having generally a mild climate, lots of shops, cafés and restaurants and some excellent walking.

35 CROWN INN

Newton-in-Cartmel, High Newton,
Grange-Over-Sands, Cumbria LA11 6JH
Tel: 01539 531793

The **Crown Inn** is situated just off the A590 in Newton-in-Cartmel which has recently been bypassed by a newly constructed road thus creating a new hidden place! Pat and David have been the proprietors since the summer of 2008, Pat has been in the hospitality industry for a while now but this property is their first together. The exterior gives off a warm and welcoming vibe, with large, colourful planters and informative notice boards. The interior only enhances this impression with a nice solid bar and stone flooring.

The bar is well stocked; there are always at least two real ales on draft, regulars are Black Sheep and Cumberland Ale. David is your excellent chef and food is served between 5.30 pm and 8.30 pm from Sunday to Saturday and between 12 pm and 3 pm on Saturdays and between 12 pm and 2 pm on Sundays. The restaurant also serves food during lunchtimes throughout the summer months but not during winter.

The inn provides accommodation as well; there are six well appointed en-suite rooms available for hire, in a mixture of sizes, and the tariff includes a hearty English breakfast! If you're lucky you will catch the variety of live entertainment on offer during the summer on Friday evenings!

159

36 THE CAVENDISH ARMS AT CARTMEL

Cartmel, Cumbria LA11 6QA
Tel: 015395 36240
e-mail: info@thecavendisharms.co.uk
website: www.thecavendisharms.co.uk

Located in the heart of this historic town, **The Cavendish Arms at Cartmel** is a picturesque establishment which dates back to the 15th century. Full of charm and character, the inn has retained many original features, including the low-beamed ceilings, a wealth of antique furniture, a blazing log fire - and creaky floorboards!

The Cavendish is much more than a Lake District hotel, but rather a charming retreat with a fine restaurant serving excellent British food using the finest of local produce. Excellent wines and traditional beers and ales presented with friendly relaxed service, together with some very comfortable rooms, ensures that you will find yourself drifting away from the hustle and bustle of everyday life into Cartmel's perfectly laid back village way of life.

In the kitchen, the staff have gone to great lengths to try and use only local produce and suppliers, thus ensuring that quality is always of a very high standard. So among the main courses you will find Cumbrian rib-eye steak, whole sea bass with a Morecambe Bay shrimp vinaigrette, and Cartmel Valley venison steak with a Cumberland sauce. Amongst the lighter meals are grilled Cumberland sausage and locally smoked duck breast with a raspberry vinaigrette. To accompany your meal, the bar offers a wide choice that includes 4 real ales - Cumberland Ale is the regular brew, plus 3 rotating guest ales from both local and national breweries.

The accommodation at the Cavendish comprises 10 en suite rooms, including one with a four poster bed. Guests enjoy the quaint low beamed ceilings and uneven floors, and there's even it is said a resident ghost. Tea and coffee and television facilities are provided in all the rooms.

If you're walking in the Lake District or simply looking for a bed and breakfast, the Cavendish Arms offers that personal and special accommodation. The area is teeming with outdoor activities. Apart from walking, there is horse riding, Cartmel races, Lake Windermere, a car museum and more. The hotel has teamed up with Black Horses Ltd to offer carriage tours of the village from just £45. If the Lake District weather has not favoured your camping or holiday cottage break, then come and unwind in these pleasant welcoming surroundings.

37 THE ROYAL OAK INN

The Square, Cartmel, Cumbria LA11 6LB
Tel: 01539 536259
e-mail: darrenallcock@btinternet.com
website: www.royaloakcartmel.co.uk

Situated in the Square in the historic village of Cartmel is **The Royal Oak Inn** where the warmest of welcomes is guaranteed. Visitors from out of town as well as locals flock here to sample the best in well kept ales along with delicious, wholesome cuisine.

This wonderfully quaint old fashioned inn is the first venture into the trade for friendly licensees, Darren and Louise Allcock. They have started as they mean to go on, making sure that all guests have an enjoyable visit whether they are just simply popping in for a drink and a bite to eat or staying overnight in one of the four en-suite bedrooms.

The cosy bedrooms are comfortable and tastefully decorated, varying in size to suit guests needs. For all the B&B guests, a full Cumbrian breakfast starts the day off perfectly. The interior of the inn is beautifully decorated and furnished with cosy fires, brass-adorned beams and comfy seating, creating a wonderful homely ambience in which to meet friends and relax.

Darren and Louise always have a great selection of Award winning draught ales including Timothy Taylor, Coniston Bluebird, Black Sheep, Hawkshead Green, Speckled Hen, Aviator and Melbreak along with a wide selection of lakeland ales.

Continuing the high standards is the traditional British cuisine served at the Royal Oak, always fresh, and prepared to the highest standards available every day. Diners can choose from a wide variety of Pub favourites and desserts with a Bar menu available for those with a smaller appetite. The lunch menu includes sandwiches filled with pan fried steak, mushrooms and caramelised onions, freshly baked jacket potatoes as well as main courses such as Homemade steak, mushroom and ale pie. The evening menu offers further delights with starters such as black pudding served on a bed of mashed potato topped with a poached egg. Main courses include slow roasted local shoulder of lamb, Cumberland sausage and grilled smoked haddock. For those with a sweeter tooth, the desserts are sure to satisfy with tempting choices such as sticky toffee pudding, chocolate fudge cake and Belgian toffee waffle.

The hidden gem of this super inn is the eye-catching rear riverside garden, secluded and well kept offering a pleasant retreat on warmer days.

The Royal Oak is only a 5 minute walk from Cartmel Racecourse, with meetings all year round this is an ideal weekend destination.

161

38 LAKELAND MOTOR MUSEUM

Holker Hall Estate, Cark-in-Cartmel,
Cumbria LA11 7PL
Tel/Fax: 015395 58509
e-mail: info@lakelandmotormuseum.co.uk
website: www.lakelandmotormuseum.co.uk

A nostalgic reminder of transport bygones, the **Lakeland Motor Museum** has more than 100 vehicles on show ranging from pioneer vehicles of the early 1900s through to the

exuberant models of the swinging 40s and fabulous 50s. As well as these classic cars, the Museum also houses a fascinating collection of "magnificent motorbikes, superb scooters, bygone bicycles and triumphant tractors!" Also amongst the 10,000 exhibits, probably the most extensive presentation of automobilia on display in the UK, are "Authentic automobilia, reminiscent rarities, micro cars and mechanical marvels". This unique and carefully maintained collection is housed in a quaint former Shire horse stable and its courtyard.

The recent recovery of Donald Campbell's *Bluebird* from the depths of Coniston Water gives an added interest to the Campbell Legend Bluebird Exhibition which pays tribute to Sir Malcolm Campbell and his son Donald who between them captured 21 world land and water speed records for Britain. Highlights of the exhibition include full size detailed replicas of the 1935 *Bluebird* car and the famous jet hydroplane, *Bluebird K7*. There's even a replica of Donald Campbell's lucky mascot, teddy bear Mr Whoppit, together with a continuous video detailing the lives, careers, failures and achievement of these two sporting celebrities. Other attractions include the Coach House Café and a gift shop.

39 THE KINGS HEAD HOTEL

14 Queen Street, Ulverston,
Cumbria LA12 7AF
Tel: 01229 588064
e-mail: info@kingsheadulverston.co.uk
website: www.kingsheadulverston.co.uk

Situated in the heart of Ulverston, **The Kings head Hotel** offers hospitality, ale and food second to none. Its olde worlde interior supports its architecture as an outstanding grade 2 listed building. At its rear it hides an enchanting beer garden backed by ivy-covered original stone walling, bursting with flowers in the summer months, a haven in which to enjoy the tranquillity of the Lake District.

Four gorgeous rooms are available to book, three twins and one double with separate power shower bathrooms nearby, and a hearty country breakfast available in the morning.

The Kings Head also offers a locally sourced menu catering for both adults and children, ranging from soup and sandwiches fresh from the local bakery to delectable Antipasti platters comprising a range of continental meats, melon, olives, feta, salad and bread, or a generous helping of homemade cottage pie. Food is served 12-2pm and 4-8pm weekdays and 12-7pm weekends in summer months, and from 4-8pm weekdays and 12-7pm weekends in the winter.

Landlord Thia Rawlinson who has put this stunning hotel back on the map prides herself on offering a choice of 4 real ales such as Jennings Lakeland Bitter, Cock-a-hoop and Cumberland Ale, with yet more rotating during the summer when the Kings Head is open all day every day. In winter visitors are welcomed from 4pm on Mon/Tues/Wed and all day Thur/Fri/Sat/Sun.

40 OLD FRIENDS

49 Soutergate, Ulverston,
Cumbria LA12 7ES
Tel: 01229 582311
e-mail: userfawcett@aol.com

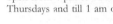

Just a short walk from the centre of Ulverston, the popular birthplace of Stan Laurel, is the traditional pub **Old Friends**. The establishment is like a Tardis, from the front it looks fairly diminutive, however it opens out inside and there is a wonderful beer garden to the rear. Gemma and Roy are your gracious hosts; they took over the tenancy over a year ago and have made themselves right at home, providing great food, drink and service.

Roy is the capable cook and the menu consists of home made pub classics. The pub is open from 4 pm to 12 midnight Sundays to Thursdays and till 1 am on Friday and Saturday.

41 GILLAM'S TEA ROOM AND RESTAURANT

64 Market Street, Ulverston,
Cumbria LA12 7LT.
Tel: 01229 587564
website: www.gillams-tearoom.co.uk

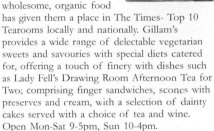

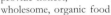

Doug and Shirley **Gillam's Tea Room and Restaurant** stands in the heart of Ulverston, built on the successful family reputation of Gillam's 1892 Grocery across the road. Their desire to provide honest, wholesome, organic food has given them a place in The Times- Top 10 Tearooms locally and nationally. Gillam's provides a wide range of delectable vegetarian sweets and savouries with special diets catered for, offering a touch of finery with dishes such as Lady Fell's Drawing Room Afternoon Tea for Two; comprising finger sandwiches, scones with preserves and cream, with a selection of dainty cakes served with a choice of tea and wine. Open Mon-Sat 9-5pm, Sun 10-4pm.

43 THE DERBY ARMS

Horse Close Lane, Great Urswick
nr Ulverston, Cumbria LA12 OSP
Tel: 01229 586348
e-mail: thederbyarms@yahoo.co.uk
website: www.gocities.com/thederbyarms

Open all day every day, **The Derby Arms** is the social hub of the picturesque village of Great Urswick which lies just off the A590 south of Ulverston. It's warm and homely appeal fully justifies

local fondness, offering a range of real ales including Hartleys, Dizzy Blond, Unicorn and a seasonal rotating brewery guest ale to tempt your tastebuds, along with light snacks for lunch on Saturday and a wholesome roast on Sunday.

Experienced licencees Judith and Stephen Davidson also offer a choice of four gorgeous rooms across the road in The Stables bed and breakfast, with two twin and two double rooms, all with ensuite facilities, television, radio, hairdryer and hot drinks. It proves an ideal retreat for a weekend break, the surrounding area being a bird watching and fishing hotspot, with easy access to many top attractions in the Lakes & Furness Peninsula. Judith's fantastic cooking also ensures that a hearty breakfast awaits you on request including bacon, sausage, tomatoes, eggs, mushrooms, all locally sourced; served from 7-8am weekdays and 9-9.30am weekends.

The Derby Arms also hosts the local darts, pool and dominoes teams, and a quiz night is open to all, children included, from 8.30pm-9pm on Mondays, ensuring a visit here is a truly welcoming one. Cash and cheque only.

42 STAN LAUREL INN

31 The Ellers, Ulverston,
Cumbria LA12 0AB
Tel: 01229 582814
e-mail: thestanlaurel@aol.com
website: www.thestanlaurel.co.uk

Starting life as a row of cottages, **The Stan Laurel Inn** is a delightful hostelry named after Ulverston's most famous son. Delightful owners, Trudi and Paul Dewar took over this quaint inn in April 2007 and over the last two years have stamped their personalities on the place winning an ever growing following among both locals and visitors to this lovely part of the world. Since then, they have created a superb rear dining room seating 20 which displays numerous photos and ornaments of the man himself – Stan Laurel. The cheerful bar offers no less than six real ales on tap with Thwaites being the regular and three ales coming from breweries within Cumbria.

Paul is a first class chef and has gained countless recommendations from local B&B's for the quality of his dishes. He uses local produce in his kitchen whenever possible and offers regular special meal deals throughout the week. Tantalising Tuesday and Wonderful Wednesday offers Two for One on all main meals throughout lunch time and the evening. Fridays deal sees fish for a fiver – served with chunky chips and mushy peas. Due to this popularity it is advisable to book at all times to avoid disappointment. The printed menu is always complemented with further choices on the specials board. Typical starters on the printed menu include platter of prawns, battered brie wedges and pork, chicken & apricot terrine-made by Paul's fair hand.

The delicious main courses are endless and from the grill include Sirloin steak served with mushrooms, onion rings and grilled tomato, Chicken Jim Jam-grilled chicken wrapped in bacon and topped with pineapple then smothered in BBQ sauce. Old favourites include house chicken curry, steak pie, chicken pepperpot and salmon and broccoli bake. Vegetarians will be delighted with options such as vegetable lasagne, veggie chilli stack and cheese and broccoli bake. For lighter appetites there is a range of freshly cut sandwiches, baguettes, and fabulous jacket potatoes not forgetting the tremendous salad selection which offers everything imaginable. Food is served Tues-Sat 12-2pm & 6-9pm and on Sundays 12-8pm.

The Stan Laurel is an ideal base for touring the area and offers accommodation comprising of three en-suite guest rooms varying in size.

Great Urswick, nr Ulverston,
Cumbria   LA12 0SZ
Tel: 01229 586394
e-mail: thegenburgoyne@aol.com
website: www.generalburgoyne.co.uk

The origin of Great Urswick is said to be around 1120, when King Alfred was on the throne of England, whilst the history of **The General Burgoyne** is somewhat shorter, there are still some tales to be told. The pub is believed to have been built at the beginning of the 17th century and several stories have been told as to how the name came about. The most common and probably the most believable, is that a soldier who fought in the U.S. War of Independence with the General came home from battle and decided to name the public house in his honour. It is certainly a unique name; there is no other pub in the UK with the same name.

The interior is warm, comfortable and functional; the bar area boasts old stone flag floors, wooden beams showing and long benches which get pretty full during the popular quiz nights! Anyone can enter the "Our Survey Said" quiz held on Sunday nights every week. The bar is extremely well stocked and there are always three real ales on offer; Hartleys XB is the regular and there are two rotating Robinson Brewery guest ales.

The main draw to this great pub however, is the excellent food; the menu consists of pub classics, cooked fresh to order, with locally sourced ingredients wherever possible. The Lake District contains several magnificent food suppliers and the General Burgoyne specialises in utilising in season foods in daily specials, one popular example is the superb Game Pie. The main menu is typified by these scrumptious choices; home made mince and onion pie, local rare breed sausage, topped with a red onion marmalade, and a massive 16oz T-bone steak. Another favourite of the menu is the General Burgoyne's Pie, Peas and Gravy for just £3.75! Food is served Monday to Friday 12 pm to 2 pm and 6 pm to 9pm, Saturday 12 pm to 9 pm and from 12 pm to 4 pm and 6 pm up 8.30 pm on Sunday. Because of the popular nature of the restaurant, it is necessary to make a reservation to dine on Friday and Saturday evenings and Sunday lunchtimes.

The General Burgoyne also has special offers on; Tuesday nights are curry nights, where you can eat as much as you can for a special price. Thursday's are 2 for 1 on the main courses. There is off road parking and disabled access.

45 THE BRIDGE CAFÉ

In the Dock Museum, North Road,
Barrow-in-Furness, Cumbria LA14 2PW
Tel: 01229 876331
e-mail: val.morley@sodexho.uk.com

The Dock Museum is one of the leading attractions in the North of England, and visitors to this superb modern museum can take a break in **The Bridge Café**.

Val Morley, who has managed the coffee shop since 2003, provides a tempting variety of home baking, snacks and made-to-order hot dishes. There are seats for 50 inside, and 24 more at picnic tables outside on the terrace.

The Museum and the Coffee Shop are open from 10 to 4.30 in season (closed Monday) and from 10.30 to 3.30 out of season (closed Monday and Tuesday). Admission to the Museum is free.

46 THE DOCK MUSEUM

North Rd, Barrow-in-Furness,
Cumbria LA14 2PW
Tel 01229 876400
e-mail: dockmuseum@barrowbc.gov.uk
website: www.dockmuseum.org.uk

One of the best attractions in the North of England, **The Dock Museum** takes you on a fascinating journey through the lives of the people who transformed what was a small farming village at the beginning of the 19th century into a major industrial town. Their story is a fascinating record of perseverance and good humour, of economic prosperity followed by years of depression, of peace, and of war. Explore the galleries and discover the entrepreneurs who dominate the town's story and how they had the vision to develop new industries. This a story told through exhibits and displays, including stunning original ship models. The Dock Museum offers a truly unique day for all the family.

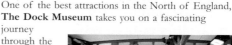

Our facilities include Cafe, Gift shop, exhibitions and events programme, Film shows, Children's playground, stunning waterfront location, extensive education service, Free Parking and Free Admission, Free guided tour for group bookings.

Open Easter to November - Tuesday to Sunday. November to Easter Wednesday to Sunday Open Bank Holidays

47 THE KINGS ARMS

Dalton Road, Barrow-In-Furness,
Cumbria LA14 1HY
Tel: 01229 836947
e-mail: bamba@thekingsbarrow.co.uk
website: www.thekingsbarrow.co.uk

The sleepy town of Barrow-In-Furness surprisingly holds one of the best entertainment venues in Cumbria, popularly graced by many well known bands from all over the world. Situated on Dalton road at one end of the long pedestrian walkway sits **The Kings Arms**; a thriving live music pub offering good food and drink all at very reasonable prices. This place is certainly a place to stop to waken you from your tranquil Cumbrian day dream as the words 'FUN PUB' emblazon the entrance to what is guaranteed to be a good night out.

Tenant Chris Bamber has been at The Kings Arms since December 2008, previously having a successful career promoting live music and other events. His expertise in this area ensures that every Friday and Saturday night there is quality live music playing late into the night. This traditional pub with a vibrant rocky injection into its décor is open until 1am from Sun-Wed, but stays open until 3am on Thurs/Fri/Sat, holding up to a staggering 250 people. But don't be put off if metal isn't your thing, there are also regular R&B nights and duke box nights where you say and the DJ plays, including a variety of quality bands from around the country.

It's also not just good music on offer here, Head Chef and Bar Manager Tony Scott-Wise who has been in the trade for 15 years ably assists Chris with a great value for money menu sampling a range of light snacks, baguettes, sandwiches, jacket potatoes and 2-4-1 offers on main meals which include a range of traditional pub cuisine like steak and ale pie, fish and chips, homemade lasagne or a range of authentic curries cooked to order by the chef, with a small selection of fine cuts of meat in dishes like lamb henry, or rump steak which are not on the 2-4-1 deal. There is also an impressive choice for vegetarians who can also take advantage of the 2-4-1 offer, a delectable dessert menu and a small children's menu. Food is served daily on Mon-Sat from 12-2:30pm. All dishes are cooked to order with local produce. A large choice of draughts, kegs, bitters, cider and stouts is also available, with Carling and John Smith's Smooth being the local favourites here. Chris and Tony ask that children be gone by 9pm, cash and cheque only.

If you are thirsty, hungry or just want to be entertained at a good price this is the ideal pub for you.

48 THE CONSERVATORY CAFÉ & QUICHE'S QUALITY CATERING

Victoria Hall, Rawlinson Street and
Carlisle Street, Barrow-in-Furness,
Cumbria LA14 1BX
Tel: 01229 827227
e-mail: l.macaulay@live.co.uk
website:
www.quichesqualitycatering@vpweb.co.uk

With an outstanding reputation for her outside catering business, Lorraine Macaulay and her husband Mike, set up **The Conservatory Café** in February of this year. Having been closed for a year previously the café, in the seaport town of Barrow-in-Furness, seats 27 people inside and 16 outside and has a five star rating from Barrow Borough Council Environmental Health Department. The outside area boasts quality patio furniture in a well kempt and spacious garden. Inside, the high ceilings and big windows add to the light and airy, spacious feel of the café. The café is exceptionally run and offers a takeaway service too, which adds to its popularity. There is a wide range of quality dishes on the menu, which include breakfasts, sandwiches, jacket potatoes, salads and a selection of delicious homemade pies. Customers can also take their pick from daily specials and a range of homemade desserts.

With more than 25 years experience in the Catering industry Lorraine places the needs of her customers at the forefront of her service and the entire team offer a friendly and hospitable service. Many customers return time after time to sample the dishes on offer, which are made with quality ingredients and executed to a high standard. OAP's get 10% off everything and with a lift the premises is easily accessible for disabled people.

The catering side of the business lends itself to every occasion. Whether it is a business lunch, wedding, children's party or funeral teas the Macaulay's are happy to provide their exceptional catering services and tailor it to customer's needs. There is an extensive selection of buffet options, which can include pastries, a range of sandwiches, filled vol au vents, cold marinated chicken drumsticks, mixed seasonal salads and tasty pork pies. Children are well catered for too and for kid's parties Children Party Variety Boxes can be arranged to make the occasion extra special. There are hot options available too including a selection of pies and hotpots all served with mushy peas, sliced onions, beetroot and gravy. A deposit of 20% is required on confirmation of booking.

All of the staff are trained to level 2 food hygiene and Lorraine, who has worked in 3 star hotels, restaurants and ocean liners has many industry qualifications. This delightful café, furnished to a high standard, is open weekdays between 9.30am-4.30pm and Saturdays between 10am-4pm.

49 THE NEWTON

2-4 Newton Road, Dalton-In-Furness,
Cumbria LA15 8LS
Tel: 01229 462399
e-mail: keir.lightfoot@yahoo.co.uk

Situated just a short walk or drive from the centre of charming town Dalton-In-Furness is the impressive Newton pub. Local couple Anne and Richard and their son Keir took over **The Newton** very recently, but they have already impressed those that visit as

their extensive experience in the pub and restaurant trade serves them well. They ensure this spacious pub is well groomed and still has all of its character, welcoming everyone, children included.

Set just back from the road, The Newton has its own gated terrace from which is quite the sun trap in the summer months. They also have a large off road car park which will no doubt be filled right up when Richard begins the delicious sounding menu proposed to start later this year. Food will be available Saturday and Sunday lunchtimes and in the summer holidays bar meals will also be available. Richard has much experience as a Head Chef so it's expected that his mouth-watering menu will go down a treat.

The Newton also offers regular draught ales, with John Smiths Smooth, Fosters, Theakstons Mild and Guinness all available on tap, ensuring that almost all tastes are catered for. Anne and Richard also run a popular quiz on Friday nights from 8:45pm, and run a vibrant live music session every other Saturday from 8:30pm to get your musical juices flowing; ring for details. The Newton also has a large pool table and plenty of seating making it the ideal place for a relaxed night out with all the family.

It's only a short walk to the town centre as well so is a great place to stop for an afternoon drink before continuing to enjoy Dalton-In-Furness's offerings. Dalton originally dates back to the Bronze Age when it was populated by the celts, and much of the fascinating history of this ancient town can be found locally, amongst which is local beauty spot Furness Abbey, well worth a quick visit. No doubt Anne and Richard's local knowledge of this pleasant old town can point you in the right direction.

50 HARTLEY'S RESTAURANT

51 Market Street, Dalton-in-Furness,
Cumbria LA15 8AP
Tel: 01229 464708
e-mail: hartleys@live.com
website: www.hartleysrestaurant.co.uk

For two years, Andrew and Lisa Turner have owned and personally run **Hartley's Restaurant**, a quality Mediterranean based establishment set in the heart of Dalton-in-Furness. The restaurant looks warm and inviting from the exterior, and the story is much the same inside, the stone floors, wooden furniture and bright décor helps create a taste of the Mediterranean in the heart of the Lake District.

Owner Andrew, is also the chef, and having been a chef for 25 years he has a very good idea of what creates a good menu. Delicious sounding examples of the extensive menu are baked fillet of salmon on a mushroom & tarragon risotto, roast rump of Lakeland lamb with hotpot potatoes and braised pork shoulder with citrus Bramley apples. There are also menus for special occasions; the Mother's Day menu offers a three course meal for just £13.50 and even the standard Sunday lunch menu is tantalising! The restaurant is open between 11.30 am and 2.30 pm and from 5 pm to late all week long, the place is very popular though, so reservations are recommended at all times to avoid disappointment.

51 FURNESS ABBEY

Furness Abbey, nr Dalton-in-Furness,
Cumbria LA13 0PJ
Tel: 01229 823420
website: www.english-heritage.org.uk

The impressive remains of **Furness Abbey** founded by Stephen, later King of England, including much of the east and west tower of the church, the ornately decorated chapter house and the cloister buildings lie just to the south of Dalton-in-Furness and just north of Barrow-in-Furness..

Originally of the Savigniac order, it passed to the Cistercians in 1147, and despite damage by Scottish raiders became (after Fountains abbey) the second most prosperous Cistercian abbey in all England. Set in the 'vale of nightshade', the romantic ruins were celebrated by Wordsworth in his Prelude of 1805.

An exhibition on the history of the abbey, with a display of elaborately carved stones, can be seen in the visitor centre.

52 ABBEY MILL COFFEE SHOP

Custodian Cottage, Abbey Approach,
Barrow-in-Furness, Cumbria LA13 0PJ
Tel: 01229 877739
e-mail: jackie.baxter@abbey-mill.co.uk
website: www.abbey-mill.co.uk

Set in idyllic surroundings in the grounds of historic Furness Abbey, the **Abbey Mill Coffee Shop** occupies what used to be the Abbot's cottage, a listed building of great character and charm with beams that have been dated to the 13th century. Owned and run by Jackie Baxter and her family, this unique café is a place to savour.

Outside, customers at the picnic tables enjoy a peaceful pastoral scene of open grassland and woodland, an ideal

place for children to play. Inside, the menu offers a good choice of appetising food, starting with a full English breakfast (or its vegetarian alternative) and continuing with an inviting selection of dishes such as home-made soup, oven-baked jacket potatoes, ploughman's, paninis and freshly prepared sandwiches. In addition to the regular menu, there are daily specials listed on the blackboard and also a separate children's menu. And you should certainly not leave without sampling one of the delicious home-made cakes.

The café seats 25 inside and many more outside. It is open from 11am to 5pm, daily in summer; and from 11am to 5pm, Wednesday to Sunday in winter.

53 THE GREYHOUND COMMUNITY PUB

Grizebeck, Cumbria LA17 7XJ
Tel/Fax: 01229 889224
website: www.thegreyhoundinn.org

With six pubs a day in the UK closing their doors, the traditional British hostelry has never been under greater threat. So, when the villagers of Grizebeck heard that their local was due to close in January 2009, the villagers decided to do something about it. Fortunately, the then licensees of the Greyhound had responded to an advert in the *Publican* from a film company looking for struggling pubs. The process of re-establishing the pub was long and involved but the efforts of local people bore fruition and on January 21st, 2009 the inn re-opened as **The Greyhound Community Pub**, staffed and run by village volunteers.

It already has a reputation for good home-made food and well-kept beers, including several real ales one of which, *New Beginnings*, is specially brewed for the pub.

The community involvement is strengthened by a monthly quiz night, an acoustic music night and there are also Saturday walks from the Greyhound leaving at 10am and back in time for lunch. The inn also offers comfortable en suite rooms. All in all, an inspiring example for others whose local is under threat.

Broughton-In-Furness,
Cumbria LA20 6ES
Tel: 01229 716272
e-mail: welcome@highcrossinn.com
website: www.highcrossinn.com

The High Cross Inn is situated high on the hills surrounding the delightful village of Broughton-In-Furness, just off the A595. It offers spectacular panoramic views of the surrounding snow-capped mountains in winter months combined with a warm and friendly environment to enjoy them in.

Leaseholders Angela and Michael have only been at the High Cross Inn since May 2009 but already are receiving excellent reviews from all those that visit. Their reputable experience in the hotel, restaurant and catering business has clearly put them in good stead as they have created a really individual environment catering for both adults and children in an informal and friendly atmosphere that doesn't forfeit quality.

Parts of the Inn date back to its status as an 18th century farm house, which later became a favoured ale house. The Inn seats up to sixty people, but manages to feel cosy with traditional log fires and farmhouse furniture. Its large dining room opens up onto a large circular bay window filling the room with natural light. From here you can enjoy the scenic views of the valley below or if you prefer, from the terrace complete with picnic tables from which to lap up the summer sun.

Open all day every day, the High Cross Inn serves 4 real ales, 3 of which rotate from local breweries and the last being regular Ennerdale brew. A delicious variety of locally sourced, seasonal food is served daily from 12-9pm. You can choose from the main menu which features a gargantuan Mixed grill (Cumberland sausage, gammon and sirloin steaks with onion rings, grilled tomato and salad) or a delicately poached salmon dish with a white wine, lemon and chive sauce served with potatoes and vegetables. A specials board is also available offering seasonal dishes. Most dishes can be cooked to half portion as a children's menu. It is recommended to book on weekends as this delicious food ensures seats fill up fast.

Accommodation is also available all year round, with seven beautiful rooms to let, currently four are en suite, but by the end of 2009 all will be en suite. Angela and Michael also offer a scrumptious breakfast in their tariff, making the High Cross Inn the perfect place to take a break in the unbeatable beauty of Cumbria. They also put on live music every fortnight, with excellent disabled access for both the bar and restaurant. All major credit cards accepted.

55 THE BLACK COCK INN

Princes Street, Broughton-in-Furness,
Cumbria LA20 6HQ
Tel: 01229 716529
website: www.blackcockinncumbria.com

Broughton-in-Furness is a very attractive little town and standing proudly in the heart is the wonderful inn, **The Black Cock Inn** provides great food, drink and accommodation. In the spring and summer,

window boxes and hanging baskets add splashes of colour to the immaculate black and white frontage and add to the history and charm of the place. The interior only enhances the property, the lounge bar hosts a roaring log fire and the low beamed ceiling provides a traditional atmosphere.

The bar is open all day, every day, for drinks, which includes a selection of five real ales; Theakston's Best and Marston's Pedigree are the regulars. That choice increases to around

15 during the inn's annual Beer Festival, which usually takes place during the first week of November. The inn also boasts a lovely secluded beer garden, and during the summer months, tables and chairs are set up at the front.

Food is served daily and the mouthwatering menu combines classic pub fare with some more exotic options. The Black Cock Inn is a great place to stay whilst exploring the Furness and Cartmel Peninsulas and the five en suite rooms include a family suite.

56 THE MANOR ARMS

The Square, Broughton-In-Furness,
Cumbria LA20 6HY
Tel: 01229 716286 Fax: 01229 716729
website: www.manorarmsthesquare.co.uk

The Manor Arms is a family run, traditional pub located in the attractive Georgian Square of the historic town of Broughton-In-Furness which lays at the foot of the spectacular wilderness of Duddon Valley.

Open all day every day this place prides itself on offering up to 8 real ales from a mixture of locally and nationally brewed sites; regular brews include Yates Bitter, Copper Dragon and Golden Pippin. A popular beer festival is held every November. The Manor Arms also offers 3 upstairs en suite bedrooms, with two doubles and one twin that can come on a room only or scrumptious bed and breakfast rate, making it a popular spot for walkers and cyclists alike. Children and dogs are welcome, all credit cards accepted apart from American Express and Diners.

Built in 1768 the bar is full of character with two log fires and a pool table and has been in the Varty family since 1988. It offers no juke box, no plasma tv – simply valuing good old conversation and atmosphere – and nestled cosily in this quiet market town with the beauty of the Lake District on its doorstep it certainly has plenty of that.

173

57 THE SUN-CONISTON

Coniston, Cumbria LA21 8HQ
Tel: 01539 441248
Fax: 01539 441219
email: stay@thesunconiston.com
website: www.thesunconiston.com

Still one of the favourite destinations in Cumbria for food, drink and holiday accommodation, overlooking the village of Coniston lies the unbeatable **Sun Coniston.**

Built in 1902 by the local brewery, a hotel extension was added over 100 years ago when the railway came in 1859. The railway has since left, however The Sun still remains and is visited from far and wide, by those wishing to experience great ales, food, accommodation and top quality hospitality.

Alan and Sharon Piper have been the owners here for the last 9 years and although having left the premises in the mid 2000's in the hands of staff, they are now back in charge and the property is becoming more and more popular on a daily basis, with locals and regulars galore.

The building is wonderful and offers a unique mix of four-star inn accommodation, conservatory restaurant, great pub and a tremendous comfortable and informal atmosphere, which is enjoyed by all who visit. Many of the original features of the property remain, including the wooden beams and roaring fireplaces and other traditional elements have been added such as the stone flooring in the bar and the beautifully provincial décor in the bedrooms. The restaurant is a beautiful accompaniment to the rest of the property, in a conservatory, surrounded by luscious greenery and beautiful views. This room is also airy with natural light, which is simply divine in fair weather.

The restaurant doesn't serve trendy food with fancy names, just good, honest, quality food that offers great taste and value. All of the meals are freshly prepared utilising the finest local ingredients, which are used in dishes such as braised shank lamb, local beef and ale pie, fish and chips and cured loin of pork glazed in a honey cherry jam. There is also an extensive wine list, over 35 wines and a whopping 8 real ales- with bluebird, hawkshead and copper dragon being the regulars, plus rotating guests, predominantly from local breweries.

The accommodation is a great end to the day at The Sun Coniston. Families with children and pets are very welcome here and the 8 ensuite bedrooms, include 3 family rooms. The tariffs are excellent value and include 5 cooked breakfast options to help you get the day off to the best of starts.

58 THE YEWDALE HOTEL

Yewdale Road, Coniston,
Cumbria LA21 8DU
Tel: 015394 41280
e-mail: peter@yewdalehotel.com
website: www.yewdalehotel.com

Located in the heart of Coniston **The Yewdale Hotel** is in the perfect location for visitors wanting to enjoy the scenic delights the Lake District has to offer. Peter and Beverley Kelly have owned the hotel for six years and being Cumbrian Peter has a lot of knowledge on the local area.

Built of local stone and slate in 1896 the hotel boasts nine comfortable en-suite rooms, which all have a TV and tea making facilities. Guests have a choice of three real ales including Old Yewdale Bitter, brewed especially for them by the Hawkehead brewery. Meals are served daily from 11.30am-5.30pm and from 6pm-9pm in the hotel bar and dining room. The owners like to use fresh seasonal produce and offer a superb Cumbrian breakfast as well as plenty of dishes for vegetarians. A good old fashioned steak and ale pie and ratatouille hot pot are among the dishes on the menu, which has something for everyone.

The surrounding area has a lot to offer, with plenty of activities to keep visitors occupied. Fishing, boating, canoeing, walking and pony trekking are all available on or around Coniston Water and those with energy to spare can tackle the climb up the 2,600 feet Old Man of Coniston.

60 BRANTWOOD

Coniston, Cumbria LA21 8AD
Tel: 015394 41396 Fax: 015394 41263
e-mail: enquiries@brantwood.org.uk
website: www.brantwood.org.uk

Brantwood is the most beautifully situated house in the Lake District. It enjoys the finest lake and mountain views in England and there is no other house in the district with such a diversity of cultural associations. The home of John Ruskin from 1872 until his death in 1900, Brantwood became an intellectual powerhouse and one of the greatest literary and artistic centres in Europe. Tolstoy, Mahatma Gandhi, Marcel Proust and Frank Lloyd Wright can all be numbered amongst Ruskin's disciples.

The house is filled with Ruskin's drawings and watercolours, together with much of his original furniture, books and personal items. The video presentation and special displays provide a fascinating insight into the work of this great man and his life in a Victorian country house. Every Thursday during the season there'll be lace making demonstrations and readings from Ruskin's writing are performed regularly in the study. An excellent bookshop specialises in Ruskin and related art and literature.

Brantwood's Estate comprises of 250 acres of gardens, pastures, ancient woods and high moors. Experience Ruskin's legacy and inspiration among eight distinctive gardens, which have been lovingly restored. Walk among beautifully scented azaleas and bluebells or marvel at magnificent views.

59 THE SHIP INN

Bowmanstead, Coniston,
Cumbria LA21 8HB
Tel: 01539 441224
e-mail: enquiries@shipinn.info

The Ship Inn is a traditional country inn standing half a mile south of Coniston in Bowmanstead. Set in a scenic location, looking down to Coniston Lake, this quaint property was built in the late 17th century and was once a popular venue for drovers.

Today the property is just as popular and having been run by the same tenants Graham and Nicola Belcher for the past 4 years, the couple have retained the buildings fine period appeal, whilst also providing all the modern comforts, which are demanded by today's visitors.

The Ship Inn provides a great base for those touring the region or just wanting to relax and enjoy the beautiful surroundings. With 4 guest bedrooms on offer, 3 doubles and one single, visitors can let the rooms on a bed and breakfast basis, for as little or as long as they require.

The building on the whole is extremely inviting, visited by many locals and visitors from further afield. The exterior of the property is bright and vibrant, with floral displays decking the façade in spring and summer- so fantastic in fact that the inn has won awards. The bar area is a delightfully relaxed and civilised space for meeting friends or making new ones over a glass or two of the real ales on offer, including Hartleys XB or Cumbria Way.

Traditional pub meals are served here daily from 12-2 and 6-8.45 (from 5.30 in high season). Meals range from family favourites such as Whitby scampi, home cooked steak and ale pie, lasagne and sirloin steak to more refined dishes of duck breast in an orange sauce, supreme of chicken in stilton and leek sauce and salmon and broccoli fishcakes and prawns with a sweet chilli dip. Always keeping in with a pub style, most of the dishes are served with chips, new or jacket potatoes and a lovely selection of vegetables, salad or coleslaw. If you are after something a little lighter, there is a lunchtime only menu, which features a large selection of sandwiches and baked jacket potatoes or even just a bowl of chips.

The Inn is closed Monday and Tuesday between November and March except during Christmas week, otherwise open daily and all day on bank holidays and school holiday weekends.

61 THE CHURCH HOUSE INN

Torver, Coniston, Cumbria LA21 8AZ
Tel: 01539 441282
e-mail: churchhouseinn@hotmail.o.uk
website: www.churchhouseinntorver.com

Dating back to the 17th century, **The Church House Inn** has a long history featuring monastic links and it even used to be a haunt of highwaymen! Found in the village of Torver, where the A593 meets the A5084, the picturesque property offers warm and comfortable rooms, good food and well kept ales. Mike and Mandy have been the proprietors for 3 years now and their experience shines through in this delightful inn, which also has a caravan park to the rear.

The five rooms available are all en suite and open for hire all year round, two of which are family sized. The reasonable rates include a fine breakfast in the mornings. Mike has been a chef for 30 years and he has crafted a great menu, genuinely home made with locally sourced ingredients and freshly prepared to order. Sumptuous

examples of the menu include Cumberland Tattie hot pot, made with slow braised Herdwick Lamb from a local farm and the Church House fish pie which features cod, haddock, salmon and prawns.

Supporting the menu is the well stocked bar, which boasts five real ales, made up of mainly locally brewed beers. The inn is open all year round, except Monday and Tuesday lunchtimes during the winter months.

63 PEPPER HOUSE

Satterthwaite, Cumbria LA12 8LS
Tel: 01229 860206
e-mail: info@pepper-house.co.uk
website: www.pepper-house.co.uk

With unbeatable views across the surrounding woodland, **Pepper House** is nestled in a beautiful valley, providing an ideal getaway for someone wanting a peaceful and relaxing break.

In an elevated position, overlooking the quiet village of Satterthwaite, the charming, traditional farmhouse boasts fantastic views over Grizedale Forest Park and is close to Lake Windermere to the east and Consiton Water to the west. Named after William Pepper, who farmed there in the early 1600s, the building is full of character with big oak beams and thick stone walls. Paul and Fran Townsend are the friendly owners of the 16th century Yeoman's Farmhouse and being keen Lakeland enthusiasts are happy to suggest walks or places to visit.

Located off the beaten track, but in easy reach of the more famous fells, the guest house boasts three tastefully decorated en-suite rooms. There are two comfortable lounges and a large dining room, which overlooks the valley, where generous home-cooked meals and breakfasts, made from local produce, can be enjoyed.

The gardens offer delightful seating areas, and walkers and bird watchers will be in their element with miles of bridleways and footpaths criss-crossing the area - perfect for exploring the Lake District, whether on foot, cycling or riding.

62 THE EAGLES HEAD

Satterthwaite, nr Ulverston,
Cumbria LA12 8LN
Tel: 01229 860237
e-mail: rnbruce@aol.com
website: www.eagleshead.co.uk

Nestling in the heart of Grizedale Forest, just a short drive west of Lake Windermere is the **Eagles Head**, boasting a truly picturesque location. Rob and Rebecca Bruce along with their Head chef Bobby McGuire have a real success on their hands with this charming establishment which has the best of facilities in all departments. Starting life in the 16th Century as a farmhouse with an attached barn, it has

been refurbished and modernised through the years while still retaining its traditional charm and warmth. Rob and Rebecca are superb hosts welcoming all with a smile into the cosy interior where guests have a fine choice of real ales on tap, including two "brewed" especially for the pub, Eagles Head (4%abv) and GrizedAle (4.8%).

The cuisine served here is second to none and has gained an excellent reputation in the area. With generous portions at reasonable prices throughout, a quality specials board and an impressive children's menu, this place speaks for itself and is hard to beat.

Talented chef Bobby uses meats and other produce from local suppliers and always cooks his dishes to order thus assuring freshness and bringing their true flavours to the fore. The stunning menu offers an excellent array of starters, main courses and desserts and includes a range of tasty vegetarian options. Special dietary needs can be catered for, given notice and Chef can adapt some dishes to cope with gluten or dairy free needs. Among the 'Eagles' most celebrated dishes are the homemade pies(which people travel miles for), the stuffed chicken and seasonal fish dishes. As mentioned, look out also for their 'specials' board, which extends their excellent food offer even further.

The lunchtime menu sees a variety of tasty lighter meals, freshly cut sandwiches and hearty soups. Booking is advised to avoid disappointment. There is a fine adjacent beer garden, with plenty of seating for those warmer summer days and evenings. Food is served from 12- 2.30pm and 7 -8.30pm Tues/Sun. No food is served on Mondays except for Bank holidays and school holidays. The quality of the cuisine and the ale here is superb and visitors to this part of the country would be foolish not to pay a visit.

64 GRAYTHWAITE FARM HOLIDAYS

Graythwaite, Ulverston,
Cumbria LA12 8BA
Tel: 01539 531351
e-mail:
enquiries@graythwaiteholidays.com
website: www.graythwaiteholidays.com

If you value fresh air, freedom, breathtaking scenery and tranquillity then **Graythwaite Country Estate** is the perfect place for you to holiday. This outstanding business offers a selection of truly stunning properties set in over 6000 acres of idyllic countryside and woodlands.

The main site is set within a Victorian farmstead where 13 properties sit cosily, beautifully converted in the nineties, gracefully decorated so that each is full of its own character and charm. They are all situated on a secluded courtyard that allows both serenity and convenience. The facilities here are second to none; nestled within the farmstead is a children's play area, indoor table tennis room, indoor heated swimming pool and its own fitness suite. The cottages are self catering and range in size from small cottages that sleep just two for a romantic break away to larger barn conversions that sleep up to ten people, perfect for a family holiday with extended family or friends. All properties have central heating, open fires or wood burning stoves with logs provided to guarantee that country feel, but all modern kitchen appliances are fitted.

The farmstead is also an ideal place to rent out for the weddings or larger functions as the properties can be hired in conjunction –family and friends can have the space and freedom to holiday together in a safe and private setting and catering and marquees can be arranged for your convenience accommodating 124 guests. The beautiful setting on the shores of Lake Windermere provides a striking back drop for any such event; see website for details.

But if it is more privacy and space you require then the Graythwaite estate still has something to offer you. There is a further eight cottages set around the spacious grounds, totally secluded with some offering stunning views of the lake themselves whilst other views are far from disappointing.

All properties are available year round and weekly bookings can be made in April, May, July, August, September, October with shorter breaks being available November, December, January, February, March and June.

Peter Whitehead has been the general manager at Graythwaite for seven years providing the warmest of welcomes to all that come, also being a font of knowledge for the surrounding area with plenty of ideas to keep you busy. He guarantees that he will never intrude on your stay but is always available to assist should you need any assistance.

65   THE RED LION INN

Mainstreet, Hawkshead nr Ambleside,
Cumbria LA22 0NS
Tel: 01539 436213 Fax: 01539 436304
e-mail: info@redlionhawkshead.co.uk
website: www.redlionhawkshead.co.uk

The family run **Red Lion Inn** is situated centrally in the charming village of Hawkshead it dates back to the 15th century when it used to be a coaching Inn, making it the oldest pub in Hawkshead. Experience licencees Paul and Lynn and their son Jake extend a cheerful and relaxed atmosphere to all their guests, warning that a sense of humour is a must! Joking aside however, the Red Lion Inn has gone from strength to strength under their management, regaining the Lion's reputation for quality in every aspect, receiving high recommendations from the locals.

The oak panelled bar complete with working traditional fireplace offers 4 real Cumbrian cask ales, with a wide range of wines and spirits and serves locally sourced food Mon-Sat 12-2.30pm/6-9pm, and Sunday 12-8pm when a succulent Lakeland roast is served with a choice of beef, pork or turkey. Dishes available include a trio of Cumberland sausage and mash with onion gravy, Homemade steak and Cumbrian ale pie served with potatoes, fresh vegetables and gravy, or a choice of tasty sandwiches including hand carved Lakeland ham with red onion chutney for smaller appetites.

Children's menus are available or half portions from the main menu or specials board can be made. All credit cards are accepted except Diners. Open all day every day, except winter Mondays (open from 3pm onwards).

Guest accommodation at the Red Lion is available all year round, each of the 8 en suite rooms has its own distinct character retaining many charming original features from their days as a coaching Inn such as oak beams, uneven floors and sloping ceilings.

Paul and Lynn are also eager to ensure that a stay at the Red Lion means a memorable trip to the Lake District so keep much up to date information on what there is to see and do in the surrounding areas. They offer informal and insightful information about local history, tourist attractions and the surprising literary history of the Lakes. They feel that they are really 'living the dream' at the Red Lion and want all those visiting to feel at home too so they invite everyone and their dogs(!) to pull up a bar stool and join in the banter.

66 THE QUEENS HEAD HOTEL

Main Street, Hawkshead,
Cumbria, LA22 0NS
Tel: 01539 436271 Fax: 01539 436722
e-mail: enquiries@queensheadhotel.co.uk
website: www.queensheadhotel.co.uk

In the heart of pretty Hawkshead, a stones throw from Esthwaite Water, close to Windermere and Coniston Water, lies **The Queens Head Hotel**, an impressive early 17th century black and white building. The beautifully traditional façade of the hotel is reflected inside as well, in the cosy bar with flag floors, oak beams and roaring fireplaces, splendid accommodation (including some impressive four-poster rooms) and fine food, which has been consistently upheld by the owners Mr and Mrs Merrick for 21 years. There is a real respect and appreciation for the surrounding lakes, forests and fells, so this is why you will find so much of the meats, fish and seafoods served at The Queens Head Hotel are seasonal, locally sourced and sustainable, to avoid any impact on this most beautiful part of England's countryside.

With this peace of mind you are free to enjoy the many delicious delicacies on offer; from the best Cumbrian Fell fed rib eye steak, served with Lancashire blue cheese mash potatoes, beer batter onion rings and red wine jus to the extensive vegetarian menu including tasty delights like the Wild Mushroom and English Asparagus Risotto, with truffle oil and parmesan shavings. They have held 1 Rosette for excellence in food for the last 7 years, and it shows in the pride of quality in their menu. In addition to this menu you can enjoy a great range of 4 real ales: Cumbria Way, Double Hop, Unicorn, plus seasonal guest ale, all from Robinsons Brewery. Food is served Mon-Sat 12-2:30pm and 6:15-9:30pm, Sun 12-5pm, and as you would expect with such an impressive menu, it is advisable to book in advance, particularly in the summer months.

Also, with an AA 2star hotel rating 75%, is their accommodation, which has a range to satisfy whatever your break requires. Be it their elegant four-poster rooms, colourful contemporary rooms (all with private bathrooms), or the self-catering cottage or studio apartment, the biggest of which sleeps four, perfect for weekend breaks. The rooms can come with a choice of Dinner-Bed-Breakfast, as well as Bed-Breakfast, so you can really relax and enjoy all The Queens Head Hotel has to offer. Although not connected to the building, you can order food from the hotel to the self-catering premises if you are tired from a day soaking in the wonderful scenery.

67 THE OLD DUNGEON GHYLL HOTEL

Great Langdale, Ambleside, Cumbria
LA22 9JY
Tel: 01539 437272
e-mail: olddungeonghyll1@btconnect.com
website: www.odg.co.uk

Visitors approaching the **Old Dungeon Ghyll Hotel** are treated to some magnificent views over the rugged scenery of the Great Langdale Valley and the stunning location is just the beginning of a truly memorable stay. This marvellous hotel was originally an inn with a farmhouse, which is the way it was run until 1949, and the oldest part is the middle section. Another part was added at a later date and the stables at the north end were converted into a dining room. The shippon at the other end became the Climbers Bar,

where the old cow stalls still stand intact. In the Hikers Bar, real ales, of which there are at least four, are served in a charming and welcoming atmosphere.

The Old Dungeon Ghyll hotel has been attracting walkers, climbers, tourists and lovers of the great outdoors for 300 years and the latest owners Neil and Jane have been the proprietors for 25 years now. Neil, a keen fell runner, and Jane have continued to improve and develop this popular family hotel whilst keeping the rustic features and charm. The hotel's reputation has grown under their care and guests come from all over the world to the hotel, which takes its name from one of the most dramatic of the Lake District waterfalls, tumbling 60 feet down a nearby fell. Neil and Jane both cook and the hearty home made dishes on the bar and restaurant menus cater perfectly for appetites sharpened by the bracing surroundings.

Guest accommodation at the Old Dungeon Ghyll comprises 14 warm, comfortable bedrooms, most with en suites and some boasting four poster beds. The resident's lounge is a great place to relax, meet the other guests to swap stories and plan the next day's activities. The hotel is amply equipped; there is even a drying room to dry those wet clothes. In the days when charabancs brought visitors from Little Langdale over Blea Tarn Pass, they would stop at the top and blow the horn, one toot for every passenger needing a meal! Over the years, the hotel has become very popular with climbing clubs and a favourite venue for club dinners, attracting many of the big names in climbing, including Sir John Hunt, Joe Brown and Don Whillans. Clubs are still very welcome and the hotel is the start point of several walks and climbs, including the famous peaks of Crinkle Crags, Bowfell and the Langdale Pikes.

68 WAYSIDE LICENSED GUEST ACCOMMODATION AND WHISKY BARN

Whitbeck, Cumbria LA19 5UP
Tel: 01229 718883
Fax: 01229 718882
e-mail: enquiries@waysidehotel.co.uk
website: www.waysidehotel.co.uk

Wayside Guest Accommodation and Whisky Barn is set at the base of Black Combe in Whitbeck, surrounded by the stunning scenery and the Cumbrian Coast. It can be found adjacent to the main A595, north of Millom towards Ravenglass. Wayside is over 400 years old and used to be a rural working farm, but has been laboriously converted into a stunning guest house with four luxury bedrooms, lounge and dining area and whisky bar.

Bought by Lynn and Steven Johns in 2004, Wayside was originally derelict but now stands beautifully renovated in traditional style, full of character, warmth and original features. Add this to the outstanding hospitality that Lynn and Steven provide and the breathtaking scenery from this beautiful corner of the world and there really is no better place for a break away.

The accommodation is open all year round, comprising of four large en suite rooms fitted with top notch facilities ensuring comfort is paramount. Each room has its own character, individually decorated, complete with high ceilings and wooden beams. There is a choice of a family room, a twin, a double or the annexe. The tariff includes a quality breakfast, and there is also the option of evening dining for guests and non residents with a choice of freshly cooked and locally sourced dishes. There is a fine range of starters, mains and desserts. You can chose from a selection that includes smoked haddock and spring onion fishcakes, chicken breast served with creamy white wine and mushroom sauce, seasonal vegetables and chefs potatoes of the day, or bilberry pie served with cream or ice cream. Food is served from 6:30-8:30pm and booking is advised at all times as even though this place has been open a mere few months it's already thriving.

The feather in the cap for this property though is the phenomenal whisky bar that sells over 250 whiskies. There is also a fine selection of other spirits, wines and a regularly changing locally brewed ale in this atmospheric bar. The lounge also sports fine décor and a wood burning stove, making Wayside the perfect place to relax after a good days windsurfing at the coast or hiking the surrounding hills.

69 THE SCREES INN

Nether Wasdale, Cumbria CA20 1ET
Tel: 019467 26262
e-mail: info@thescreesinnwasdale.com
website: www.thescreesinnwasdale.com

The outstanding and picturesque **Screes Inn** stands in the stunning post card location of Nether Wasdale. Found just off the main A595, it's just a stone's throw from the famous Wastwater Lake and Scafell Pike.

A former Temperance hotel, becoming a country inn back in the early 1960's, this property is stunning. Traditional and charming, this business has plenty of character, which draws visitors from far and wide. Tenants Karen and Speedy have only been here since the start of 2009 but already they're getting a reputation for quality hospitality and fine facilities.

Karen has been in the trade in Ireland for 10 years prior to this venture and her partner Speedy is still a local fireman, bringing some intrigue and conversation in to the building.

Open all day, everyday there is a great selection of beverages on offer, including 4 real ales, which are all from the Robinson's brewery range. They include hatters, dizzy blonde and double hop, as well as a rotating guest ale.

The food is also splendid here, with something to offer those with a wide variety of differing tastes. The Chef is a vegetarian, so there is a great selection of quality vegetarian dishes always available, including goats cheese strudel with roast parsnips, celeriac and leek and apple, which is served with a white wine and mustard sauce, Screes vegetarian chilli and a splendid spinach, sweet potato and coconut curry. For those who enjoy meat dishes there is a stunning menu of Gill Unsworth's home baked steak and kidney pie, marinated shoulder of local lamb, grilled fillet of salmon with a fresh herb butter and home made lasagne. As well as this there is also tagliatelle with a creamy mushroom pesto sauce with an option of smoked salmon or smoked crispy bacon and a fabulous dessert menu, with homemade sticky toffee pudding, bread and butter pudding and a scrumptious hot chocolate fudge cake.

The Screes Inn has everything, including accommodation. There are currently 5 ensuite bedrooms available to hire all year around, each of which are comfortable and are available in a variety of sizes. The tariff is competitive and ranges from £43 per night for a single up to £80 per night for a family. The tariff includes a hearty breakfast, fit for a king.

70 THE VICTORIA HOTEL

Station Road, Drigg,
Cumbria CA19 1XQ
Tel: 01946 724231
e-mail: enquiries@thevicatdrigg.co.uk
website: www.thevicatdrigg.co.uk

The Victoria Hotel is a family run country hotel with a warm and welcoming atmosphere from the moment you enter. Situated in the village of Drigg on the west Cumbria coast, the Vic, as it is known locally, was built in about 1885 to service the Furness railway which still runs along the coast from Barrow-in-Furness to Carlisle. Drigg is known for its sand dunes which form, what is believed to be, the largest nesting sites in Europe for black headed Gulls and is also a sanctuary for rare Natterjack toads. Tenants Sandra and Peter are Cumbrian born and bred and took over at the Victoria in 2008. While this is their first venture into licensing, they have been in the catering industry for nearly 20 years.

The Victoria was extensively renovated in 2006 and features six quality en suite rooms, all with digital colour televisions and tea & coffee making facilities. The hotel is named for Queen Victoria and in keeping with this tradition, the rooms are all named after her children: Leopold, Louise, Alice, Beatrice, Edward and Alfred. The room rates are very reasonable, the doubles are £40 a night and the family room just £52 a night. The tariff includes a hearty English breakfast in the mornings.

The hotel also features a very popular restaurant which offers good traditional home cooked food made to order on the premises. Sandra cooks alongside an employed chef using food sourced from local suppliers. For example, the meat is sourced from Wilson's Butchers of Egremont and the delicious ice cream is supplied from Hartley's of Egremont. Favourite dishes include the sumptuous steaks from Victoria's Grill and the local Cumberland sausage; the home made pies are extremely popular as well. The menu also features a variety of all day breakfasts, fish dishes, a vegetarian selection and a range of sandwiches. The restaurant is open for service from 12 pm to 2 pm and 6 pm to 9 pm all week long and there is a sample menu available on the excellent website.

The bar is open every afternoon and evening session and all day Friday, Saturday and Sunday. The bar is very well stocked and features 2 real ales, Jennings Bitter and a rotating guest ale. Once a fortnight there is a quiz on Friday night from 9 pm and all are welcome to participate.

71   GOSFORTH HALL INN

Wasdale Road, Gosforth,
Cumbria CA20 1AZ
Tel: 01946 725322
e-mail: info@gosforthhallinn.co.uk
website: www.gosforthhallinn.co.uk

Gosforth Hall Inn is located on the western edge of the Lake District National park, close to Wastwater (the deepest Lake in England) and Scafell Pike (the highest mountain in England). Built back in 1658, the year of Oliver Cromwell's death, the Grade II* listed building retains many of it's original features, including the Coat of Arms dated back to 1673, located in the bar which CAMRA recently voted West Cumbria Pub of the Season for Spring 2007. The Hall stands next to St Mary's Church with its famous

15 feet tall Viking Cross and is an excellent base for visiting the Eskdale Valley, Ravenglass, Muncaster Castle and Whitehaven. Rod and Barbara Davies, who took over the Hall in 2002, greet every guest as a friend, and take great pride in the accommodation, food and drink they provide at this superb place.

Their well-kept real ales, wide range of drinks, including a fine wine cellar and choice of meals keep the guests coming back time and time again. The restaurant is open for evening meals seven nights a week, although diners have the option of eating in the bar, lounge, restaurant or beer garden. The seasonally changing menu takes its inspiration from home and abroad with dishes ranging from creamy garlic mushrooms, devilled kidneys & black pudding, steaks and seasonal game to kleftiko, chicken fajitas and spinach & brie pancakes. Barbara's signature dish, the chicken melt, is a very popular favourite. A recent addition to the menu is a selection of home made pies, these are well liked and in the first year, they sold over 2000!

The nine beautifully appointed guest bedrooms include the superb Suite, which boats a four-poster bed and a truly vast en suite bath, favoured as a bridal suite, it has to be seen to be believed.

The hotel is an ideal base for touring the unspoilt Western Lake area and discovering the many scenic and historic delights of coast and countryside. Walking can be anything from a stroll by the lake to tackling the 3 Peak challenge - or guests can just sit back and relax in a walled beer garden where they might even catch a glimpse of the resident Barn Owl. A recent archaeological dig took place in the front beer garden and post holes dating to AD 920 were found, these were verified at nearby Lancaster University and correspond with the supposed age of St. Mary's Church.

72 BLACKBECK HOTEL AND BREWERY

Egremont, Cumbria CA22 2NY
Tel: 01946 841661
e-mail: drink@blackbeckbrewery.co.uk
website: www.blackbeckbrewery.co.uk

Having been extensively furnished in recent years the **Blackbeck Hotel and Brewery** is a delightful hotel situated alongside the main A595, just a couple of miles out of Egremont towards Easforth. Boasting 20 quality en-suite rooms and with a spacious dining room and outside area it has gone from strength to strength since the current owners, Ken and Belinda, took charge and is known as one of the best hotels in the area. The couple also brew their own beer in their own brewery with business partner Johnnie Taylor. Blackbeck brewery opened this year and guests can choose from two of their delicious ales, Trial Run and Blackbeck Belle.

The rooms vary from standard to executive grades and prices include a hearty breakfast. Six of the rooms are located on the ground floor making them easily accessible for disabled or elderly guests.

Quality, locally sourced, food is available from the hotel's extensive menu from 12pm-2pm and from 7pm-late. Barnsley lamb chops on a bed of herb mashed potato with a rich mint gravy, served with tomatoes stuffed with cheese and herbs as well as chicken Thai red curry are among the dishes guests can choose from. Meals are served in the beautifully laid out and spacious dining room and guests can also enjoy a relaxing drink in the patio area. The outside space has a contemporary and relaxing feel to it – perfect for enjoying a drink after a long day exploring the local area.

Ken and Belinda welcome children and are happy for guests to bring their dogs. Keen walkers will be in their element with many nature reserves, rivers, lakes and open countryside to explore. Cyclists will also be able to enjoy the scenery and historic castle. For those interested in the history of the area there are underground mine trips that can be had and there is also a mining heritage museum, genealogy centre and art galleries to browse. Guests staying at the Blackbeck Hotel and Brewery are just a few miles away from the traditional market town of Egremont, which has a long historical and industrial heritage.

There is a wide range of activities and attractions close by and being situated at the foot of Uldale Valley and Dent Fell there are some stunning views to take in. If it is a quality service you are after, run excellently, with top facilities then this is a good choice.

73 THE RUM STORY

27 Lowther Street, Whitehaven,
Cumbria CA28 7DN
Tel: 01946 592933 Fax: 01946 590595
e-mail: dutymanagers@rumstory.co.uk
website: www.rumstory.co.uk

Located in the original cellars and warehouses of 1785, **The Rum Story** tells the colourful tale of Whitehaven's involvement in a trade that attracted pirates, smugglers, slavers, gangsters and Nelson's navy. During your visit you will discover the origins of the town's dark slave trade, and hear rum tales of Blackbeard and piracy on the high seas. After your tour, enjoy a browse around the themed Gift Shop for a selection of really special souvenirs. Then relax in the Courtyard Café and sample a delicious home-made meal. And for special occasions, there's the Vault function suite which provides a truly unique dining experience. Booking required.

76 THE SHEPHERDS ARMS HOTEL

Ennerdale Bridge, Cumbria CA23 3AR
Tel: 01946 861249
e-mail: shepherdsarms@btconnect.com
website: www.shepherdsarmshotel.co.uk

The Shepherds Arms Hotel is the ideal base for discovering a wonderful part of the country. Located in the centre of Ennerdale Bridge, on Wainwright's famous Coast to Coast walk, the hotel is loved by many visitors to the area. It is also an extremely popular haunt for locals to enjoy a drink or meal in the wonderfully decorated and traditional panelled Georgian restaurant or bar.

Owned and run by Malcolm Thomas-Chapman for the last 3½ years, the business just gets better with age. Old beams and open fires create a cosy atmosphere in the 400-year old building, creating the perfect atmosphere to enjoy 1 or more of the 5 real ales available here- Jennings Bitter being the regular.

There are 8 bedrooms located upstairs, 6 of which are ensuite, two with private bathrooms and they are available all year round on a B&B basis.

Malcolm has recently taken over at The Fox and Hounds, located close by, in the same village and has refurbished the property to produce a bistro style eatery as well as bed and breakfast accommodation.

Main Street, St. Bees, Cumbria CA27 0DE
Tel: 01946 822287
e-mail:
enquiries@queenshotelstbees.co.uk
website: www.queenshotelstbees.co.uk

The quaint coastal village of St. Bees is well known throughout Cumbria for having a medieval church and a four hundred year old public school. The picturesque village is also home to the **Queen's Hotel**; a 17th century Inn that has recently been renovated to its former glory by Mark and Sue Smedley. Unfortunately, this classic inn had been closed for some time until Mark and Sue purchased it in June 2008, spent a great deal of time and money restoring it to a very high standard and reopened it to the public in August 2008. The premises have gone from strength to strength since reopening and the inn's reputation is now second to none in the area.

The classic black and white exterior is very well kept and brightened up by colourful hanging baskets and window boxes that adorn the walls. Inside the décor is well chosen, warm and relaxing colours mean that you feel comfortable and at home. The cosy pub atmosphere is enhanced by the exposed wooden beams and roaring log fire. The 14 rooms are comprised of singles, twins, doubles and family suites. All of the rooms have en suite facilities and are extremely well appointed, stocked with everything you could need or want from this very reasonably priced hotel. The tariff even includes a fine breakfast and packed lunches can be supplied for those visiting on walking holidays.

The pub is open all day every day for business and the bar is remarkably well stocked, boasting a fine collection of wines, a vast array of spirits and between 3 and 4 real ales at any one time, Jenning's Bitter and Cumberland Ale are the regulars with the others being guest ales. Delicious food is available at Queen's Hotel all year round, all daily form 11 am to 9 pm during the season and some lunchtimes and every evening during the off season. Due to the popular nature of the restaurant, it is necessary to make a reservation to dine on Fridays, Saturdays and Sundays to avoid disappointment. The excellent menu is filled with classic pub fare, garnished with some more exotic choices, for example, there is the stunning home made Steak and ale pie made with local ale from the classic menu or home made spiced beef and coriander koftas for a slightly more exotic option.

75 HARTLEY'S BEACH SHOP & TEA ROOM

Beach Road, St Bees, Cumbria CA27 0ES
Tel: 01946 820175
Fax: 01946 820456
website: www.hartleys-ice-cream.co.uk

Set in an unbeatable location overlooking the foreshore at St Bees, **Hartleys Beach Shop & Tea Room** is one of the most popular places in the region for enjoying a snack. It's a long, single-storey building which has been around for 20 odd years and its reputation ensures locals, tourists, walkers and holidaymakers alike all swarm like bees to a honeypot. As the premises are situated more or less at the beginning of the famous coast to coast walk across the Penines, and of course much-needed refreshment for those at the end of the walk. The sunny yellow colour scheme brightens up even the most overcast of days and the warm welcome received by the Richardsons only add to the atmosphere.

The tea room is open daily from 9 to 5, with hot food served until 4 o'clock. The food choice runs from made-to-order sandwiches with generous fillings like tuna savoury, corned beef & onions and chicken mayo, to soup, beans on toast and home-made cakes, teacakes and scones. Very few summer visitors leave without trying one or more of the delicious ice creams, which are made by the firm established by the Hartley family in 1931 in Egremont, where they are still made. The ice creams come in more than 60 flavours, with some diabetic varieties and also eight flavours of sorbets. They are sold to the public and to the retail and catering trades in tubs from 125ml to 10 litres, and freezer packs are a speciality. They are made fresh every day in the Church Street creamery in

Egremont, and new lines include semi-freddo desserts - a perfect way to end a meal. The actual ice-cream store is situated on Church Street in Egremont and is open between 11 am and 5 pm from January to March and until 7 pm in the busier summer months. To drink, guests can choose from cold soft drinks, milkshakes, tea and a variety of coffees.

The business was taken over in 1981 by the Richardson family, who run the beach shop with friendly, hardworking staff. The tea room has seats for 48 inside, and when the weather is kind, tables and chairs are set outside.

Hartleys at St Bees also has a gift shop and mini-mart selling walking and camping essentials.

77 THE COCK AND BULL

**7 South Street, Cockermouth,
Cumbria CA13 9RT
Tel: 01900 826922**

Situated in the heart of Cockermouth in South Street, you'll find the ever so impressive **Cock And Bull**. During the course of the properties lifetime, the business has had many different names, however the old fashioned Cock And Bull really suits it.

The pub has been run since November 2008 by couple Helen and Dave; they have many years experience in the trade between them and Dave is a first class Chef, meaning that the food on offer here is simply divine.

Open all day, everyday, there are 3 delicious real ales to enjoy, with Cumberland ale being a regular and several guests rotating. The food is served daily, except for Tuesdays and is available from 12-3pm and 6-8.30pm. With a wonderful array of spectacular dishes to choose from, there is something for everyone to enjoy. The starters are lovely, with splendid soups, bbq meatballs and half pint of shell on prawns for those wishing to have a tantalising light bite. There are also platters to share, light meals of baguettes or rustic rolls, with a large variety of fillings such as bacon with stilton or brie, steak, onion and French mustard, chicken, grapes and mayonnaise and a lovely tuna mozzarella melt. The mains are wonderfully prepared and see Cock And Bull kebabs, served with couscous, crisp salad and homemade jack daniels bbq sauce, homemade chicken kiev's served with homemade chips and a splendid Chef's homemade pies, which sees the specials board change daily.

This is supplemented by a menu dedicated to children, with healthy options and child favourites such as soup, Chef's homemade burger with chips, sausages, mash and gravy and a large selection of sandwiches. The food is so good here and David is extremely well known for his homemade pies - so much so that he has won awards during the national pie week. All of David's food uses produce that has been sourced from within the country and everything is freshly prepared, which is obvious from the spectacular taste of the dishes.

As well as the lovely food and drink on offer there are also poker leagues, pool tournaments, quiz nights and open mic night throughout the week - something that everyone can enjoy.

78 ROOK GUEST HOUSE

9 Castlegate, Cockermouth,
Cumbria CA13 9EU
Tel: 01900 828496
e-mail: sarahwaters1848@btinternet.com
website: therookguesthouse.co.uk

Cockermouth is a beautiful Georgian market town on the edge of the Lake District and has plenty to offer. It is here that visitors will be delighted to find **The Rook Guest House.**

This charming early 18th century property with exposed beams and stonework oozes character and provides comfortable, high-quality bed and breakfast accommodation close to the Castle. There are three stylish en-suite bedrooms, each with TV and beverage tray. Friendly owner, Vicky Waters, has been here for more than 10 years, and is always on hand to see that her guests are

enjoying their stay. Children are welcome, (dogs are also welcome by prior arrangement) and Vicky makes sure that the day starts with a hearty breakfast for everyone. Vicky will also provide guests with a tasty packed lunch if required. Cockermouth has a wealth

of history to discover and Rook Guest house is an ideal base for tourists, walkers and cyclists, with plenty of bars, restaurants and shops all within walking distance.

80 JUNIPERS RESTAURANT & CAFÉ BAR

11 South Street, Cockermouth,
Cumbria CA13 9RU
Tel: 01900 822892
website: www.junipersrestaurant.co.uk

Renowned for its contemporary food, **Junipers Restaurant & Café Bar** is a popular haunt, located in the centre of Cockermouth. Having been refurbished in 2004, the interior is clean cut and contemporary, with contrasting colours being used throughout, in order to give an eye-catching and vibrant atmosphere.

Debbie and Lee have been at Junipers for the last 6 years and their previous experience in the restaurant industry has enabled them to produce a top-notch business here. Chef Lee has been cooking for 30 years and creates wonderful dishes of home roast ham on buttered cabbage, seared smoked salmon and beef bourguignonne. They also specialise in tapas, inspired from Spain, 15 dishes in total all accompanied by a large selection of wines imported from around the world.

Set over two floors, the café/ bar on the ground floor is used at lunchtimes for light bites, sandwiches etc and in the evenings for tapas and drinks. Upstairs the spacious 50 seat restaurant serves an array of dishes in a relaxed atmosphere. Everything is cooked by the chef/owner Lee and supervised by Debbie in front of house, thus ensuring the quality and consistency that junipers is well known for.

192

79 THE BUSH

Main Street, Cockermouth,
Cumbria CA13 9JS
Tel: 01900 822064
e-mail: joesf@btinternet.com

Whatever brings visitors to Cockermouth – the Castle, the museums, Wordsworth's house, Castlegate Gallery – it's always well worth pausing awhile at **The Bush Hotel** to get a real flavour of the local brews, the local characters and the local atmosphere.

Leaseholder Joe Fagan and Bar Manager Jim Weldon, all with considerable local experience, have an equally warm and genuine welcome for familiar faces and first-time visitors at this appealing former coaching inn. The arched entrance to the courtyard used by the old stage coaches still stands, and behind the striking black and white frontage the inn has an inviting old-world atmosphere, with comfortable chairs and settees, upholstered stools, carpets and a handsome old brick hearth.

The food here is second to none, and a monthly changing menu, using locally sourced produce, assures that even the most frequent of visitors will still have something new to try. Available at lunchtimes only, diners can expect to see dishes such as salads, hot and cold sandwiches, homemade lasagne, homemade steak pie, gammon steak and baked potatoes. The desserts are equally as tempting, with chocolate fudge cake and sticky toffee pudding the firm favourites.

The inn is open all day, everyday for drinks on a long list that starts with a selection from the local Jennings Brewery, including Jennings Bitter, Cock a Hoop, Cumberland Ale and Snecklifter; add to these a monthly Jennings guest ale and a rotating nationally brewed ale and visitors will be spoilt for choice. There's also a good range of other draught and bottle beers and lagers, stout and cider. This is definitely one of the best places in Cockermouth to socialise over a drink, with a convivial atmosphere created by the management, the staff and locals and visitors of all ages and from all walks of life who come here for the good beer and the good conversation. Children and dogs are made welcome and all major credit cards are accepted. When the weather is kind, the beer garden, with heaters for cooler evenings, is a popular spot for alfresco sipping. The Bush also hosts occasional music nights; please ring for more details.

81 | BEATFORDS COUNTRY TEA ROOMS

7 South Street, Lowther Went, Cockermouth, Cumbria CA13 9RT
Tel: 01900 827099

Renowed throughout Cockermouth and beyond as being one of the best known places to dine, is a delightful tea rooms known as **Beatfords Country Tea Rooms**. Situated in the quaint town of Lowther Went, nestled between the main street and the town's biggest carpark, Beatfords offers the perfect place to meet for a drink and a fine choice for a meal. Attentive owner Eileen Jackson has over 30 years of experience in the catering industry and it really shows. The atmosphere here is relaxed and friendly allowing visitors to escape the stresses and strains of everyday life and enjoy a little 'me' time.

The edible options here are truly delicious, and will leave visitors spoilt for choice. Using locally sourced produce from within the county, everything on offer is homemade, from the tempting cakes and scones to the hearty hot meals. There is something for every appetite and palette with toasted tea cakes, freshly baked scones, fruit pavlova and homemade fruit pie just a few options to satisfy a sweet tooth. The lemon merange pie is a firm favourite and melts in your mouth! For those wishing to satisfy a savoury craving, jacket potatoes with a choice of 12 fillings, open sandwiches, salads and toasted sandwiches are sure to do just that.

An ever changing specials board is also available to keep the regular visitors satisfied. Beatfords offers a comprehensive choice of beverages to accompany your meal or enjoy alone, with hot chocolate, coffee, ice-cream milkshakes, freshly squeezed orange juice and a range of cold drinks all ready to quench the thirst. For visitors who love their morning brew, Beatfords has 10 different types of tea to choose from allowing you to have a different tea for everyday of the week.

Open Monday to Saturday 9am – 5pm (closed on Sunday). Children are made to feel welcome and all major credit cards are accepted.

82 THE HALL PARK HOTEL

23 Carlton Road, Workington,
Cumbria CA14 4BX
Tel: 01900 602968 Fax: 01900 65949
e-mail: susan.fryer@tesco.net
website: www.thehallparkhotel.co.uk

The quality, **Hall Park Hotel** is located on the outskirts of the centre of Workington, across the road from the well-known Helena Thompson Museum. A free house and comfortable hotel, run for the past 3 years by Paul and Susan Fryer, the couple have plenty of years experience in the trade, with Susan having worked in the catering business previously for 15 years.

Dating back to the turn of the 20th century, this Victorian premises is traditional, with good quality furnishings as well as bright and airy décor, perfect for unwinding. The Hall Park Hotel prides itself on the accommodation and it is very popular with businessmen and workers, working away from home, as well as tourists interested in the surrounding history.

The hotel comprises of 14 bedrooms, 11 of which are ensuite, in a variety of sizes- single, twin, double and family. The prices vary from £40, without an ensuite to £85 for a superior room with ensuite. All tariffs include a hearty breakfast, available between 7 and 9am and it is simply delicious, with extremely generous helpings.

83 THE LAKE DISTRICT COAST AQUARIUM

South Quay, Maryport,
Cumbria CA15 8AB
Tel: 01900 817760
e-mail: info@ld-coastaquarium.co.uk
website: www.lakedistrict-coastaquarium.co.uk

The Lake District Coast Aquarium was built in 1997 using private funding with support from the European Regional Development Fund. It has a wonderful position on the South Quay of Maryport Harbour, affording views out across the Solway Firth to Scotland on most days. The harbour area has received substantial public investment from the mid 1980's onwards as part of a regeneration programme following the closure of local coal mining, steel making and shipbuilding, and tourism was seen as having a vital part in this.

The Aquarium is privately owned and not part of a national chain, and is the size of a typical modest Sea-Life Centre that most of the public are familiar with. The 45 displays that make up the live exhibition all contain local or Irish Sea species, as well as a wide variety of shellfish and invertebrates. It is rated as being one of the best places to go to see native sealife now that most other aquariums have diversified into being eclectic selections of world wide species.

In order to broaden the appeal of the attraction and make it possible to stay all day, there is a highly rated integral café overlooking the harbour, a well stocked gift shop, a 12 hole crazy golf course , a radio control boat pool and water cannon game, and an extensive adjacent free adventure play park run by the local authority.

It is open every day year round from 10-5 except on the 25th and 26th of December, and all admission tickets are valid for re-entry on the day of issue so that people can take advantage of the scheduled fish feeding demonstrations.

84 THE MINERS ARMS INN

Church Road, Broughton Moor, Maryport,
Cumbria CA15 7RY
Tel: 01900 810131
e-mail: broughtonminers@aol.com

This friendly establishment has had several names over the years but currently functions under **The Miners Arms** and is open every session and all day Thur-Sun. It's found just off the A594 between Maryport and Cockermouth is a real asset to the area.

The inn itself dates back to the early 19th century but current licensees Andy and Mandy only took over in May last year. This hard working pair have changed the Miner Arms Inn back into the thriving pub it once was creating a warm and friendly environment for both locals and tourists all year round. The facilities are second to none and a visit here guarantees that you will leave satisfied.

Andy is the chef here providing delicious food for all to sample from 12-2pm Thurs-Sun and 6-8:30pm Tues-Thurs. There is small but well thought out menu with a range of starters, mains, desserts, sides and children's options to fill you up. The local favourites here are the Cumberland sausage and black pudding, and the steak options which include a handsome surf and turf dish with whole tail scampi. Other options include breaded mushrooms, lasagne, or pan fried chicken breast. Truly delicious puddings can be chosen fresh each day, and Andy also caters for small parties, christenings, birthdays, weddings, making any occasion

hassle free, tasty and memorable. On Sundays a scrumptious lunch is available but it's necessary to book as it's very popular. 95% of produce here is sourced locally so you will get a real taste of Cumbria here.

The bar here also lives up to the finest Cumbrian standards with up to 4 real ales to enjoy – regulars include Jennings Bitter and Dark Mild with others rotating from local micro-breweries. In the summer months the atmospheric patio at the rear of the Inn is the perfect place to enjoy them and the annual beer festival held each May.

Andy and Mandy also put on live music every Saturday from 8:30pm with either a soloist or a duet to serenade you, making the Miners Inn well worth a visit. All major credit cards are accepted with cash back also available.

85 THE BEECHES CARAVAN PARK

Gilcrux, Wigton,
Cumbria CA7 2QX
e-mail:
henry@beechescaravanpark.com
website: www.thebeechescaravanpark.com

The Beeches Caravan Park is situated between the A595 and A596 just 5 miles north of Cockermouth and just over 3 miles from the Solway Coast at Allonby. Set in two acres of picturesque grounds are the 12 modern caravans owned and maintained by Henry Airey who has been providing a quality service to caravaners since 2002. The site is open all year round and there is a minimum of two nights stays onwards.

The park is renowned for not only its location which looks towards Scotland, making it an ideal place for touring both the northern and western Scotland, but it's on site facilities which include a post office, shop, laundry and even its own restaurant and bar complete with log fire and takeaway service which opens every evening and weekend lunchtimes and is also open to non-residents. Caravans are equipped with WC, shower, full kitchen, colour TV and gas fire, sleeping 6 with a wonderful children's playground on site also on their doorsteps making this a hassle free holiday for any family.

86 THE SHIP HOTEL

Main Street, Allonby, Maryport,
Cumbria CA15 6QF
Tel: 01900 881017
e-mail: THESHIPALLONBY@aol.com
website: www.theshipallonby.co.uk

With stunning views stretching across the Solway Firth, towards Scotland, **The Ship Hotel** offers the ideal place to relax. Located in the attractive village of Allonby, an area of outstanding natural beauty, visitors can enjoy the beautiful backdrop of the Lake District fells. The hotel itself is a grade II listed building, which was once a 17th century coaching inn, and offers visitors a comfortable stay in a peaceful, seaside village.

The Cumbrian Coastal Way is right on the hotel's doorstep – perfect for walkers and cyclists and with a golf course five miles in either direction and water sport facilities in the village there is something for everyone. Children can enjoy miles of beaches and dogs are welcome to stay too.

The hotel offers mostly en-suite bedrooms, which are traditionally furnished with real wood furniture. The exposed beams and real fires add to the authenticity of the hotel, where Charles Dickens and Wilkie Collins stayed in 1857.

The owners, Steve and Val Ward have been there for nine years and a lot of the food on offer is locally sourced or home-made with meals served in the quaint dining room.

Bed and breakfast prices start from £28 per person per night and £12 for children.

87 TANGLEWOOD CARAVAN PARK

Causeway Head, Silloth-on-Solway,
Cumbria CA7 4PE
Tel: 016973 31253
e-mail:
tanglewoodcaravanpark@hotmail.com
website:
www.tanglewoodcaravanpark.co.uk

Located on the fringes of the Lake District is the wonderful family-run caravan park **Tanglewood**. A quiet and friendly campsite, ideal for those who wish to experience a relaxing, laid back and memorable holiday, surrounded by picturesque views and greenery await visitors here. Set just a mile inland from the pleasant small port and seaside resort of Silloth-On-Solway, this caravan site is surrounded by natural beauty of the countryside, offering something for everyone. For those wishing to experience a relaxing holiday or for those who enjoy long hikes or cycling.

Having been established for over 30 years, Mike and Jen Bowman, along with their parents Elaine and Norman pride themselves on the quality service that they provide. They currently house 58 static caravans on site, 9 of which are for hire. They also have 21 pitches for touring caravans, all with electric hook-ups and water/drainage facilities. There are 10 pitches for tents for all the campers out there, with plenty of wash facilities, including showers and toilets, with underfloor heating, as well as a fully equipped laundry service, giving you a home from home experience.

Tanglewood's large modern holiday homes are 32 feet x 12 feet and are planned for spacial living, fully equipped for premium comfort. The bedrooms are of a good size and house all mod cons you would expect to find in a self-catering property- gas fire, cooker, microwave oven, fridge and colour TV but to name a few. There is also a parking space next to each plot, with convenience in mind.

The main coach house has been converted into a licensed lounge bar, which is open to all park clients and the public daily from 8pm and from lunchtime on Saturdays and Sundays. There is also a children's games room adjoining the bar and the site has a play area with swings and a sandpit, ensuring that this site is perfect for families.

The tariff is reasonable, ranging from £250 per week for 2 people, varying from time of year and how many people will be sharing. Tanglewood is open all year round, excluding the month of February and is one of the best of its kind. Approved by many Associations, including the British Tourist Authority, this business is excellent.

88 SILLOTH CAFE

2 Station Road, Silloth,
Cumbria   CA7 4AE
Tel: 01697 331319

Situated in the leisurely peaceful town of Silloth, the popular **Silloth Café** offers great food and unbeatable hospitality to anyone exploring this charming old port and seaside resort. In this substantial building on a corner site, attentive owner Alison Henderson and her niece Amanda offer a warm and friendly welcome to all who pass through the door.

Amanda offers a good selection of snacks and meals and also prepares a range of special dietary dishes such as gluten free. Traditional fish & chips head the menu, and other choices run from filled rolls to Cumberland sausage, haggis and home-made pies and patties –
something for
everyone and
the majority of the produce is sourced locally. A hearty roast dinner is added to the menu on Sunday which has proved to be a real success. If you are looking for a something to satisfy a sweet tooth the cakes are a real treat! Children are made to feel very welcome and there's a special junior menu with high chairs available on request.

This delightful café is open from 11.30am to 2pm for lunches and 4.30 to 8pm for evening meals. Closed Wednesday. Cash and cheque only.

89 JOINERS ARMS COUNTRY INN

Newton Arlosh, Wigton,
Cumbria   CA7 5ET
Tel: 016973 51470
e-mail: dmaddiso@rocketmail.com

Situated in the picturesque village of Newton Arlosh, found on the B5307 between Abbeytown and Carlisle is the **Joiners Arms Country Inn** – renowned throughout Cumbria as a fine establishment for excellent food,
real ale and hospitality.

Owners Darren and Angela have been running the Joiners Arms since October 2008 and locals say they have made a very successful start, giving them back their beloved village Inn. This place is the heart of the community, serving Cumberland Ale, open every day and offering a fine selection of food every lunchtime from 12-2pm and Wed-Sun evenings from 6-9pm.

We suggest booking on Saturday evenings as Darren and Angela have made the Joiners Arms a popular place to dine out serving traditional homemade locally sourced favourites such as poached salmon, steak and ale pie, a large range from the grill including lamb rump and duck breast. There is also a good selection for vegetarians including a nut roast, and the lunch menu has a varied selection of starters, mains and desserts and a selection of light lunches for the smaller appetites.

This handsomely decorated wood panelled Inn is in picture perfect setting and also offers a homely double en suite room with hearty breakfast included so that the area and this stunning Inn can be fully appreciated.

90 BRYSON'S OF KESWICK

42 Main Street, Keswick,
Cumbria CA12 5JD
Tel: 01768 772257   Fax: 01768 775456
e-mail: debra@brysonsofkeswick.co.uk
website: www.brysonsofkeswick.co.uk

A highlight of a visit to Keswick, **Bryson's of Keswick** have been in trading for over 60 years now and they are still going strong; Debra has been here for 3 years and is ably carrying on the excellent Bryson's reputation. Bryson's craft bakery started baking bread from locally milled flour more than 60 years ago on the same site that the shop and bakery stand today. A family business then as well as now, Bryson's is the place to go for high quality confectionery for that special treat!

Open between 8.30 am and 5.30 pm normally and between 9 am and 5 pm during the winter months, there is seating for 80 upstairs and another 30 outside if the weather is agreeable. The menu is extensive, offering everything from a snack to a full meal

to an afternoon tea. As you would expect from such heritage, all of the ingredients are sourced locally and all of the bakery products are created daily to ensure freshness. Downstairs, Bryson's also sells a vast range of locally made preserves, chocolates, biscuits etc and there is an area to buy takeaway goods made on site, e.g cakes, pies and pastries to enjoy on the move.

92 THRELKELD MINING MUSEUM

Threlkeld Quarry, Keswick,
Cumbria CA12 4TT
Tel: 017687 79747/01228 561883
website: www.threlkeldminingmuseum.co.uk

The Threlkeld Quarry & Mining Museum is situated three miles east of Keswick, in the heart of the breathtaking Lake District in Cumbria. The quarry and museum have been lovingly run by knowledgeable and dedicated staff for more than ten years, and the site continues to expand through the dedication of the staff and volunteers.

The quarry itself is a RIGS site and displays contacts between the "Skiddaw Slate" and the granite intrusion, as well as other fascinating features.

The museum now has a new mining section which has been developed with the help and cooperation of the Cumbria Amenity Trust Mining History Society and a number of individuals.

The Mining Room contains artefacts, plans and photographic records of explorations of many local mines, which, in this area, exploited copper, iron, lead, zinc, tungsten, graphite, barites and fluorite. A representative display of local minerals can be seen and there is a new section on lighting, drilling and explosives.

The museum offers activities for all the family, from budding geologists to hopeful prospectors, including an underground tour of a realistic mine, a quarry site with a unique collection of machinery and mineral panning.

There is ample free parking, a shop and refreshments available. Open 7 days a week from Easter to October.

200

91 WHITE HORSE INN

Scales, Keswick, Cumbria CA12 4SY
Tel: 01768 779883
e-mail: bj9er@yahoo.com

One that may be easily missed, but definitely worth the journey is the **White Horse Inn.** Situated just off the A66 the White Horse Inn is located at Scales and has beautiful surroundings. Dating back to 1610, the building has character, style and charm, equally traditional, historical and with a hint of modernism, brought about by the new tenants. Starting off life as a farmhouse and then alehouse, eventually becoming an inn in the early 18th century, the property was once a meeting pace for highway men and smugglers; today times have changed, but the social hub of the inn is still the same, with locals and tourists gathering to enjoy a real ale or two in a pleasant and warm environment.

Barry and Katy McGeachy, along with business partner Matthew Hall, bar supervisor Philip and head Chef Mike took over the reins here in March 2009 and already the recommendations for quality hospitality and service are arriving by word of mouth and by the number of customers returning time and time again. All of the aforementioned names in the team have past experience in licensing or catering and are like family, all getting on very well with one another.

Open every session and all day Saturday and Sunday there are 3 real ales to enjoy, Camerons Strongarm being the regular, with two rotating guest ales on offer. Food is also available, being a massive part of the inn's business. Served daily from 12-3pm and 6-9pm, with bar snacks being served all day Saturday and Sunday as an extra, head Chef Mike produces quality cuisine, using local produce and local suppliers wherever possible; however prime Aberdeen Angus beef is always used.

Snacks see nachos, homemade chips and bacon or sausage baps on the menu, whereas for lunch you may fancy a breakfast bun, white horse burger or venison pasty, all of which are served with homemade chips, providing great value for money. Throughout the evening there is a fabulous hot and spicy pork steak on offer, as well as Cumberland pie, which is black pudding and lamb in a hand made pie and grilled salmon fillet with a lemon sauce. Food can be eaten throughout the inn, creating a warm and sociable atmosphere and children are more than welcome, meaning that the White Horse Inn is great for families.

93 THE MILL INN

Mungrisdale, Penrith,
Cumbria CA11 0XR
Tel: 01768 779632
e-mail: info@the-millinn.co.uk
website: www.the-millinn.co.uk

The Mill Inn is set amongst some spectacular scenery in the heart of the Lake District, situated at the foot of Souther Fell in the lea of the Blencathra range and the picturesque Mungrisdale Valley.

Helen and James are proud to welcome you to this 17th century inn which provides warm comfortable beds, well kept ales and home cooked food. Approaching the Inn gives a welcoming first impression; the white and black exterior is adorned with farming paraphernalia and hanging baskets that provide bursts of colour. Inside is just as impressive; the décor manages to combine traditional features with modern comforts, most notable is the large open log fire, which warms even the coldest of hands in the winter.

There are six rooms available in this inn, 3 doubles and 3 twins, all of which are en suite and well appointed. In addition to the lounge bar and restaurant, there is an upstairs residence lounge and a games room, complete with a pool table and dartboard. The in house restaurant is very popular with locals and visitors alike; the menu is extensive and is comprised of classic pub fare, cooked with the finest of local produce.

94 SWALEDALE WATCH

Whelpo, Caldbeck, Cumbria CA7 8HQ
Tel: 016974 78409
e-mail: nan.savage@talk21.com
website: www.swaledale-watch.co.uk

For the last 25 years **Swaledale Watch** has been offering bed and breakfast accommodation in a gloriously unspoilt location set within the Lake District National Park.

Arnold and Nan Savage have been welcoming families, couples and friends in to their family home, providing guest accommodation, which is shared between the main house and the nearby annex, a stylishly converted cowshed. There are 5 rooms on offer, each of which are luxuriously furnished and include a family room, and 4 (all ensuite) rooms. The tariff is competitive and includes a generous cooked breakfast, which is enjoyed by many repeat visitors.

The property is set in wonderful grounds on a working sheep farm and guests are free to wander around the 300 acres, taking in the breathtaking views and experiencing the birth of lambs (lambing season is the highlight of the year). With many activities to do near by, Arnold and Nan are happy to recommend nearby walks and places of interest. They also supply books, games and puzzles for those rainy days, making Swaledale Watch perfect for everyone.

95 PONDEROSA GUEST HOUSE

Uldale, Wigton, Cumbria CA7 1HA
Tel: 01697 371805
website: www.ponderosakeswick.co.uk

Nestled among the fells and valleys of the northern part of the Lake District National Park is a truly remarkable guest house. **Ponderosa Guest House** sits in its own grounds on a working sheep and dairy farm, and provides a perfect retreat from the hustle and bustle of everyday life. With over 25 years experience in welcoming bed and breakfast guests, there's no one better to look after you during your stay, than Margaret Wilson. She has lived in Uldale for over 40 years and is always on hand to offer guests help where needed. For those wishing to explore the local area Ponderosa offers the perfect base with an unbeatable host.

Guests can choose between two luxuriously furnished en suite bedrooms with fantastic views across the

countryside. A hearty full English breakfast starts the day and guests can enjoy a traditional home-cooked dinner if pre-arranged with Margaret. Children over the age of 12 are more than welcome but the house cannot accept dogs.

The self-catering accommodation, for up to five guests, is in an adjacent cottage equipped with all the mod cons. Both the B&B and the self-catering facilities are perfect for touring or walking holidays, and an ideal stopover between England and Scotland.

96 SNITTLEGARTH LODGES

Snittlegarth, Ireby, Wigton,
Cumbria CA7 1HE
Tel: 01697 371235
e-mail: green_snittlegarth@hotmail.com

Country roads lead from the A591 and A595 to the quiet village of Snittlegarth, where friendly couple, Roddy and Ros Green provide superior self-catering accommodation in two luxurious pine lodges. Situated in an isolated and picturesque location **Snittlegarth Lodges** offer the perfect opportunity to relax and unwind in a peaceful setting. The popular lodges were created and opened in January 2007 and have already won many repeat guests. Open all year round, they have superbly appointed interiors that contain everything needed for a relaxing, come-as-you-please holiday.

Each lodge sleeps up to four guests, and short breaks are available at certain times of the year.

The woodland setting is home to abundant wildlife, including red squirrels, and this whole area, at the top end of the Lake District national Park, is great walking country and offers easy access to most of the Western Lakes, major towns and beyond. The attractions hereabouts are many and varied: rambling and bird watching around Bassenthwaite Lake, climbing on Skiddaw, spectacular scenery and Trotters World of Animals, providing a great day out for all the family.

The Wheatsheaf @ Embleton,
Cockermouth, Cumbria CA13 9XP
Tel: 01768 776408

The Wheatsheaf is a great inn situated amongst some stunning scenery in the Lake District. Set in the quaint village of Embleton, home to around 300 people, the pub is within easy reach of the A66 and the nearby town of Cockermouth. From the pub, excellent views of the surrounding countryside can be admired, the Cumbrian hills creating a magnificent backdrop for this establishment. The premises are clean and welcoming on approach, the white walls are set off by the black framed windows and a little wooden porch provides a wonderful entrance. Mother and son team Evelyn and Jonathon Hill took

control of the Wheatsheaf in December 2008 and have 7 years experience in the hospitality industry. On arrival, they set about improving this already good inn, a complete refurbishment was the result and the premises are now in a superb condition. As a result of the refurbishment, the interior is just as nice as you would expect with comfortable dining areas in well decorated surroundings.

The bar is very well stocked and hosts 2 to 3 real ales at any one time; Jennings Bitter and Cumberland Ale are favourites among the friendly locals. The pub is open every evening Sunday to Saturday and for lunchtimes on Saturday and Sunday. The Wheatsheaf serves food every evening between 6 pm and 9 pm and between 12 pm and 2 pm on Saturday and Sunday lunchtimes.

Due to the popular nature of the restaurant, it is essential to make a reservation to dine on Saturday evening or Sunday lunchtime to avoid disappointment. Evelyn and Jonathon employ professional chefs to cook all the food to order, all the ingredients are sourced within Cumbria where possible and as tantalising as the menu is, there is even a daily specials board to choose from. The menu is composed of good old classic pub fare, cooked to perfection by the professional chefs. Examples of the great menu are wholetail Whitby scampi, served with home made chips, garden peas, tartare sauce and a dressed salad; local Cumberland sausage, served with fried egg and onion rings and, not to be missed, the home made steak and ale pie with home made chips. For those lucky enough to visit on Sunday, there is a choice of local beef or leg of lamb roasts with all the accoutrements!

98 RAVENSTONE LODGE

Bassenthwaite, Nr Keswick,
Cumbria CA12 4QG
Tel: 01768 776629 Fax: 01768 776638
e-mail: enquiries@raventonelodge.co.uk
website: www.ravenstonelodge.co.uk

Ravenstone Lodge is a privately owned hotel situated amongst magnificent Lake District scenery beneath Skiddaw and between Bassenthwaite Lake and Ullock Pike and just a few miles from Keswick. The great location means that the hotel is a perfect base for guests exploring the beauty of the Lake District. The stone built property stands in six acres of woodland and pastureland and appears warm and inviting as you approach, with the interior only adding to the pleasant atmosphere.

The hotel boasts 9 rooms, all en suite and named for various features found on nearby Skiddaw. The rooms are available in a range of shapes and sizes to suit every need and budget. All of the rooms have a TV and radio, hair dryer and tea & coffee making facilities. Internet connections are available through the hotel's wifi broadband.

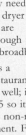

There is a fabulous restaurant in the hotel as well; it only seats 25 so it is essential for non-residents to make reservations to avoid disappointment. For breakfast, guests are able to choose from the simple and healthy options or the hearty full English! The restaurant is open for lunchtime and evening service all year round.

99 LAKELAND COTTAGE HOLIDAYS

Melbecks, Bassenthwaite, Keswick,
Cumbria CA12 4QX
Tel: 017687 76065 Fax: 017687 76869
e-mail: Info@lakelandcottages.co.uk
website: www.lakelandcottages.co.uk

Covering a wide range of holiday accommodations in a wide range of differing locations, **Lakeland Holiday Cottages** has a large portfolio of 'many years standing' beautiful and historical properties available to hire. Introducing a variety of new properties within the Northern Lakes area, the buildings are stunning, offering a number of different facilities, depending on your requirements.

Each property is chosen by the business' owners Jo and David Burton, who are dedicated to ensuring customer satisfaction and overall enjoyment throughout visitors stay. The owner's first hand knowledge of each property means that they can recommend the perfect property to suit your needs, whether it be Derwent Farmhouse, sleeping 6, with a quiet courtyard or

Whitesde, sleeping 4 in a lovely, modern apartment.

Each property is independently graded by the English Tourism Council and have been awarded a 'Quality Star' rating. The couple are in charge of about 60 properties sleeping from 2 to 8 or 9, all combining period charm with up to date comfort and amenities. The area covered by Lakeland Holiday cottages covers from Borrowdale and Newlands to Penruddock and Keswick. England and Scotland.

101 DALEGARTH GUESTHOUSE AND CAMPSITE

Hassness estate, Buttermere,
Cockermouth, Cumbria   CA13 9XA
Tel: 01768 770233
e-mail: dalegarthhouse@hotmail.co.uk

Dalegarth Guest House and Campsite stands in Buttermere surrounded by thousands of acres of picturesque countryside filled with forests teaming with wildlife and the stunning Buttermere lake. You'll find it just off the B5289 between Seatoller and Lorton.

Dalegarth's owners James and Kelly took charge of this glorious site in June this year but their reputation for quality facilities and outstanding hospitality is spreading the length of Cumbria day by day. This lovely couple have been coming to the area for many years, getting married locally and making

it a dream to one day own and run the property themselves. James and Kelly are currently living that dream and are making others come true too. This place is a real haven for any holiday maker with the option of staying in the main house which holds nine rooms, four of which are en suite. Four are located on the ground floor but there is a good variety of size with all rooms including doubles, family and twin rooms all of which have their own tea and coffee making facilities for your convenience. The house also sports a large spacious and comfortable living room complete with its own real log fire and a good selection of books, games and music to use at your leisure. All the room tariffs include a hearty full English breakfast with a continental and vegetarian option also available.

For those of you that prefer the outdoor lifestyle Dalegarth also sports a large 35 pitch campsite which has its own cold storage area, drying room, lockable garage space for motorbikes and cycles with hot showers. The pitches are laid out over four flat terraces just two minutes walk from the edge of the serene Buttermere lake, nestled below the peak of Robinson making this an ideal area for walkers of all ages and abilities as one of the most spectacular fell walking areas in England. Buttermere is also a haven for bird watchers and animal lovers alike as its home to woodpeckers, cuckoos, golden eagles, deer, foxes, badgers and otter families. Families with smaller children can rest assured however that there are plenty of attractions nearby and James and Kelly will also provide packed lunches full of homemade treats.

Whatever your reasons for visiting this stunning area of Cumbria, sightseeing, walking or just relaxing Dalegarth is the perfect choice.

103 ASHNESS FARM

Borrowdale, Keswick,
Cumbria CA12 5UN
Tel: 01768 727364
e-mail: enquiries@ashnessfarm.co.uk
website: www.ashnessfarm.co.uk

The six mile long valley that forms Borrowdale is thought to be the most beautiful in the Lake District and 750 acres of this spectacular scenery belongs to **Ashness Farm**. Dating back to the 16th century, this impressive farmhouse boasts unrivalled views of the surrounding mountains and countryside, including

Derwent Water and the famous Ashness Bridge. It is from this farmhouse that Anne and her family farm the 750 acres of land, mainly Herdwick sheep and Belted Galloway cattle, as well as a number of differing breeds of pig. The farm is in a great location, close to the A66, which is found on junction 40 of the M6. With easy access to the rest of the Lake District, Ashness Farm is the ideal base from which to explore the area, be it by foot, bike or car. For those out and about, Anne and her family will happily provide a packed lunch to take away, to ensure you won't be hungry.

On approach, the large stone building with slate roof looks like a typical farmhouse, however, as you step inside it is clear that the place has been decorated with comfort and practicality in mind. That is not to say it has lost its traditional values; there are ancient wooden beams exposed everywhere and the large log fire will warm even the coldest of cockles! There are five superior en suite rooms in the farmhouse, which are available to hire all year round, except for Christmas and New Year. All of the rooms have been named for local features; Amboth, Catbells, Causey Pike, Grisdale Pike and Maiden Moor. The rooms are all upstairs, three of them have baths and the other two have walk-in shower units. Guests have the use of several facilities on site, including a resident's lounge, an outdoor play area for children and fishing.

Included in the very reasonable price is a hearty breakfast, and it is hearty, the breakfast has to be seen to be believed as it is fit for a king! You start with a huge range of cereals, juices, yoghurts etc and then follow it up with a farm produced breakfast. Bacon, sausages, and eggs, all from Anne's farm are the highlight and ensure you won't be going hungry!

100 WHINLATTER FOREST PARK

Braithwaite, Keswick,
Cumbria CA12 5TW
Tel: 017687 78469
e-mail: whinlatter@forestry.gsi.gov.uk
website: www.forestry.gov.uk/
northwestengland

Whinlatter Forest Park is an ideal venue for all sorts of outdoor activities. There are walking and orienteering routes, and the more energetic can walk through the forest and out onto the surrounding fells. Or bring your bicycle and cycle on the traffic free forest roads - provided you don't mind the hills!

The forest also provides excellent opportunities for photography, sketching and painting, botany, or bird watching. Of particular interest to birdwatchers are the Bassenthwaite Ospreys, which have nested on Bassenthwaite Lake since 2001. The award-winning Lake District Osprey Project provides viewing facilities for these magnificent birds at Whinlatter on the giant screens with up close and personal images of the nest. Nearby, Dodd Wood view point offers fantastic panoramic views of the birds natural environment where you may be lucky enough to see them catching fish on the lake, during the breeding season, April to the end of August.

At Whinlatter children are also catered for too, the gigantic walk in badger sett , the Rabbit Run and Fox Trot trails and the adventure playground will keep them entertained for ages. Supporting your visit to Whinlatter, the Visitor Centre includes an attractive gift shop and Siskins café.

Opening hours: 10am - 5pm daily in summer and 10am - 4pm daily in winter. Closed Christmas and New Year.

102 SEATOLLER FARM

Borrowdale, Keswick, Cumbria CA125XN
Tel: 017687 77232 Fax: 017687 77232
e-mail: info@seatollerfarm.co.uk
website: www.seatollerfarm.co.uk

Located at the head of the stunning Borrowdale valley amidst the towering fells is **Seatoller Farm,** a traditional Lakeland 16th Century working hill farm. The 1000 acre farm and surrounding area is owned by the National Trust and has been a mecca for walkers for generations with its superb location. Unbeatable scenery is to be found in every direction so there is no shortage of first class walks from the farm.

Offering an oasis in which to relax and recharge ones batteries, guests have a choice of B&B accommodation, self-catering or camping. Whatever choice is preferred, dedicated hosts Christine and Stephen will certainly ensure that all guests have a warm, friendly and enjoyable stay. There are three comfortable en-suite rooms available on B&B basis and guests are offered tea/coffee and homemade baking upon arrival. The hearty cumbrian breakfast consists of local produce where possible and will set

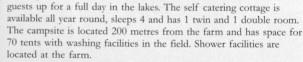

guests up for a full day in the lakes. The self catering cottage is available all year round, sleeps 4 and has 1 twin and 1 double room. The campsite is located 200 metres from the farm and has space for 70 tents with washing facilities in the field. Shower facilities are located at the farm.

There are plenty of activities on the doorstep for the whole family to enjoy including Keswick climbing wall, Keswick museum, Cumberland pencil Museum and Honister slate mine.

104 AGRICULTURAL HOTEL

Castlegate, Penrith, Cumbria CA11 7JE
Tel: 01768 862622
e-mail: info@the-agricultural-hotel.co.uk
website: www.the-agricultural-hotel.co.uk

The Agricultural Hotel is a friendly, convivial family run inn close to the centre of the historical town of Penrith. Just a two minute drive from the M6 and a minute's walk from the train station, the hotel is in a great location for those requiring a base from which to explore the Lake District. This large, handsome building has a well documented history; built in 1807, the hotel was one of the first places in the world to hold a cattle auction. There is still the hatch where farmers would bring their cattle up to the bar with them as they got a beer!

This family run hotel, featuring parents Gary and Wendy, son Paul and daughter Heather, boasts 6 en suite rooms, comprised of 3 twins and 3 doubles. The reasonable rates include a hearty breakfast and the rooms are well stocked with everything you could need. Food is served in the popular restaurant daily between 11 am and 9 pm, son Paul is the head chef and the menu is packed full of classic pub fare cooked using the best of local Lake District produce. The bar is always full of locals trading stories and enjoying the well kept real ales on offer, a feature recognised by CAMRA.

106 RHEGED DISCOVERY CENTRE

Redhills, Stainton, Penrith,
Cumbria CA11 0DQ
Tel: 01768 860018   Fax: 01768 868 002
website: www.rheged.com

Penrith's most spectacular visitor attraction, **Rheged Discovery Centre**, dedicates itself to "a celebration of 2000 years of Cumbria's history, mystery and magic - as never seen before".

Open all year round, the Centre is housed in the largest earth-covered building in Europe, and is carefully designed to blend harmoniously with the surrounding fells. Although it is built on 7 levels, from the outside Rheged looks like just another Lakeland hill. Inside, babbling brooks and massive limestone crags replicate the Cumbrian landscape but the centrepiece is a 6-storey high, giant cinema screen, 60 feet wide and 48 feet high, showing up to 5 spectacular movies daily.

Only a couple of minutes drive from Exit 40 of the M6, Rheged also offers visitors a permanent National Mountaineering Exhibition, 12 carefully selected shops, restaurants, children's indoor play area, gateway tourist information centre with regular daytime and evening events.

105 SCOTT'S FISH BAR & STEAKHOUSE GRILL

34 Burrowgate, Penrith,
Cumbria CA11 7TA
Tel: 01768 890838
e-mail: dharding66@btinternet.com

Scott's Fish Bar and Steakhouse Grill is located centrally in popular Penrith, in Burrowgate. Offering an array of chip shop classics, wonderful steaks and a few other mouth-watering dishes, this business is well known in the area as one of the best places to dine for fast food, with a difference.

At Scott's fish bar all the food served is homemade daily, using only the finest and freshest local produce. There is a large range of fantastic fish dishes available as well as award winning Lakeland steaks, which are cooked to your liking. All the meats used in the dishes are sourced from within Cumbria and the fish is brought daily from North East Ports.

Owner Dave Harding and his son Dan have been here since 2008 and have made this property one to put on the map. The father and son duo have previous experience in the trade and still run a chip shop in the town, linking the two businesses nicely. The premises offers something for everyone as not only is there the main restaurant, but adjacent there is also a takeaway, so you can enjoy the splendid food from the comfort of your own home.

This very popular place to dine is open 7 days a week between 11.30am-2pm and 4.30pm-8pm, with extended hours on Thursdays, Fridays and Saturdays until 10pm. With seating for 54, the restaurant is of a good size and is licensed so you can enjoy a few beverages from the menu, lagers and beers, spirits and wines.

The menu is vast with a lunchtime menu, served until 1.30pm, including dishes such as speciality fish cakes made with either smoked haddock, tuna and mozzarella, salmon and dill or Thai cod and mash. There is in addition a large array to choose from, something to tantalise the taste buds and satisfy even the fussiest of tastes. Seafood lasagne, crispy coated camembert and calamari rings are available to start, followed by wonderfully prepared fish dishes of poached salmon fillet, breaded plaice and a delicious crispy coated fish medley. There is also crispy chicken breast served with two sides, steaks, cooked to your liking and vegetarian meals of three-cheese and broccoli pasta bake. All meals are of a reasonable price, meaning that visitors return again and again.

107 BROUGHAM CASTLE

Brougham, Penrith, Cumbria CA10 2AA
Tel: 01768 862488
website: www.english-heritage.org.uk

Picturesque **Brougham Castle** was begun in the early 13th century by Robert de Vieuxpont, near the site of a Roman fort guarding the crossing of the River Eamont. His great keep largely survives, reinforced by an impressive double gatehouse and other 14th-century additions made by the powerful Clifford family, Wardens of the Marches. The castle thus became a formidable barrier to Scots invaders.

Though both James I and Charles I stayed here, Brougham was in poor condition by the time of the Civil War. It was thereafter restored as a residence by the indomitable Lady Anne Clifford (see also Brough Castle and the Countess Pillar): she often visited with her traveling 'court', and died here in 1676.

Today, the site features an introductory exhibition, including carved stones from the nearby Roman fort. The site has good wheelchair access to entry point, toilet, shop and small introductory exhibition. There is a wheelchair route to the castle ruins, which enables visitors to make a circuit of the site and read the interpretation panels. The keep is not accessible to wheelchairs.

108 HORNBY HALL COUNTRY GUEST HOUSE

Brougham, Penrith, Cumbria CA10 2AR
Tel: 01768 891114
e-mail: enquire@hornbyhall.co.uk
website: www.hornbyhall.co.uk

Located on a working farm within a peaceful, rural setting yet only three miles from Penrith is **Hornby Hall Country Guest House**, offering the very best in gracious country house accommodation. This attractive property, built of local red sandstone by Edward Birbeck, is Grade 2 listed and dates back to 1550. Guests today will find a perfect combination of original features, antique furnishings and up to date amenities.

The premises have been recently refurbished by present owner Christine Westropp, adding further charm to this delightful guest house. Within the main house there are five superb en suite rooms with a further two enchanting singles in the tower, reached via a spiral staircase. All the rooms are south facing and overlook the stunning grounds. The Great Hall with its sandstone floor and large open fireplace is extremely eye catching and the perfect place to dine. Guests are welcome to

stay on B&B only or dinner, B&B. Christine's cooking is second to none and her breakfasts will keep guests going all day! Her evening meals are a must as she uses local produce, some from the estate, and organic produce whenever possible.

Fishing is available on the River Eamont and the guest house can be booked for fishing/shooting parties. Hornby Hall provides that special ambience for private parties and special occasions and is guaranteed to delight all who visit.

211

109 THE BEEHIVE

Eamont Bridge, Nr. Penrith,
Cumbria CA10 2BX
Tel: 01768 862081
website: www.thebeehivepenrith.co.uk

Built in 1727, **The Beehive** is an 18th century inn offering all the best in hospitality as well as providing a warm and friendly atmosphere, perfect for relaxing with friends and family. Enjoyed thoroughly by all who visit, the beehive is a wonderful family run business, offering great food and drink throughout the day.

Run by Martyn and Samantha Swaby, the young and enthusiastic couple have really put their stamp on the place. The property is becoming ever so popular with both locals and tourists and there is always a hospitable buzz surrounding the bar, inviting to all.

Food is served daily from 12-9pm and there are a range of sandwiches, jacket potatoes and salads, as well as pub classics of whole tail scampi, three cheese pasta bake, homemade steak and ale pie and large mixed grill, which comes from 21 day mature beef, which has been selected from locally sourced meat. There are also main courses of suet pudding, chicken and bacon melt and a delicious homemade creamy mushroom strogonoff. All of this can be washed down with one of two lovely real ales always on tap.

110 THE CROWN HOTEL

Eamont Bridge, Penrith,
Cumbria CA10 2BX
Tel: 01768 892092
e-mail: crownhotel@msn.com

Located only 1 mile from Penrith town centre but set in the beautiful Eden Valley, **The Crown Hotel** at Eamont Bridge is a welcoming former coaching inn dating back to 1707. For the past sixteen years, owner Wendy Graham-Weston, has worked tirelessly in her beloved Inn and has consequently established a glowing reputation for the quality of the appetising home-made food served here.

The chalkboard menu offers a cosmopolitan selection of dishes, including Indian, Chinese and Italian, along with home-grown favourites such as smoked BBQ chicken and minced beef pie. Vegetarian choices might include a Broccoli & Pasta Bake or a vegetarian tikka masala. Extra special meals include choices such as duck a l'orange and lamb Henry. Only locally sourced meats and vegetables are used. Food is served every lunchtime and evening during the week, and all day on Saturday and Sunday and bank holidays. A tasty carvery with a choice of roasts is added to the menu on Sundays, as these are extremely popular it is wise to book ahead. Great value continues with children eating free when one adult purchases a main dish.

The Crown also has 15 beautifully appointed guest bedrooms, 6 of which have en suite facilities. The tariff includes a delicious breakfast. All major credit cards apart from American Express and Diners are accepted. There is plenty of parking for guests convenience.

112 THE SUN INN

Newton Reigny, nr Penrith,
Cumbria CA11 0AP
Tel: 01768 867055
e-mail: thesuninn@talktalkbusiness.net

The pretty village of Newton Reigny, a couple of miles west of Penrith, is home to the marvellous **Sun Inn**, a popular, traditional free house dating from the 17th century. Tenants Adrian and Carolyne Stevenson-Jones took over here in January 2007, moving from a public house in Glasson Dock.

With over 34 years of joint experience in the trade, tenants Keith and Liz decided that The Sun Inn should be their next venture and took over the premises in 2007. With so much experience and knowledge of the trade, it comes as no surprise that this inn is such a popular choice for visitors and locals alike.

Open all day everyday, food is served from 7am through to 10pm, and Liz prepares traditional pub food with a modern twist. Using locally sourced produce as much as possible, Liz has created a menu that offers something for everyone; with lemon sole, daubes of beef, venison steak, stuffed chicken, nutters steak pie and vegetarian chilli being just a few of the options.

The bar offers the usual selection of hot and cold drinks as well as three real ales from the Thwaites brewery range, Wainwrights Bitter being the regular. A garden at the back of the inn runs down to a picturesque stream, providing a very pleasant spot in the summer months. The Sun is not only a delightful place for a drink and a meal, it's also the perfect base to relax, unwind and discover all the attractions of the region.

The accommodation comprises 5 well appointed upstairs rooms, four of them with en suite facilities and one of them a family room with its own private bathroom. Children are very welcome, and the inn can cater for private functions and parties – even a dance floor is available. A quiz night is held every Wednesday from 9pm and all are welcome to join in the fun.

The scenery hereabouts is truly beautiful, and the inn itself is as pretty as a picture in the summer, when the award-winning gardens and hanging baskets are in full bloom. Penrith is close by and the Lake District National Park is on the doorstep. Ullswater is six miles away, and other places to visit include Aira Force Waterfall, Whinlatter Forest Park, Dove Cottage, Eden Ostrich World and Trotters Wold of Animals. This is also excellent walking country, and golf, riding, pony trekking and fishing are all available nearby.

111 KINGS ARMS

Stainton, Penrith, Cumbria CA11 0EP
Tel: 01768 862778
e-mail: adakeman@sky.com

The purpose built inn the **Kings Arms**, was constructed in 1721 and this impressive property has been a popular haunt for locals and visitors since. Open every session and all day on Saturdays the inn boasts three well kept real ales Courage Best, Black Sheep and a rotating guest ale.

Good quality, home cooked food is available every lunchtime and evening with guests choosing from the extensive menu or the specials board, which varies on a daily basis. The menu is punctuated with classic pub favourites, such as an excellent steak and kidney pie and locally made Cumberland sausages with mash potato and onion gravy.

Situated just off the A66 and close to junction 40 of the M6, the Kings Arms is in a very good position. The exterior is well kept and welcoming and the interior is spacious and traditional, while outside there is a small garden to the rear and patio seating out the front. Leaseholders Richard Jakeman and his son Adam have many years experience in the hospitality trade, providing truly excellent food, drink and service to all of their guests.

113 BOOT & SHOE

Greystoke, Penrith, Cumbria CA11 0TP
Tel: 01768 483343
e-mail: info@bootandshoegreystoke.co.uk
website:
www.bootandshoegreystoke.co.uk

The picturesque village of Greystoke, long known for being the ancestral home of Tarzan, is situated about 5 miles west of Penrith on the B5288 and it is here you can find **The Boot & Shoe**.

This former coaching inn and post house is now over 400 years old and has seen many tenants over its long history. The latest tenants, Jan and Ban Mandale have been the proprietors for 2 years and the premises are doing a roaring trade. The stone building has planters and hanging baskets littered around the exterior giving bursts of colour and giving a great first impression. The interior is much the same, wrought iron furniture and a large inglenook fireplace promote the warm welcome received as you enter the place.

The bar is very well stocked, open all day every day, there are three real ales on offer, Black Sheep as well as two rotating guest ales, normally from local brewers if possible. A major draw to the establishment is the food, available between 12 noon and 3 pm and 6 pm to 9 pm daily, the menu consists of classic British pub fare, cooked extremely well using the best of local produce. The Boot & Shoe also offers accommodation in the form of four en suite rooms; the reasonable tariff includes a breakfast.

114 THE HORSE AND FARRIER

Dacre, Penrith, Cumbria CA11 0HL
Tel: 01768 486541
Fax: 01768 486764
e-mail: office@thehorseandfarrier.co.uk

Dacre is a classic Cumbrian village filled with picturesque cottages, a castle, an unusual church and a thriving community pub - **The Horse and Farrier**. It is situated in the heart of Dacre, just off the main A66 or A592, just south of Penrith.

The olde worlde interior of The Horse and Farrier supports its 18th century status, as it used to stand on a former Drovers Road. The warm combination of original stone walling and a wood panelled bar and cottage feel helps create the cosy atmosphere the Horse and Farrier is renowned for. Leaseholders Susi and Alistair only took over in February this year, but already are attracting return tourists and visitors and are a hit with the locals who are thrilled to have their village pub back to its old self again.

Susi and Alistair are proud to serve two real ales, Deuchers IPA and Cumberland Ale and they plan to add a guest ale before too long. They also serve a good variety of other beers, wine, spirits and soft drinks. But this stunning pub is also a fantastic place to dine at any time of the day. Head Chef Shirley serves up a wonderfully tempting menu from between 12-3pm and 6-9pm. The lunch menu offers a variety of homemade soup, sandwiches, ciabatta, jacket potatoes, or light main meals such as smoked bacon or Mediterranean vegetables carbonara with penne pasta. The evening menu also has a hearty variety to choose from with starters like the trio of salmon with salad and honey mustard dressing, and a range of sumptuous meaty dishes such as the marinated lamb henry served on caramelised red onion mash with minted gravy and seasonal veg, and a selection of homemade puddings to finish off. On Sundays there is a hearty range of traditional Sunday dishes with a twist, and a specials menu each day ranging from smoked mackerel pâté with cheesy oatcakes to black pudding, smoked bacon and apple terrine with a creamy wholegrain mustard sauce and salad garnish or homemade pork and apple pie served with chips, garden peas and cider gravy. There really is a fantastic choice for everyone (half portions are available for children) and it is all locally sourced wherever possible. There is room for 45 people in the separate dining area with large French windows opening onto the countryside beyond. We advise booking from Thurs-Sun, all major credit cards accepted apart from Amex and Diners.

115 POOLEY BRIDGE INN

Pooley Bridge, Lake Ullswater,
Cumbria CA10 2NN
Tel: 01768 486215
e-mail: stay@pooleybridgeinn.co.uk
website: www.pooleybridgeinn.co.uk

Situated in the heart of picturesque Pooley Bridge, on the banks of Lake Ullswater (and a convenient 5 minute car journey from Penrith station), the **Pooley Bridge Inn** is a must-visit spot for locals and visitors alike. This family-run Inn has an ever-growing reputation for their excellent food and service, which can only be due to the work of the licensees Keith and Carolyn Wray, and their head chef Steve Angel all of whom ran a very successful public house before taking over the Pooley Bridge Inn and really putting it on the map. Although in appearance it is a traditional late 19th century Inn, it has all of the mod-cons to ensure your every comfort, including free Wi-Fi connection and colour TV.

In the bar area, with its beautiful fireplace and original timber ceiling, you can kickback and enjoy a glass of one of the rotated real ales (one usually coming from a local micro-brewery) and a locally supplied homemade meal. These include delicious dishes such as Traditional Homemade Pie of the Day and Hunters Chicken (chicken breast wrapped in bacon, topped with mozzarella and BBQ sauce). In addition to their menu, which also includes options for children, there is always a specials board to give a great range of choice. On Sundays a traditional roast is added to this menu, where the indecisive among you are able to have up to 3 different meats on one plate! If the weather is fine, there is an outdoor seating area in the stable courtyard, which is the perfect place to relax and enjoy your meal.

The Pooley Bridge Inn offers comfortable accommodation upstairs; all rooms are en-suite with either shower or bath and boast central heating, a colour television and tea and coffee making facilities. Seven of the eleven rooms have a balcony out onto the front of the Inn. Accommodation prices start from a very modest £75, although if real luxury is your aim then there are several elegant four-poster beds available (all of which are also rooms with balconies). The prices for all of the rooms include a hearty breakfast.

For the accommodation it is advisable to book in advance in order to avoid disappointment. Food is served daily between 12 noon to 8.30pm. There is a large off-road car park to avoid any worries about parking, and disabled access to the bar area.

116 PARK FOOT

Howtown Road, Pooley Bridge, Penrith,
Cumbria CA10 2NA
Tel: 017684 86309
Fax: 017684 86041
e-mail: holiday@ parkfootullswater.co.uk
website: www.parkfoot.co.uk

One of Cumbria's premier holiday parks, **Park Foot** offers the very best in caravan, camping and self-catering accommodation. Set in 40 acres of picturesque grounds looking down on Ullswater, the park was created in 1949 and is still owned and run by the same family. The caravan and camping area is superbly equipped with a full range of amenities, including a shop and licensed bar. Some caravans are available for sale.

If you prefer self-catering, Park Foot has a total of 15 different properties to choose from. Blanton House is a handsome stone building recently converted to a high standard into 2 separate holiday cottages, each of which can sleep up to 6 people. Then there's Parklands, a lovely detached bungalow which can accommodate up to 10. Woodside Cottages is a small row of 5 cottages, each of which sleeps between 4-6 people. Also available are 2 lodges, 4 log cabins and 'Beckside', a stone-built cottage with disabled access which can accommodate up to 6 people. It is located next to the shop and tennis court, and opposite the clubhouse and reception. Out of season, short breaks are available in the self-catering properties

117 THE WHITE LION INN

Patterdale nr Penrith,
Cumbria CA11 0NW
Tel: 01768 482214

The White Lion Inn has a tradition of hospitality that dates back over two centuries. It enjoys a peaceful setting in scenic Patterdale at the edge of Ullswater on the sweeping road leading to the Kirkstone Pass, the Lake District's highest pass open to motor traffic, offering breathtaking views for miles around. Visitors and their dogs are assured of the warmest welcomes from owner Rita Dawes and licensee-managers Alastair and Mandy Howard-Carter.

They provide an extensive menu sampling traditional light snacks and lunches, seasonal fish dishes and a choice of hearty dishes including Beef in Guiness, an 8oz sirloin steak simmered in rich Guinness sauce with onions, mushrooms and peppers served with peas, Lamb Henry or Mediterranean Vegetable Risotto delicately flavoured with white wine, herbs

and sun-drenched tomatoes. Food is served from 12-9pm, sandwiches and

breakfasts are served until 6pm. The bar is open all day every day also offering two real ales, one from the Cumbrian Tirril Brewery and a rotating guest ale.

The White Lion Inn also offers seven guest bedrooms, five ensuite, the others with private bathrooms, which provide a quiet comfortable base for a relaxing break away in the beauty of the Lake District.

118 THE QUEENS HEAD INN

Lower Green, Askham,
Cumbria CA10 2PF
Tel: 01931 712225
e-mail: parkL702@aol.com
website: www.queensheadaskham.com

Located in the heart of the picturesque village of Askham, **The Queens Head Inn** is a traditional village inn. The inn, owned by Keith and Lynne Park, dates back to 1672 and is a grade II listed building within the Lake District National Park. Originally tourists to the area themselves they enjoyed it so much that in November 2008 they took over the inn, which gets more popular by the day. The experienced owners, who had worked in bars and restaurants on the border of Scotland previously, offer an excellent menu, serving lunch and dinner every day with daily specials that change regularly to take advantage of local and seasonal variety.

"The Queens" as it is known by locals is popular with tourists and local people alike because of its warm and friendly atmosphere. Two open fireplaces in the main bar, which offers a range of fine ales, keep visitors warm on winter nights.

Visitors can eat, to suit their mood, in the main bar or the newly refurbished dining room. Keith and Lynne pride themselves on the quality of the food they serve, which is available daily between 12pm-2.30pm and 6pm-9pm. They have just taken on a new chef, who will work alongside Lynne, to create an exciting new menu. Roasts are served daily along with many mouth-watering choices, including Crofters Pie – made with real haggis. The inn, which is open all year round, offers two real ales and visitors can enjoy a game of pool in the pool room.

The Queens Head has four tastefully furnished en-suite bedrooms, one which boasts a four poster bed. The Inn welcomes children and pets and has a secure rear car park. Located three miles south of Penrith off the A6 and on the western bank of the River Lowther there are numerous off-site activities for visitors to enjoy, including, fishing and shooting, which have to be pre-arranged. Close by is the River Lowther, which provides some of the best wild brown trout fishing in England. Accompanied red deer and roe deer stalking is available on the Lowther Estate, along with various other forms of rough shooting. Keen walkers are close to the fells, which give views of nearby Ullswater. Askham offers plenty of footpaths and bridleways through woods, pastures and open fells.

119 THE GREYHOUND HOTEL

Main Street, Shap, Cumbria CA10 3PW
Tel: 01931 716474
e-mail: info@greyhoundshap.co.uk
website: www.greyhoundshap.co.uk

A famous Westmorland hostelry, **The Greyhound Hotel** has been dispensing hospitality for almost 330 years. Way back in 1680, newly-weds Richard and Ann Whinfel extended their recently inherited property and opened The Greyhound as a coaching inn where the "New Times" horse-drawn coaches used to stop. Business must have been good since Richard and Ann extended west in 1684 and at the same time built Green Farm on the opposite side of the main road to supply the inn with its fresh produce. Their son William extended the inn to its present size in 1703 - a date stone on the outside of the building commemorates this new building. The stone has the initials AW and WW with the date 1703 and a crude depiction of a greyhound. Some 40 years later, it is recorded that Bonnie Prince Charlie stayed at the inn on his march south with his Highlanders in 1745.

Today, mine host at the Greyhound is Rob Furber who has more than 25 years experience in the hospitality business. He has made good, quality food based on locally sourced ingredients a priority. At lunchtime, you'll find a good choice of hot and cold sandwiches, salads and baguettes, as well as old favourites such as Whitby scampi, Cumberland sausage, steak & ale pie, and fresh cod and chips. For vegetarians, there's a tasty dish of roasted Mediterranean vegetables topped with a slab of grilled Mozzarella and served with braised rice.

A somewhat different menu is available in the evening and includes locally reared rump steak, the Greyhound's own confit of duck (a long term favourite), and a slow-cooked Lamb Henry. Children have their own menu and some of the dishes are available in small portions for those with lighter appetites.

To accompany your meal, the bar stocks a comprehensive range of alcoholic beverages, including up to 8 real ales during the summer months with Black Sheep and Lancaster Ale as the regular brews.

The Greyhound also offers comfortable accommodation in 12 en suite rooms, some of which have recently been refurbished to a de luxe grading. The hotel's location has made it a welcome stopover for walkers along Alfred Wainwright's famous Coast to Coast walk, and also for travellers along the M6 whose junction 39 is just a mile away.

120 THE GEORGE HOTEL

Front Street, Orton, Penrith,
Cumbria CA10 3RJ
Tel: 01539 624229
e-mail: thegeorgehotel-orton@hotmail.co.uk
website: www.thegeorgehotelorton.com

The George Hotel stands in the picturesque village of Orton, to be found where the B6260 meets the B6261 and just a short drive from junction 38 on the M6. Located in the heart of the beautiful Eden Valley, it is the perfect place from which to explore the whole of the stunning Lake District and Cumbria. This impressive establishment has been personally run by Marc and April since the beginning of the year. With sheer hard work, determination and heaps of enthusiasm, this talented young couple are putting The George back on the map and bringing plenty of life and character back into the place. It is open every session during the winter and all day, every day in the summer months with a choice of three real ales to choose from, Cumberland the regular plus two rotating guest ales.

Good food is always an attraction and it's certainly the case here. Marc has sixteen years experience as a chef and people are flocking back to the George to sample his superb cuisine which is served everyday 12-3pm & 6-9pm. To tantalise the tastebuds, the starters menu includes Garlic mushrooms, Thai chilli prawns and Hot wings served with a sour cream dip to extinguish the fire! Main courses include Marc's renowned steak and ale pie, Cumberland sausage, sirloin steak and an ever changing fish of the week. Vegetarian choices include mushroom stroganoff and vegetable jalfrezi . Children are made very welcome and can choose from their own menu or have a small portion from the main menu choices. Booking is advisable from Thursday through to Sunday.

The George Hotel's accommodation consists of eight upstairs rooms. Six are ensuite with the remaining two rooms sharing a bathroom which has a Jacuzzi. Guests are welcome to come on Bed and Breakfast only or Dinner, bed and Breakfast. During the winter, special rates are offered so please ring for details. All major credit cards are accepted except A/Express and Diners.

121 THE BLACK BULL HOTEL

38 Market Street, Kirkby Stephen,
Cumbria CA17 4QW
Tel: 01768 371237
e-mail: jalex5463@aol.com
website:
www.blackbullkirkbystephen.co.uk

Situated on the main street in Kirkby Stephen on A685 south of Brough close to the north Yorkshire National Park is **The Black Bull Hotel**. This fine building dates back to the 18th century in parts and is a real success.

John and Denise Alexander have put their heart and soul into this business, giving the bull a new lease of life making a very popular pub and hotel. They offer nine upstairs en suite rooms all year round with their own baths and a hearty Cumbrian breakfast included.

Homemade food is available daily from 12-9pm, ranging from favourites like steak and kidney pie, salmon fishcakes and pasta in red pepper sauce.

Alongside our favourites menu we also offer a regularly evolving seasonal menu. All our food is prepared and cooked on the premises by our team of dedicated chefs and wherever possible, locally sourced.

The bar is well stocked with locally brewed cask ales and wines from around the world. So why not sit by the open fire and enjoy a cold drink.

Booking is advised Saturday evenings and Sunday lunchtimes as despite being open all day every day the Black Bull is always full of satisfied customers.

122 STOUPHILL GATE

Ravenstonedale, Cumbria CA17 4NN
Tel: 01539 63653
e-mail:
info@accommodationkirkbystephen.co.uk
website:
www.accommodationkirkbystephen.co.uk

Stouphill Gate is located in a glorious setting with spectacular views and offers a wonderful choice of bed and breakfast as well as self-catering accommodation in a traditional Cumbrian farmhouse that takes its name from nearby Stoup Hill.

Gillian and Martin Wainhouse are the owners here and provide lovely B&B rooms in a relaxing atmosphere with beautiful views of the country. They provide the perfect getaway to unwind and act as an ideal base for discovering the many scenic and historic delights of the surrounding area.

Gillian is a superb cook and caters to her guests, providing a hearty and splendid breakfast for all who visit. She also produces delightful homemade jams and chutney, which are made in small batches on the farmhouse Aga. All these jams and preserves are served at breakfast, however they can also be purchased from the property itself.

There are two bed and breakfast rooms, one of which is fully wheelchair accessible, these have very comfortable beds and en-suite bathrooms. There is an adjacent cottage, suitable for larger groups and

this offers old world charm, character and everything that you may need for a memorable and relaxing self-catering holiday home for up to 5 guests. There is a separate laundry room for use by guests.

123 THE MIDLAND HOTEL

25 Clifford Street,
Appleby-In-Westmorland
Cumbria CA16 6XY
Tel: 01768 351524
e-mail: midlandmagnay@hotmail.com
website:
www.themidlandhotelappleby.co.uk

Situated five miles from the centre of Appleby lies the welcoming 18th century **Midland Hotel.** Located across the road from Appleby's railway station, this inn offers good pub food, great real ales and 5 guest rooms, which are tastefully decorated. Paul and Leigh have been the licensees here for 18 months and have continued to provide great service, as well as improve the food, which is deliciously prepared by fantastic cook Leigh. Food is available daily until 8pm.

HIDDEN PLACES GUIDES

Explore Britain and Ireland with *Hidden Places* guides - a fascinating series of national and local travel guides.

Packed with easy to read information on hundreds of places of interest as well as places to stay, eat and drink.

Available from both high street and internet booksellers

For more information on the full range of *Hidden Places* guides and other titles published by Travel Publishing visit our website on

www.travelpublishing.co.uk
or ask for our leaflet by phoning
01752 697280 or emailing
info@travelpublishing.co.uk

124 TUFTON ARMS HOTEL

Market Square, Appleby-In-Westmorland,
Cumbria CA16 6XA
Tel: 017683 51593
Fax: 017683 52761
e-mail: info@tuftonarmshotel.co.uk
website: www.tuftonarmshotel.co.uk

Set in the main square of the busy market town of Appleby lies the splendidly traditional and charming **Tufton Arms Hotel.** Appleby is regarded as the jewel of the northwest towns and this small, intimate and luxurious hotel in Cumbria, does not let this statement down.

The Tufton Arms Hotel started life in the 16th century as a coaching inn and is now a grade II listed building, which was rebuilt in Victorian times with tall ceilings and grand features, creating a sense of space and elegance. The building keeps in with the Victorian era, which can be seen in the interior of the building. Attractive patterned wallpapers, engravings and prints, heavy drapes and old fireplaces are combined with contemporary fabrics, soft muted tones and modern lighting in order to create a sophisticated yet classic look, which is calming, enabling you to unwind and enjoy the wonderful surroundings.

The Milsom family have been the owners here for many years and provide a relaxing destination for an enjoyable break in the heart of the beautiful Eden Valley. Guests are welcomed upon their arrival by hospitable staff, who genuinely want to help make the stay a memorable one.

There are 22 ensuite bedrooms available, all beautifully decorated tastefully in a traditional style, with a contemporary flair. Each room has its own charm and character, with furnishings that include the occasional antique piece from the Milsom farmhouse.

After great hospitality, food and drink is at the top of the list. The award winning team of Chefs seek out the best and freshest local produce in order to prepare spectacular meals, once again traditional but with a modern twist. The menu consists of seared tuna steak, roast rack of Eden Valley lamb, pan fried breast of chicken and a scrumptious homemade steak and ale pie. There is also a specials menu with favourites, enjoyed by all and desserts that have something to tempt even the sweetest tooth. All of these meals are served in the elegant conservatory restaurant, overlooking the cobbled mews courtyard, which may remind you of times gone by.

The standard of quality at the Tufton Arms Hotel is second to non; you really will find the best of everything here and there are often special offers available as well as discounts for booking online.

125 SANDFORD ARMS

Sandford, nr Appleby-In-Westmorland,
Cumbria CA16 6NR
Tel: 017683 51121
Fax: 017683 53200
e-mail: sandfordarms@hotmail.com
website: www.sandfordarmscumbria.co.uk

The **Sandford Arms** is a superb conversion of 18th century farm buildings into a beautiful residential inn, lounge and restaurant. Located in a picturesque and pleasant location, just a mile or so off the A66 in a charming village by the River Eden, this country inn provides splendid food, drink and guest accommodation.

Owned and run by hosts Stephen and Nicola Porter for the last 3 years, the couple have a combined experience in the trade of 18 years and their hospitality and knowledge of what visitors want is 100%. The Sandford Arms has a warm and friendly atmosphere, heightened by the endless rapport that the hosts build with their visitors and the relaxing and traditional décor of the building, including the local stonework and the profusion of oak beams, only makes the visit more enjoyable.

The property, which is enjoyed by both locals and visitors alike often enjoy one of the 3 real ales on offer, black sheep being the regular plus rotating guest ales from either the Tirril Brewey or the Hesket Brewery, which are both in Cumbria. Food is also enjoyed daily from between 11.30am-2.30pm and 6pm-8.45pm. All the produce used is from local suppliers, wherever possible and the ingredients are used to produce many dishes, including the Chef's specials of minted lamb henry, Sandford chicken, homemade lasagne and local pork fillet and black pudding. There is also a fantastic menu, suitable for vegetarians, which sees stuffed aubergines, vegetable balti, mushroom and red pepper stroganoff and a lovely selection of freshly prepared salads, such as blue Wensleydale cheese and smoked bacon and salmon and prawn. There are in addition plenty of starters, side orders and a menu dedicated to children, with all of their favourites in tow.

The Sandford Arms has 3 ensuite bedrooms available to hire throughout the year and each room offers real comfort, tasteful furnishings and good value for money. With the rooms offering views across the meadows towards the romantically named fells, "Roman Fell" and "Murton Pike", this accommodation is great for a relaxing and unwinding getaway.

The tariff is reasonable with prices ranging from £42.50 for a single room to a double or twin being £65. There are great rates for the family rooms, as well as special rates on offer for a weeks stay.

126 CHOFH'S TEAROOM AND TAKEWAY

New Road, Brough,
Cumbria CA17 4AS
Tel: 01768 342800

Hidden away just yards from the busy A66 on the edge of the centre road to Brough is **Chofh's Tearoom and Takeaway**, a hotspot for hungry cyclists, walkers and tourists and is of course well loved by the locals. Chofh's has been a well established tearoom in Brough for many years now, current owner Jennie Dawson had worked here for 3 years when she fell in love with the place and bought it for herself and husband John.

It's clean and friendly country décor aids the feeling of traditional tearooms, and lives up to standards serving a quality range of homemade cakes. There is room for 22 people to dine inside and room for 8 more outside, with a choice from a delicious locally produced menu and daily specials board, though the specialties are Jennie's famous bacon sandwiches and filling all day breakfasts – perfect to keep you going all day on your trip around the scenic area of Brough.

Brough is set on the ancient Roman site of the fort of Verteris, on the road that used to be the Roman gateway across country, and is filled with some interesting historical buildings, including St Michael's Castle dating back to Norman times and Brough castle built in the 11th century. If history isn't what interests you however, there is plenty to attract those looking for a country ramble, as the area surrounding Brough is filled with enchanting walks along beautiful stretches of old railway lines, some of which even take a wander to the local nature reserve. Chofh's makes the perfect start for such a day.

Chofh's is open Monday-Friday 7.30am to 4pm and Saturday 8:30am-3pm, but in the summer months on Thursdays doors are open right through until 8:30pm. Closed on Sundays. Booking is advised for larger parties as Chofh's is a local favourite, and seats can fill up fast. Cash only please.

And if your after more than just tea and a scrumptious Cumbrian snack, you might be interested in John's other talents which include being local toastmaster and master of ceremonies, available to book for weddings, private parties, corporate functions, charity auctions or commentating!

Morland, Penrith, Cumbria CA10 3AZ
Tel: 01931 714310

The village of Morland is in some spectacular surroundings, set in the heart of the Eden Valley, the scenery around creates some great walks and days out. For that well earned break, **The Crown Inn** offers tasty food for the hungry and delicious ales for the thirsty. Morland can be found just of the A66 or the A6 close to Penrith; originally the Saxon capital of the Kingdom of Cumbria, Penrith boasts several impressive buildings and monuments to that bygone era.

In this day and age, a pub which has no ties to a brewery is a rare place and The Crown Inn does not disappoint. Shaun Brennand has owned and personally run this free house for the past four years now and the establishment has gone from strength to strength in his capable hands. From the exterior, the Crown Inn looks warm and cosy, the stone built building decorated with colourful hanging baskets and planter pots outside the entrance. Inside the décor is convivial and welcoming with knick knacks adorning the shelves and pictures of days gone by on the walls to look at. The dining area is lit by a large bay window and the whole pub is light and airy. Supporting the already large dining area is a patio outside for those balmy summer evenings, it is perfect for enjoying a nice pint; The Crown Inn has two real ales on offer, Deuchars and a rotating guest ale.

A major draw to this great pub is the food, served Thursday, Friday, Saturday and Sunday evenings and during the afternoon; 12 noon to 2 pm on Saturdays and Sundays. The menu specialises in classic British pub fare, taking the popular favourites and cooking them extremely well, using local produce where possible. Examples of this sumptuous menu are the local Cumberland sausage served with egg, onion rings, home made chips, salad, vegetables and coleslaw, deep fried camembert served with a redcurrant jelly and the 16oz gammon steak served with egg, pineapple and onion rings.

The pub also put on special nights, steak nights are always popular and there are also occasional special offers; 2 courses for a cut price for example. The Crown Inn does schedule entertainment, live music etc, for more details, please contact the pub.

128 EDEN VALE INN

**Bolton Village, Appleby,
Cumbria CA16 6AU
Tel: 01768 361428
e-mail: theedenvale@googlemail.com**

Located in the heart of the stunning Eden valley lies the delightful **Eden Vale Inn.** Dating back to the mid 1700's, this inviting old hostelry has plenty of warmth and character, offering splendid food, as well as a sociable environment, suitable for families.

Nigel and Richard took over the lease here in the summer of 2006 and together with Nigel's 20 years experience in the hospitality business and Richard's talents as a Chef, the two

have transformed this property in to a destination for discerning dishes. The imaginative menu offers tantalising dishes of lamb shoulder, homemade steak and kidney pudding, baked avocado stuffed with goats cheese and a lovely spinach and ricotta cannelloni, suitable for vegetarians. Children are very much welcome and there is also an early bird menu. The regular menu is supplemented by a good choice of daily specials, such as venison and swordfish steaks. Not only can does the Eden Vale Inn offer wonderful food, 3 real ales and a splendid beer garden, there are also 4 recently refurbished ensuite guest bedrooms available throughout the year.

130 EDENHALL COUNTRY HOTEL & RESTAURANT

**Edenhall, Penrith, Cumbria CA11 8SX
Tel: 01768 881454
Fax: 01768 881266
e-mail: info@edenhallhotel.co.uk
website: www.edenhallhotel.co.uk**

Set in the beautiful Eden Valley but just 4 miles from junction 40 of the M6, **Edenhall Country Hotel & Restaurant** provides its guests with the opportunity to indulge in that rarest of modern activities - a well-earned rest. Owners Paula and Wayne Williams are both Cumbria born and bred and take great pride in the quality of local produce. So, in their stylish restaurant, the proud holder of an AA Rosette, you will find the finest British food expertly cooked with flair and imagination.

In the hotel bar, you can sample one of the many fine malts or one of the real ales from the local Turril Brewery, sit by a roaring fire, or admire the superb gardens from the conservatory. The newly refurbished bedrooms at Edenhall offer guests the highest standards in traditional furnishing and modern en suite convenience. There are 17 rooms in all, one

of which is on the ground floor and has been adapted for the disabled.

During the day, visitors can enjoy a tranquil stroll along the 'Ladies Walk' beside the River Eden; the thrill of a shoot, or a day's fishing on one of England's premier rivers.

129 THE NEW INN COUNTRY PUB

Brampton, Appleby-In-Westmorland,
Cumbria CA16 6JS
Tel: 01767 351231
e-mail: info@thenewinnbrampton.co.uk
website: www.thenewinnbrampton.co.uk

Standing in the village of Brampton, off the main A66, a few miles north of Appleby is the traditional and charming **New Inn Country Pub.**

The building, which dates back to 1730 is absolutely wonderful, exuding its history and classic features. There are open fires in the bar and restaurant, flagstone floors, beamed ceilings and old artefacts adorning the walls. There is also a huge beer garden at the rear of the property, with its own beer bar, providing visitors with an enjoyable experience both inside and out.

Licensee's Gary and Robert Pallas, along with their parents Bob and Carol have now been here for 2 years and they offer a relaxing and friendly atmosphere, whilst also providing great food and drink, an ideal place to unwind and enjoy the surrounding areas.

The bar is open all day, everyday of the week and among the favourite tipples are the real ales from the local Tirril Brewery, including old faithful and red barn. Alongside this, the hosts prepare exceptional food, which is served from 12-9pm Monday to Saturday and 12-6pm on Sundays. Amongst the menu are spectacular dishes such as New Zealand greenlip mussels steamed in white wine, crispy bacon and black pudding tower, traditional mince and leek dumplings, steak and old faithful pie and beer battered haddock. As well as this there are medallions of venison, pair of duck legs and Thai king prawn curry from the à la carte menu. For those wishing to have a lighter bite, there is a selection of sandwiches with far from traditional fillings. The food is enjoyed widely here and is busy most of the time, with those wishing to enjoy a top quality meal, using local produce. It is recommended to book at weekends, in order to avoid disappointment.

The New Inn Country Pub also houses 3 guest bedrooms, including one double ensuite, a further double room and one twin that share a toilet and shower facilities. The comfortable rooms provide an ideal base to explore the surrounding area of Appleby. The bedrooms are tastefully decorated and minimalist, creating a relaxing and tranquil environment.

The tariff is between £25 and £30 a night, per room, with breakfast being a further £5.50 per head, which is served from 8am-10.30am.

131 BRIEF ENCOUNTER

The Old Station, Langwathby, nr Penrith,
Cumbria, CA10 1NB
Tel: 01768 881902
e-mail: geeedgar@aol.com
website: www.briefencounterlangwathby.co.uk

This beautifully quaint café-restaurant is situated in a station building on the north platform on the Settle-Carlisle line. **Brief Encounter** is run by Gordon and Elsie Edgar, a couple passionate about maintaining the wholesome traditional flair of times past; something you can really taste in their homemade jams, preserves, own label biscuits and confectionary all available to buy on the premises.

A great range of award winning light lunches and evening meals (traditional roast available on Sundays) are served using certificated Cumbria-sourced produce. Who could resist the mouth-watering steak & ale pie, made with Newcastle Brown Ale? Or why not just drop in for a morning coffee or afternoon tea to soak up the atmosphere, which is as elegant and romantic as the 1945

film *"Brief Encounter"* gains its name from. Opening times are Apr-Oct (7days) 9am-5pm

Nov-Mar 10am-4pm (closed Mondays), it is advisable to book, particularly in the busy seasons and for larger groups. A delicious takeaway service is available all year on Wednesdays 4:30pm-7pm.

Adjacent to Brief Encounter is a lovely craft and gift shop, which would complete any trip to this superb dining establishment. This is the perfect place to get that special gift for someone else, or for yourself. Opening times are Thurs pm and Fri-Sun 10am-4pm.

132 HIGHLAND DROVE INN

**Great Salkeld, Penrith,
Cumbria CA119NA
Tel: 01768 898349
e-mail: highlanddrove@kyoles.co.uk
website: www.kyloes.co.uk**

In the picturesque village of Great Salkeld, among pleasant 18th century cottages and farmhouses in red sandstone in the lush pastures of the Eden Valley, sits the **Highland Drove Inn**, a place renowned for its cosy traditional atmosphere, delicious food and great hospitality. The Highland Drove has hundreds of years of hospitality behind it, which father and son Donald and Paul Newton, have been consistently upholding since 1998.

The great food is at the real heart of the Highland Drove Inn; favourites such as haddock & chips, Ploughman's and steak and ale pie are served alongside such creative mouth-watering dishes as Nile Perch on stir-fried vegetables with mussels and a creamy curry sauce. For a light bite or quick early evening meal Downstairs at the Drove offers a reduced menu of good hearty pub food, with all the style of Kyoles chefs. Opening hours for serving food are Tuesday to Friday (and also Sunday) lunchtime 12-2:30pm, evening meal 6- 9pm. On Saturdays they are open all day but only serve food within these hours and on Mondays the Highland Drove is not open for lunch, but is for the evening meal. Also, if you are reluctant to leave the cosy atmosphere, there are several rooms available, all of which are en-suite and have that same snug traditional quality as the rest of the Inn.

Also run by Donald and Paul is **The Cross Keys**; a short drive from Penrith on the A686, in the nearby village of Carleton. Both of these premises now come under the name of Kyoles Inns, which, as described by them, is "named after the highland cattle from the Western Isles that were driven across the narrow Kyles to the mainland, (and) has become a byword for innovative and high quality food." This is something that The Cross Keys has in abundance, fuelled by the popularity of The Highland Drove, the fine food and ales on offer in this beautifully fully-refurbished establishment have already forged a reputation among locals and visitors since its open in Dec '08.

Dishes such as the locally sourced Cumbrian lamb hot pot with braised red cabbage or the "Kyloes" 16oz T-bone steak (not for the meat-shy!) can be enjoyed Mon – Sat 12noon to 2:30 and 5:30 to 9pm and Sun 12noon to 2:30 and 6 to 8:30pm. For nice weather there is a balcony leading off of the main dining area, where you can dine outside and enjoy the superb views.

133 HARTSIDE TOP CAFE

Hartside, Alston, Cumbria CA9 3BW
Tel: 01434 381036

At 1893 feet above sea level the famous **Hartside Top Café** is England's highest cafe, with a truly magnificent view looking out over the Great Gable, Skidaw, Helvellyn and the Scottish Criffel. Situated in total wilderness adjacent to the A686 between Penrith and Alston, Hartside brings travellers from all over to sample the truly glorious combination of hearty food, warm hospitality and stunning views.

Owners Kath and Colin Renwick accompanied by their right hand lady and in house baker Jayneann Burrow have created a buzzing business over the last 7 years serving a variety of very reasonably priced breakfasts, homemade cakes, snacks and hot and cold lunches such as hot turkey bap with stuffing and cranberry, or the hearty vegetable and ham homemade broth. Most of the produce is locally sourced. A small selection of hot and cold drinks made to taste are also available.

A popular stop off point for coaches, families or adventurous hikers, Hartside opens its doors daily from 9am-5pm all year apart from in the winter months. It seats a surprising 100 people inside, with room for at least 50 more on its terrace and garden area where the beauty of Cumbria can be soaked up along with the sunshine in the summer months.

The café isn't just popular with enthusiastic ramblers, it has gone down in biking history as one of the best places in the country to enjoy some good food, a cuppa and a chat as it sits in the middle of one of England's best loved motorbike routes, famous for its tight and twisty chicanes leading up to an altitude of 1904 feet and fast bends sweeping all the way down the valley at the bottom.

Hartside also has good disabled access and toilets, but only accepts cash and cheque. Biker or not, this gem of an eatery is well worth a pitstop, with views and hospitality second to none.

134 THE CUMBERLAND INN ⅋ ⊨

Townfoot, Alston, Cumbria CA9 3HX
Tel: 01434 381875
e-mail: helenguy@aol.com
website: www.cumberlandalston.com

In their mid-Victorian hotel at the foot of the main street, hospitable owners Guy and Helen Harmer provide a warm family welcome to all their patrons. **The Cumberland Hotel** is a place of wide appeal where visitors arrive as guests and leave as friends. It offers a convivial spot to meet for a drink, a fine choice for a meal at any time of day and a comfortable base for both leisure and business visitors. In the two licensed bars, four real ales, including Yates Bitter and guest local brews, can be enjoyed over a chat, and when the sun shines the patio is a pleasant alternative; this area overlooks the quoits pitch, used by the players in the summer local league.

Guy prides himself on using the best local produce in his dishes and uses local suppliers to assure his food is as fresh as it can be. Dishes such as chicken & mushroom pie, steak & ale pie, minced beef & thyme dumpling and homemade pork mince lasagne adorn the menu, and can be enjoyed daily between noon and 9 in the evening. Booking is recommended on Saturday evenings and Sunday lunchtimes. The hotel is a popular venue for

birthday parties and other special occasions. The accommodation comprises five well-appointed rooms, all en suite, sleeping up to 14 in total; they can be block-booked for families or groups of friends.

Alston is an important centre at a major crossroads, and numerous visitor attractions are within easy reach, including the Gossipgate gallery in town, the Nenthead Mines Heritage Centre, Ashgill Force Waterfall, the Pennine Way and Hartside Pass with views of the fells and Solway Firth.

135 NENTHEAD MINES HERITAGE CENTRE 🏛

Nenthead, Alston, Cumbria CA9 3PD
Tel: 01434 382037
e-mail: administration.office@virgin.net
website: www.npht.com

The 200-acre centre at Nenthead, in the North Pennines, is in an Area of Outstanding Natural Beauty. It offers a unique insight into the lives of the miners who transformed these fells. Visitors have the chance to experience the underground world through guided trips in Carr's Mine, last commercially worked for lead in 1920.

There is the huge "Power of Water" interactive area, where visitors can open sluice gates to operate water wheels and drive machinery. *Brewery Shaft* is an impressive 328 feet deep, with a viewing platform for visitors to gaze down into the depths and be amazed at the courage of anyone daring to descend. Around the centre are various restored buildings, which contain exhibitions and interactive displays about the geology of the area, the local wildlife and social history of the area.

The site includes woodland walks, mountain streams and a waterfall, whilst the surrounding area is ideal for walkers of all ages and gives access to the spectacular scenery of the North Pennines. There is a café where people can rest their legs and take refreshments, and a well-stocked shop where they can purchase postcards, books and gifts.

136 THE FOX AND PHEASANT INN

Armathwaite, Cumbria   CA4 9PY
Tel: 01697 472400
e-mail: info@foxandpheasantinn.co.uk
website: www.foxandpheasantinn.co.uk

The river Eden runs through some spectacular scenery as it winds it way through the Lake District, it is on the banks of this river, in Eden Valley, that you will find **The Fox and Pheasant Inn**. Situated in the quaint village of Armathwaite, which is ideally set approximately halfway between Carlisle and Penrith and just 10 minutes drive from the M6, this inn makes the ideal base. The Fox and Pheasant Inn started life as a 16th century coaching inn and was later extended to incorporate a former shooting and fishing lodge.

Tenants Sarah and Billy Hunter have over 20 years experience in the hospitality trade and since taking over at the end of 2007, The Fox and Pheasant has gone from strength to strength. A recent refurbishment of the bedrooms has ensured that the quality associated with this great inn is now assured throughout. There are five bedrooms available for hire, all with full en suite facilities. The rooms are comprised of doubles, twins and single and are well stocked with everything you could expect of high quality accommodation. Breakfast is included in the reasonable tariff and the restaurant will provide you with a packed lunch to sustain you during the day's activities.

Adjoining the main accommodation, the converted barns now house the stable barn bar and restaurant, which boasts exposed stone, wooden beams and sandstone floors. The main bar always has a great atmosphere, the flagstone floors and inglenook fireplace creating a warm and welcoming place to share stories. Indeed, the bar is a popular meeting place for local fishermen, gamekeepers and ghillies, all swapping stories as they enjoy the well kept ale. The bar offers a minimum of three ales, and up to five during busy periods, the regulars are Unicorn and Dizzy Blonde from the Robinson's Brewery.

The restaurant is well thought of; dishes can be chosen from the standard printed menu or from the specials board which changes regularly, all of the food is created fresh to order using local produce wherever possible. Food is available daily, Monday to Friday between 12 pm - 2 pm and 6 pm – 9 pm and all day between 12 pm and 9 pm on Saturday and Sunday. Although you can eat anywhere within the inn, reservations are recommended at the weekends to avoid disappointment. For a more special occasion, the Victorian dining room can be hired out, which offers a luxurious culinary experience in wonderful surroundings.

137 THE DUKES HEAD INN

Armathwaite nr Carlisle,
Cumbria CA4 9PB
Tel: 01697 472226
e-mail: info@dukeshead-hotel.co.uk
website: www.dukeshead-hotel.co.uk

Found just east of the A6 between Penrith and Carlisle in the heart of the Eden Valley at Armathwaite is the historic Dukes Head Inn. Helen and Henry Lynch who have been running the Dukes Head for 19 years pride themselves on offering great hospitality in a homely setting where a quality experience is assured.

The cosy bar and dining room complete with open log fires provide the perfect setting to sample some of the best food in Cumbria. Available from 12-2pm and 6:30-9pm daily is a tantalising selection of starters, mains, specials, homemade sweets and cheese including venison, pheasant and rabbit hotpot; black pudding, sausage, chorizo and poached egg salad topped with mustard vinaigrette; and refreshing orange and pineapple in a honey mint and passion fruit syrup with lemon sorbet. We advise booking at all a time as the cuisine here comes highly recommended and it's always busy. The bar also offers good quality with three local rotating real ales.

Accommodation here offers 5 upstairs rooms with private bathrooms, all full of character and comfort to make a truly enjoyable stay. Helen and Henry also offer to make up flasks and lunches for guests and there is ample outdoor space to enjoy the beautiful blossom filled gardens in summer.

138 DENTON STREET CAFÉ

Denton Street, Carlisle,
Cumbria CA2 5EL
Tel: 01228 599926

Denton Street Café makes up for its small size in hospitality and fine home cooked food. Just a short walk from Carlisle's city centre you will find a charming café serving a variety of hot and cold snacks and drinks with the real speciality being the "pick your own breakfast" where you can chose from a vast array of locally sourced items to create the perfect start to your day. Everything is reasonably priced but doesn't lose out on quality as the dedication of owners Richard and Jane have made this business a real success. The hard work renovating this delightful venue combined with experience and great cooks ensures that all 26 seats are in demand. Open to all Mon-Sat 9am-3:30pm. Cash only please.

HIDDEN PLACES GUIDES

Explore Britain and Ireland with *Hidden Places* guides - a fascinating series of national and local travel guides.

Packed with easy to read information on hundreds of places of interest as well as places to stay, eat and drink.

Available from both high street and internet booksellers

For more information on the full range of *Hidden Places* guides and other titles published by Travel Publishing visit our website on

www.travelpublishing.co.uk
or ask for our leaflet by phoning
01752 697280 or emailing
info@travelpublishing.co.uk

139 NO. 10

No. 10 at Eden Golf Club, Crosby-on-Eden, Carlisle, Cumbria CA6 4RA
No. 10, Eden Mount Stanwix, Carlisle, Cumbria CA3 9LY

Paul and Sarah Minett owners of the popular **No. 10** restaurant in Stanwix have created a second No. 10 at the Eden Golf Club in Crosby-on-Eden which has proved an equally successful venture.

This second property overlooks the well kept fairway at the Golf Club, providing an experienced menu created by Paul, chef of 20 years available to both members and non-members of the Golf Club from 10am-9pm in the summer months and from 10am-4pm in the winter months. There is a well stocked bar with a healthy range of wines, spirits and beers plenty of comfortable seating opening onto a beautiful patio by the fairway. In the evenings on Fridays and Saturdays it turns into a bistro from 6:30-9pm serving delectable dishes with all produce sourced locally within the county. We advise booking as the elegant setting matched with fine food and experience keeps both keen golfers and more coming all year round.

The original No.10 is open from 7pm 5 days a week serving up a delicious choice of à la carte and set

menus. The classic décor and unbeatable service have set No.10 up as one of the finest eateries in Carlisle. It's located just a short drive from the city centre from the J44 off the M6.

140 THE WATERLOO

Aglionby, Carlisle, Cumbria CA4 8AG
Tel: 01228 513347

The Waterloo is a traditional Cumbrian Inn that stands adjacent to the main A69, set back from the road half a mile from junction 43 on the M6. This inn dates back to the early 19th century when it was originally a working farmhouse.

The Waterloo is tenants June and Keith Nelson's first venture in the licensing trade and they have been creating a warm and welcoming atmosphere since March this year. June is an extremely talented self taught cook – the evidence is their custom; visitors and locals are returning every day to sample her food and say that The Waterloo has been given a much needed new lease of life by this couple.

On offer from 12-8pm Wed-Sat and 12-6pm Sun-Mon is a tasty selection of traditional pub cuisine with a choice of starters and main dishes that include special recipe scampi, half roast chicken and pork and black pudding in red wine gravy. There is also a range of baguettes, desserts, children's menu and an extensive steak selection. All produce is sourced locally. On Sundays a roast is served from 12 until it runs out so make sure you get in quick!

On Saturday evenings an easy listening singer plays from 9pm to help you relax followed by Bingo and a raffle, and if the weather is nice all this can be enjoyed from the beer garden complete with its own stream. Cash only please, open all year round (in winter closed on Mondays).

141 WILLOWBECK LODGE

Scotby, Carlisle, Cumbria CA4 8BX
Tel: 01228 513607
e-mail: info@willowbeck-lodge.com
website: www.willowbeck-lodge.com

Standing in 1½ acres of superb gardens, with a pond to the front of the building lies **Willowbeck Lodge.** Purpose built by an award-winning local architect, this boutique hotel nestles among mature willows, beech and oak and is within easy travelling distance of the Lake District.

Offering top quality bed and breakfast accommodation, Willowbeck provides 'home away from home' comfort. Upon arrival you are greeted by a grand and contemporary property, with plenty of glass and exposed beams.

Owned and run by John and Liz McGrillis, this property was built 5 years ago on what was and still is the couple's own grounds. They have done a superb job with this building as the premises oozes class and style in each and every area. The interior is light and airy, with contemporary furnishings, finished to a top quality standard.

There are 6 ensuite bedrooms available here, 5 of which overlook the front grounds and the pond, creating a relaxing and tranquil feel, perfect for unwinding and taking in the wonderful surroundings. Each bedroom is comfortably furnished in a modern style, with flat screen TV, broadband connection, hairdryer and tea making facilities. 4 of the bedrooms are located in the main house and the other 2 rooms have been built in the attached extension.

The tariff is reasonable and is reflected in the quality services that are on offer here, as well as the high standard and 5 star gold award rating. Prices start from £110 per room, based on two people sharing, up to £130. All prices include a wonderfully prepared breakfast, with dishes suiting even the fussiest of palettes. Fresh fruit juices, cereals and fruit salads are on offer, as well as traditional full English or continental breakfasts. If you would prefer something in-between you may decide to opt for scrambled egg with smoked salmon, kippers or scotch pancakes. Evening meals are also available upon request, in advance. Each evening meal is a set menu, with a choice of starters and desserts.

Whether a group of business people, couple or friends wishing to get away for a few days, Wellowbeck Lodge is happy to arrange activities for you, in order to make your stay worthwhile and memorable.

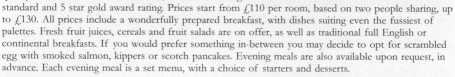

142 COUNTRY KITCHEN

5 The Square, Dalston, Carlisle,
Cumbria CA5 7PJ
Tel: 01228 711431
Mobile: 07706874541
e-mail: jcountrykitchen@aol.com

As you walk through the Square in the village of Dalston the tempting smell of homely baking wafts from the doors of the **Country Kitchen**, a quality tea room and coffee shop serving a surprising variety of treats. You'll find Dalston on the B5299 just south west of Carlisle off the main A595 and only a short drive from junction of 42 of the M6.

This cosy tea room makes you feel right at home, with an eye catching display of crafts dotted around available to purchase as a memoir of you time in Cumbria. Local lady Joyce has been in the catering business for over 20 years and her experience shows in the fine produce available here. Joyce's daughters Wendy and Tracy help her run the Country Kitchen and she needs it – Joyce's culinary skills have kept this business busy each day.

There are 22 seats inside with room for 4 more outside that have a pleasant view of the square. Joyce opens from 9:30am-3:30pm and booking is advised at lunchtimes due to the kitchen's popularity. You can choose from the main menu or the daily specials board, both of which are cooked using local produce where possible. Choices on the main menu include Scampi, Cod, lasagne, curry & rice, Cumberland sausage and egg and a variety of chicken dishes. There is also a range of light snacks in baked potatoes, salads, rolls and toasties.

The real attraction here according to locals and visitors alike is Joyce's range of home baked cakes and scones. Each day there is at least 5 different choices of cake, all of which are truly melt in your mouth – and the scones are said to rival Devonshire cream teas! But if you are an early bird looking for a hearty breakfast to start your holiday then have no worries - the Country kitchen is also the place for you. Combine a full English breakfast with a hot cup of coffee and you will be set for the day. Cash and cheque only, plenty of parking adjacent to the building.

237

143 CROSBY LODGE COUNTRY HOUSE HOTEL & RESTAURANT

High Crosby, Crosby-On-Eden, Nr.
Carlisle, Cumbria CA6 4QZ
Tel: 01228 573618
Fax: 01228 573428
email: enquiries@crosbylodge.co.uk
website: www.crosbylodge.co.uk

Delightfully situated in lush grounds of plenty is the spectacular **Crosby Lodge Country House Hotel & Restaurant.** With its grand exterior and splendid scenery, this property is designed to make you unwind, relax and recharge those batteries.

Only a short distance away from the River Eden, the building has a fine view of the Vale of Eden and

distant mountains, providing a tranquil and relaxing atmosphere. Having been regarded as one of the region's most outstanding country house hotels, it is not hard to see why this hotel is so popular with all whom visit.

The building oozes history and charm and dates back to the first decade of the 19th century. Previously built as a stately home for the Deputy Lieutenant of Cumberland, the building, which is now Grade II listed, entices those with an interest in British history.

Acquired by the Sedgwick family in 1970, the hotel underwent a substantial, yet sympathetic refurbishment, keeping many of the original features, as well as providing the height in comfort, service and hospitality. Still in the family, Patricia Sedgwick is the owner of Crosby Lodge and she offers tremendous accommodation, which can be booked on a bed & breakfast or dinner, bed & breakfast basis throughout the year.

There are 9 beautifully appointed rooms, each of which are ensuite and individually designed and furnished with an impeccable style and taste, which is consistent throughout this building.

As well as the comfortable and luxurious bedrooms, there is an elegant restaurant on site, serving the very best in fine cuisine. The table d'hôte and à la carte menus make excellent use of fresh ingredients in classic British and Continental dishes ranging from Gressingham duck breast and seared pork loin with black pudding to haddock and chips, toad in the hole and award winning Cumberland sausage on bubble and squeak. There is also a delectable array of Crosby Lodge delicious desserts, including homemade ice creams and a choice of British cheeses, which are a pleasant accompaniment to any main meal.

The fine food is also complemented by an equally distinguished wine list, which is compiled by Phillipa Sedgwick wines, who have a wine warehouse in the courtyard.

144 HOUSE OF MEG TEA ROOMS

Mumps Ha, 4 Hall Terrace, Gilsland,
Cumbria CA8 7BW
Tel: 016977 47777
email: houseofmeg@yahoo.co.uk

House Of Meg Tea Rooms is an outstanding tearoom situated at Gilsland, close to Hadrian's wall. The building is homely, with top quality décor and furnishings, oozing class and ultimate comfort.

Formerly an alehouse run by the historic Margaret Teesdale and with an ill repute, the property has a very different atmosphere today. The business, which is now named after Meg, a recluse that once lived on the moors in the area is now anything but lonely. There is an array of sofas to slump in, unwind and enjoy a brew or a bite to eat with friends and family.

Owned and run by Andrew Keen for the last 2½ years, Andrew was born and bred in the village and has 8 previous years experience in the trade. He entices

visitors and locals with a lovely selection of paninis, all day breakfasts, baguettes and jacket potatoes as well as offering hot and cold beverages, with hot chocolate, served with cream and marshmallows being a favourite. There is also a wonderful array of scrumptious cakes on offer on the specials menu, changing daily. .

146 KIRKSTYLE INN

Slaggyford, Brampton,
Northumberland CA8 7PB
Tel: 01434 381559
Fax: 01434 381711

Owners Julie and Andrew Beaumont-Markland have been here since November 2007 and in that time have improved the property and the food and drink on offer. One of the most popular guides for Pennine Way walkers says it all: "Pennine Wayfarers are always looking for an excuse to stop at **The Kirkstyle Inn**. From the choice of beers to the tasty bar menu and the atmosphere this place has evrything walkers go for."

Julie has been a professionally qualified Chef for 12 years, so she knows what discerning customers want and how to provide it. Staples on her menu include such as homemade chicken curry, horseshoe gammon and pineapple or huge beer battered cod with handcut chips. She also offers an everchanging "specials" board and a house speciality; a Northumbrian sausage menu featuring special sausages

made for her locally; reflecting her preference for fresh, local ingredients.

Adjacent to the pub is a cosy, self-catering,cottage sleeping two which can be rented at any time of year.

145 GREENHEAD HOTEL & HOSTEL

Greenhead, Brampton CA8 7HB
Tel: 016977 47411
e-mail:
daveandsuegreenhead@btconnect.com
website: www.greenhead-hotel.com.uk

Set in the dramatic countryside of Hadrians Wall in a small village is the ever so popular and thriving business **The Greenhead Hotel And Hostel.** The hotel is wonderfully historic and has plenty of charm, enticing all who visit. Made of brick, the building is grand, with large doorways and windows, bringing in plenty of natural light and displaying the beautiful scenery.

The interior of the building is traditional, with a combination of exposed beams and brickwork as well as bright white walls, complimenting the traditional features. The newly refurbished bar is warm and welcoming, with a large hugh fire, perfect for winter nights and intimate atmosphere. Overall the façade and décor of the property is outstanding and finished to a very high standard.

Dave and Sue have been the licensees here since October 2008 and you would never believe that this is the couple's first venture into this type of business. Sue has been in the catering business for over 7 years, so naturally she is in charge of producing the lovely food, which is available daily between 12 and 8.30pm. There is a selection of meals available such as sirloin steak, whole tail Whitby scampi, butterfly chicken with Stilton sauce and creamy mushroom pasta. There is also a daily specials board, which is definitely worth looking out for. The local butcher is used, as well as local farms to source all the meat and produce that features in each meal, meaning that each dish is prepared with the finest ingredients and of the best quality.

The hotel here has 4 ensuite bedrooms, with 3 doubles and one twin, with slight variations available, such as an additional single bed. The rooms are tastefully decorated, with everything that you may require in order to make your stay as comfortable and relaxing as possible. The tariff is very reasonable at £33.50 per night, including a full English breakfast.

Located across the road in a former Methodist Church is the Greenhead Hostel. With 40 beds, split between 6 dormitories, 4 x 6 and 2 x 8, this accommodation is available throughout the year at a competitive rate and has facilities such as a common room, self-catering kitchen and showers.

Tourist Information Centres

ALSTON MOOR

Town Hall, Front Street, Alston,
Cumbria CA9 3RF
e-mail: alston.tic@eden.gov.uk
Tel: 01434 382244

AMBLESIDE

Central Buildings, Market Cross, Ambleside,
Cumbria LA22 9BS
e-mail: amblesidetic@southlakeland.gov.uk
Tel: 015394 32582

APPLEBY-IN-WESTMORLAND

Moot Hall, Boroughgate,
Appleby-in-Westmorland, Cumbria CA16 6XE
e-mail: tic@applebytown.org.uk
Tel: 017683 51177

BARROW-IN-FURNESS

Forum 28, Duke Street, Barrow-in-Furness,
Cumbria LA14 1HU
e-mail: touristinfo@barrowbc.gov.uk
Tel: 01229 876505

BOWNESS

Glebe Road, Bowness-on-Windermere,
Cumbria LA23 3HJ
e-mail: bownesstic@lake-district.gov.uk
Tel: 015394 42895

BRAMPTON

Moot Hall, Market Place, Brampton,
Cumbria CA8 1RW
e-mail: ElisabethB@CarlisleCity.gov.uk
Tel: 016977 3433

BROUGHTON-IN-FURNESS

Town Hall, The Square, Broughton-in-Furness,
Cumbria LA20 6JF
e-mail: broughtontic@btconnect.com
Tel: 01229 716115

CARLISLE

Old Town Hall, Greenmarket, Carlisle,
Cumbria CA3 8JE
e-mail: tourism@carlisle-city.gov.uk
Tel: 01228 625600

COCKERMOUTH

Town Hall, Market Street, Cockermouth,
Cumbria CA13 9NP
e-mail: email@cockermouth-tic.fsnet.co.uk
Tel: 01900 822634

CONISTON

Ruskin Avenue, Coniston, Cumbria LA21 8EH
e-mail: mail@conistontic.org
Tel: 015394 41533

EGREMONT

12 Main Street, Egremont, Cumbria CA22 2DW
e-mail: email@egremont-tic.fsnet.co.uk
Tel: 01946 820693

GRANGE-OVER SANDS

Victoria Hall, Main Street, Grange-over-Sands,
Cumbria LA11 6DP
e-mail: grangetic@southlakeland.gov.uk
Tel: 015395 34026

KENDAL

Town Hall, Highgate, Kendal, Cumbria LA9 4DL
e-mail: kendaltic@southlakeland.gov.uk
Tel: 0153 979 7516

KESWICK

Moot Hall, Market Square, Keswick,
Cumbria CA12 5JR
e-mail: keswicktic@lake-district.gov.uk
Tel: 017687 72645

KIRKBY LONSDALE

24 Main Street, Kirkby Lonsdale,
Cumbria LA6 2AE
e-mail: kltic@southlakeland.gov.uk
Tel: 015242 71437

KIRKBY STEPHEN

Market Street, Kirkby Stephen,
Cumbria CA17 4QN
e-mail: ks.tic@eden.gov.uk
Tel: 017683 71199

MARYPORT

Maryport Town Hall, Senhouse Street, Maryport,
Cumbria CA15 6BH
e-mail: maryporttic@allerdale.gov.uk
Tel: 01900 812101

MILLOM

Station Building, Station Road, Millom,
Cumbria LA18 5AA
e-mail: millomtic@copelandbc.gov.uk
Tel: 01229 774819

PENRITH

Middlegate, Penrith, Cumbria CA11 7PT
e-mail: pen.tic@eden.gov.uk
Tel: 01768 867466

RHEGED

Rheged, Rheged, Penrith, Cumbria CA11 0DQ
e-mail: tic@rheged.com
Tel: 01768 860034

SEDBERGH

72 Main Street, Sedbergh, Cumbria LA10 5AD
e-mail: tic@sedbergh.org.uk
Tel: 015396 20125

SILLOTH-ON-SOLWAY

Solway coast Discovery Centre, Liddell Street,
Silloth-on-Solway, Cumbria CA7 5DD
e-mail: sillothtic@allerdale.gov.uk
Tel: 016973 31944

SOUTHWAITE

M6 Service Area Southwaite, Carlisle,
Cumbria CA4 ONS
e-mail: southwaitetic@visitscotland.com
Tel: 016974 73445

ULLSWATER

Main Car Park, Glenridding, Penrith,
Cumbria CA11 0PD
e-mail: ullswatertic@lake-district.gov.uk
Tel: 017684 82414

ULVERSTON

Coronation Hall, County Square, Ulverston,
Cumbria LA12 7LZ
e-mail: ulverstontic@southlakeland.gov.uk
Tel: 01229 587120

WHITEHAVEN

Market Hall, Market Place, Whitehaven,
Cumbria CA28 7JG
e-mail: tic@copelandbc.gov.uk
Tel: 01946 598914

WINDERMERE

Victoria Street, Windermere, Cumbria LA23 1AD
e-mail: windermeretic@southlakeland.gov.uk
Tel: 015394 46499

WORKINGTON

21 Finkle Street, Workington,
Cumbria CA14 2BE
e-mail: workingtontic@allerdale.gov.uk
Tel: 01900 606699

Towns, Villages and Places of Interest

TRAVEL PUBLISHING ORDER FORM

To order any of our publications just fill in the payment details below and complete the order form. For orders of less than 4 copies please add £1.00 per book for postage and packing. Orders over 4 copies are P & P free.

Name:

Address:

Tel no:

Please Complete Either:

I enclose a cheque for £ _____ made payable to Travel Publishing Ltd

Or:

Card No: Expiry Date:

Signature:

Please either send, telephone, fax or e-mail your order to:

Travel Publishing Ltd, Airport Business Centre, 10 Thornbury Road, Estover, Plymouth PL6 7PP

Tel: 01752 697280   Fax: 01752 697299   e-mail: info@travelpublishing.co.uk

	Price	Quantity		Price	Quantity
HIDDEN PLACES REGIONAL TITLES			**COUNTRY LIVING RURAL GUIDES**		
Cornwall	£8.99	....	East Anglia	£10.99	....
Devon	£8.99	....	Heart of England	£10.99	....
Dorset, Hants & Isle of Wight	£8.99	....	Ireland	£11.99	....
East Anglia	£8.99	....	North East	£10.99	....
Lake District & Cumbria	£8.99	....	North West	£10.99	....
Lancashire & Cheshire	£8.99	....	Scotland	£11.99	....
Northumberland & Durham	£8.99	....	South of England	£10.99	....
Peak District and Derbyshire	£8.99	....	South East of England	£10.99	....
Yorkshire	£8.99	....	Wales	£11.99	....
HIDDEN PLACES NATIONAL TITLES			West Country	£10.99	....
England	£11.99	....			
Ireland	£11.99	....			
Scotland	£11.99	....			
Wales	£11.99	....	**TOTAL QUANTITY:**		
OTHER TITLES			**POST & PACKING:**		
Off the Motorway	£11.99	....			
Garden Centres & Nurseries	£11.99	....	**TOTAL VALUE:**		

READER REACTION FORM

The *Travel Publishing* research team would like to receive reader's comments on any visitor attractions or places reviewed in the book and also recommendations for suitable entries to be included in the next edition. This will help ensure that the *Hidden Places series of Guides* continues to provide its readers with useful information on the more interesting, unusual or unique features of each attraction or place ensuring that their visit to the local area is an enjoyable and stimulating experience. To provide your comments or recommendations would you please complete the forms below and overleaf as indicated and send to:

**The Research Department, Travel Publishing Ltd,
Airport Business Centre, 10 Thornbury Road, Estover, Plymouth PL6 7PP**

Your Name:

Your Address:

Your Telephone Number:

Please tick as appropriate:

Comments ☐   Recommendation ☐

Name of Establishment:

Address:

Telephone Number:

Name of Contact:

READER REACTION FORM

COMMENT OR REASON FOR RECOMMENDATION:

....

....

....

....

....

....

....

....

....

....

....

....

....

....

....

....

....

....

Index of Advertisers

PLACES OF INTEREST